ABOUT THE AUTHOR

IAN JACKMAN is the coauthor of *The We~ ~cial Companion*. He is the author of *The Artist's . ~ ~spiration from the World's Most Creative Minds*, and *E~ ~his!: 1,001 Things to Eat Before You Diet*, among other books.

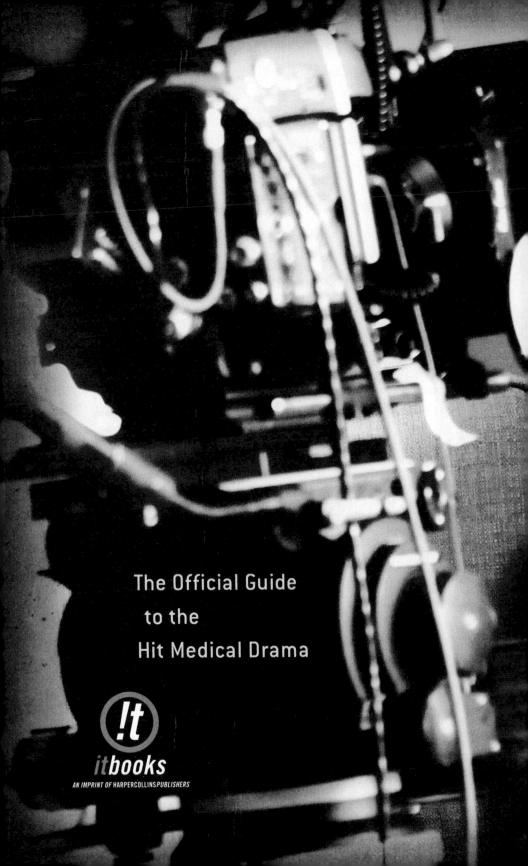

The Official Guide
to the
Hit Medical Drama

!t

*it***books**

AN IMPRINT OF HARPERCOLLINS PUBLISHERS

[H]OUSE M.D.

IAN JACKMAN

With a Foreword by Hugh Laurie

itbooks

HOUSE, M.D.: THE OFFICIAL GUIDE TO THE HIT MEDICAL DRAMA. © 2010 Universal City Studios Productions LLLP. *House, M.D.* is a copyright of Universal Network Television LLC. Licensed by NBC Universal Television Consumer Products Group. All Rights Reserved. Printed in the United States of America. No part of this book may be used or reproduced in any manner whatsoever without written permission except in the case of brief quotations embodied in critical articles and reviews. For information address HarperCollins Publishers, 10 East 53rd Street, New York, NY 10022.

HarperCollins books may be purchased for educational, business, or sales promotional use. For information please write: Special Markets Department, HarperCollins Publishers, 10 East 53rd Street, New York, NY 10022.

FIRST EDITION

Designed by Janet M. Evans

Library of Congress Cataloging-in-Publication Data is available upon request.

ISBN 978-0-06-187661-5

10 11 12 13 14 DIX/WCF 10 9 8 7 6 5 4 3 2 1

CONTENTS

FOREWORD

This is not only a foreword to a book but also an afterword to a large chunk of my life.

As I write, in 2010, it's more than a tenth: for Jennifer Morrison and Jesse Spencer, bless their creamy complexions, it's a fifth. I think it's time for an explanation, and one of these old ink-and-paper type deals seems a good spot for it.

I was in a Starbucks once and overheard a woman say to her companion: "I had a very interesting blueberry muffin yesterday." At the time, I was struck by her descriptor, "interesting." It interested me. There were, and still are, plenty of adjectives available to describe a blueberry muffin—"good," "bad," "stale," "crumbly," "kosher," "laced with LSD," or "shaped like Richard Nixon," among others—but "interesting"? It mystified me. Now, looking back, I think I know what she meant.

Before sunrise on most mornings of the last six years—let's say a thousand mornings, give or take—I have presented myself at the Fox Studio Lot in Los Angeles, a tiny principality on Pico Boulevard with its own police force, fire department, courtiers, peasants, stalwarts, and thieves. It has no established religion, but there is a giant bust of Rupert Murdoch in the central square, about two hundred feet tall, made from the bones of fallen enemies. (I might have imagined this.) Here, on stages 10, 11, 14, and 15, I have immersed myself in a fictional character, in a fictional place, in a fictional world, with an hour for lunch. My experience has been so weirdly shrink-wrapped that I couldn't even tell you what happens on stages 12 and 13, much less the outside world. Come to think of it, I don't even know where 12 and 13 are. Like hotel floors, maybe there is no 13? I know little of Californian weather, or which party is in power, or what the chances are that this hip-hop thing will catch on. I've used metal cutlery about a dozen times since I got here.

It's been interesting, all right, but not in the way you might expect. The interest has come not from the breadth of the experience but the narrowness; the exclusion of all thought outside the immediate word, blink, breath, moment—a moment that has far exceeded its normal duties, eventually stretching to a full six years and thereby risking the loss of its Momentary credentials.

But look, I'm getting ahead of myself. Let's go back (if you ever catch me using the word "rewind" to mean anything other than "rewind," I want you to shoot me, dead) to see how all this works.

....

An Englishman is summoned to Los Angeles. On the strength of a scratchy piece of video tape, he has apparently put himself in contention for a major television role. To advance to the finals, he must jump through hoops, kiss rings, and swear oaths—all of which he does, and gladly. He is chosen. He travels to Vancouver, city of ... I don't know ... buildings, and there he makes a one hour show, which he lays at the feet of the Gods. The Gods show it to a focus group. It scores highly enough to earn thirteen episodes. The Englishman packs a few shirts, kisses his family good-bye, and flies to Los Angeles. (He emphatically does not "jet into" Los Angeles as the British tabloids would have it, as if everyone else travels in steam-powered Dakotas ... but wait, if I start on the tabloids, we'll never get out of these parentheticals.)

His expectations at this point are low. He knows that American television is a fiercely competitive arena, and that one hour dramas follow the same actuarial arc as spermatozoa—gushing toward the giant Nielsen ovum in a spasm of excitement, a few moments of frantic wriggling, then oblivion. And yet, miraculously, the show survives those first weeks, grows stronger, gathers momentum, until it's careering, tumbling downhill, and the Englishman's suspenders are trapped in the door and his little legs are scrambling to keep up. Time disobeys its own nature—speeds up, slows down, bends, goes sideways—the days become windowless and weird, filming stories that aren't real mixed up with photo shoots, red carpets, and talk shows that are even less so. The result, inevitably, is madness. Late one night the Englishman is found wandering the Pacific Coast Highway, naked, carrying a .45, and reciting the Psalm 23.

His name was Ronald Pettigrew and the show was, of course, *Wetly Flows the Mississippi*. It ran for two seasons on the Trump Network.

Although I haven't taken it quite as hard as the Pettigrewster, there have certainly been times when I've found it intense. Has it been as intense as fighting in Afghanistan or stealing a base against the Yankees (whatever that means and whoever they are) or running a successful brothel? I've no way of knowing. Some of you may be thinking "come on, it's only a television show" and that's true—in the sense that you can attach the word "only" to any human event, as long as you're calibrated correctly. Nuclear Armageddon will "only" lead to the end of the human race, a geologist or astrophysicist might say.

But here's the paradox: If those of us who work on *House* had ever behaved as if it were "only" a television show, then it wouldn't be a television show. It would be a canceled television show. An ex-television show. Like most people in the entertainment business, we are professionally disproportionate. Intensity exists in the mind, as Marcus Aurelius might have said if you translated him badly, and when disproportionate people decide that a thing is intense, and devote all their physical and mental energies to it, then it becomes so. Well, that is what we did with *House*, for better or worse. It may seem comical to some; but I hope the Some don't live in glass houses, because those things are ridiculous. The heating bills alone.

....

But hard work, on its own, doesn't explain why *House* has become the most watched TV show on the planet. (This is not my claim: I read it in a trade journal recently, and have no idea how the writer arrived at his conclusion. I don't plan on finding out, either.) There has to be something else. Of course, one could say that the show is more than the sum of its parts, but that's true of almost everything outside the field of pure mathematics. Try driving to work in the pile of parts that make up a Honda Civic. One could say that House's aversion to the genteel, the euphemistic, gives an older audience some relief from the mealy-mouthed political correctness of our time; you could also say that he appeals to a younger crowd because he is anti-authoritarian, which is how young people like to think of themselves, but very rarely are. On top of that, House is a healer, a fixer of problems, a savior—not usually an unattractive quality. All of these things may have contributed in some way to the show's survival into baggy middle age. But, for my money, it's the jokes.

I think House is enormously funny. I become vexed when people describe him as grumpy or sour or a jerk because I feel those people are missing the good bits of both the show and the character. I find House playful, quick-witted, and thoroughly good company. I like spending time with him. But more than that, I believe his funniness is intrinsic to his character and profession. Let me explain.

(Of course you don't have to let me explain at all. You can, if you want, just slam this book shut and move on to the DIY section of the store. Or you can skip to the pictures of Olivia Wilde, that's fine, too.)

There are few things more tedious than a discourse on the nature of humor or why a joke is funny, but let's quickly get a rough definition under our belts so we can move on. Most jokes depend, in essence, on the yoking together of two apparently dissimilar things. The sudden recognition of a previously hidden similarity is the laugh. (Ugh. I feel unclean describing the delicate beauty of humor in such crude, mechanical terms. But there it is. The butterfly is pinned.) The joke, then, comes from the metaphorical area of the brain that produces and deciphers similes, analogies, and the rest. It is House's habit, from time to time, to describe a medical condition in metaphorical terms. This performs the convenient function of explaining to a lay audience (within the show, it's typically the patient, while outside, it's, well, the lay audience) the technicalities of what's going on. But underneath that function, House's metaphorical skill is also what makes him exceptional at what he does. His facility for dismantling problems with metaphorical tools (I used one, while describing one—this is what we call a high-protein sentence) allows him to see things more clearly, more analytically, than his peers. The funny part of House's brain is the same as the diagnostic part, which is also the part that expresses his attitude to death.

House is an atheist. (I don't have paperwork from David Shore authorizing me to say this, but I will take a chance and declare it anyway. If House finds God in season 9, I'll rewrite this bit.) And what does an atheist choose when faced with the cold, empty cosmos? He can jump in a river; he can pursue happiness, as someone memorably put it; or he can make jokes. For House, the atheist, I believe the joke is actually rather sacred. It is the defining essence of his humanity. The alleviation of suffering, the doing of the Right Thing, these are the rules by which House is forced to play; but he does so grudgingly, uncertainly, suspecting that the game is worthless, and that all is vanity. The joke, on the other hand, that's a cry of joy, a spark of the divine, a way of poking the encroaching cosmos in the eye. House, basically, laughs at death. Which is an option, kids.

....

Now, the more practical, tire-rotating, removing-leaves-from-gutters, readers among you may be wondering what any of this has to do with the workings of a typical American hospital. Do real doctors metaphorize, make jokes, carry on in any way like House, Cuddy, or Wilson? And if they do, is it worth remarking on?

Well, first of all, anyone who thinks Princeton-Plainsboro is a typical hospital must have spent most of their life in rude good health. It isn't typical or realistic, and wasn't ever meant to be. To me, Princeton-Plainsboro has always been an enchanted forest, where patients come to be cured of allegorical complaints. The treatments are metaphorical, the dialogue is dialectic. Of course, any drama must obey the laws of its own universe—the characters can't fly or travel through time—and the show achieves as much verisimilitude as it can afford with the time and money available (with the obvious exception that, in the world of *House*, there's no TV show called *House*). But still, the characters and events are not real. More than that, it's imperative that they aren't. Because real is random, and stories are not. Stories are how we impose structure, morality, and meaning on the blank universe. Beauty, too. The English landscape artist Joseph Turner was once upbraided by a critic who pointed to one of Turner's paintings and sniffily remarked that he, the critic, had never seen a sunset like that, to which Turner replied: "But don't you wish you had?" Well played, by the artist.

There is a prop on the set of House's inner office, a piece of stage dressing. It's a granite square—a coaster, I suppose—on which are engraved the words "A MERE COPIER OF NATURE CAN NEVER PRODUCE ANYTHING GREAT." I've never liked it much, too pompous, too snobbish, and why engrave it? What's wrong with a Post-it note? But I still think the statement is true.

And if the reproduction of reality on-screen is undesirable, it also happens to be impossible. At least, it's never been done, as far as I know. Movie cops don't look or behave like real cops, movie lawyers like real lawyers, or movie starship captains like real starship captains. Strangest of all, the film business can't even accurately represent the film business. Every time you see a movie within a movie—and I mean every time—a director will rip off his headset and angrily scream "CUT!"—causing a harassed assistant to flap his hands and call "TAKE 5 EVERYONE!" In thirty years of acting, I have never seen this happen.

Now it sounds as if I'm defending the show against criticism, and perhaps I am. (The chance to settle a few scores was one of the attractions of this assignment. Well, come on, wouldn't you?) I'm not going to name names—apart from rumpygirl518, may she be unreasonably detained in a foreign customs hall without access to a lawyer or a working lavatory—but I do want to defend, if not the show, then the people who make it. They are an extraordinary bunch, and their talent and dedication is a marvel to behold. I wish you could see them in action, really I do.

They would take your breath away. The mistakes we make on *House*—and, of course, we make them all the time because that's the nature of the thing—are never the result of carelessness or a lack of pride; they are the sort of mistakes you make when trying to do your taxes while falling down stairs. That's how it feels sometimes. Decisions come down on the crew like hailstones, and yet they march on, hour after hour, month after month, with skill, guile, muscle, and good humor—the sort of blend of qualities you can imagine taking Normandy. They are, in short, a fine outfit.

So there, I've said it. Score settled. Rumpygirl, you may have your phone call now. No, I don't have any damn coins.

....

It's been suggested that I provide some detail, some texture, so let me take you through a typical Monday.

6:00 A.M.

I pull in at the studio, repeating to myself the phrase "I really don't understand," over and over. This is my American accent warm-up. If the word "really," containing adjacent r and l sounds, doesn't come out right in the car, it's going to be a bad day. The slight diphthong on "stand" is also a good exercise.

At the gate, I am greeted by Lawrence, a blue-uniformed Cerberus who informs me that the power is within and that I must strive to find grace on this very special Monday. Sometimes, he reads me some of his poetry. Other times, it's just a long, slow smile, as if it's all so obvious, it doesn't need to be said. We finish with an exchange of fist and elbow bumps—whose significance I will never understand though I live a thousand years. Lawrence carries a gun.

I go to my trailer, which has increased in length every season, like an old man's ears. This year, I rented out the back half to a very nice Korean family. I eat a pint of chewy espresso coffee and skim through the "call sheet," a menu of the day's work and its ingredients. As with a menu, I can't help glancing down at the price—in this case, the total page count for the day. If it's more than seven pages, it's going to be hard. If it's more than nine, it's going to be a brain-scrambler. That may sound like a minuscule amount— maybe five minutes of screen time per day—but keep in mind that in the sumptuous world of feature films, two pages is about as much as the poor dears can handle before their feet start hurting.

Yep, that espresso sure is bitter.

6:10 A.M.

I'm sitting in the hair chair, where the talented Lori Rozman conceals my incipient baldness with her own special mixture of fiberboard and acrylic paint. I've always believed that cinema is 50 percent hair. And I don't mean cool hair; I mean good hair. Good hair means a good character, the way a good drummer means a good band.

6:30 A.M.

Crew call. Onto the set to rehearse the first scene. This can be a simple mechanical business—I'll stand here, you stand there—or a complicated physical and psychological puzzle: how best to express the information of the scene and the underlying music between characters. But simple or complicated, we have to keep moving. Like a shark, if we stop, we asphyxiate. (The production resembles a shark in no other way.) When the scene is staged to everyone's satisfaction, the technicians are summoned for a final rehearsal, where the actors' movements are marked on the floor with colored tape. I'm green.

7:00-ISH

Back into the makeup chair, where Marianna Elias, the Greek goddess, shellacks my wrinkled visage. Considering I'll be eighty-one in June, she does a pretty fine job.

Meanwhile, on the set, the cinematographer Gale Tattersall is weaving his own cat's cradle of light, bouncing it off sheets of muslin, white card, and copies of *Auto Trader*. The camera operators, Tony Gaudioz and Rob Carlson, are perfecting their framing; the dolly grip, Gary Williams (seven feet tall, moves like a ninja, hasn't made a mistake in the four years he's been here) times the dolly to the pace of the stand-ins; Ken Strain the boom operator is working out how the heck he can record dialogue without the mike booms being reflected in the fifty panes of glass that make up the hospital rooms, and so on.

Or they may all sit around playing gin rummy until I get back. I can't be sure.

Visitors on the set, any set, often observe that there seem to be a lot of people "just milling around." That is certainly how it appears. But then it's also how an ant colony appears until you've watched it for long enough to understand the ebb and flow of work. Film sets are ba   ing to the outsider because there are no uniforms. Everyone wears jeans and sneakers, and no one's trade is signified by their clothes, apart from grips and electric who need gloves to handle red-hot lights and the actors who wear white coats to handle red-hot dialogue. (Of which that was conspicuously not an example.)

The above process is repeated for six hours, until lunch—which isn't lunch at all, but the only time in a fifteen-hour day that crew members can call their bank, their plumber, their children's teacher, or their divorce attorney. They pace the lot with cell phones clamped to their ears, pleading, cajoling, threatening, or being threatened. You can usually tell straight after lunch whose calls have gone well and whose have gone badly.

For the actors, lunch might involve a table-read of a new script or a looping session, where lines have to be re-recorded because of a dog barking, airplane noise, or a bad performance—or it might be spent doing an interview with a journalist who's come to write about how people on a film set seem to be just milling around. If it's none of these, then it's sleep—which I do standing up, like a horse, to save on a hair rebuild in the afternoon.

And that's basically it. Repeat until mad. Or until the audience finds something shinier somewhere else. Six years in, it's hard to believe that our efforts are still being received, and received well, here and overseas. I was screamed at in Italy and chased in Spain. Chased, I tell you. I think they might have chased me in France, too, if it hadn't risked spoiling the crease in their trousers. The foreign response is particularly surprising, given the show's densely verbal, idiomatic texture. I can understand the global appeal of cop shows, where a lengthy line of dialogue might be "get in the car"—but what on earth does a Turkish translator do with "I promise you, the next knitting injury that comes in here, we're on it like stink on cheese"? I suppose I will never know. One of our regular directors, Juan Campanella (Academy Award this year—oh yes, we run with the right people) told me that he'd seen a translated film in his native Argentina, where the word "chip" (as in "chip on his shoulder") was rendered as "microchip." I mean, What?

Ah well. I have probably detained you long enough. The amuse-bouche is over. If you're still standing in the bookstore, trying to decide whether this book is worth the cover price, I think you now have more than enough information. I say, go for it. It's not much more than a bag of blueberry muffins, and you never know—you might find it interesting.

HUGH LAURIE
New Rochelle, New York
April 2010

INTRODUCTION

One Out of One-Three-One

Everybody lies. Go back and watch the first few minutes of the pilot of *House,* which aired on November 16, 2004, and see how quickly this basic tenet of Dr. Gregory House's universe is established. In the teaser, the scene setter that comes before the first credit, a young woman teacher, Rebecca (Robin Tunney), rushes into school as the bell rings for class. She runs into a colleague who teasingly implies Rebecca is late because she was with a guy the night before. No, I didn't sleep with him, says Rebecca. You're lying, the friend says, lightheartedly. "I wouldn't lie to you," says Rebecca. Now, with six seasons of *House* under its belt, the audience knows better. Suddenly, as she chats to her kindergarten class, Rebecca loses control of her speech and collapses. The first mysterious ailment presents.

Soon we're walking the halls of Princeton-Plainsboro Teaching Hospital (PPTH). Wilson says he wants House to look into Rebecca's brain cancer diagnosis because she's his cousin. We find out later that Wilson and Rebecca are not related. That makes one verifiable untruth and one probable fib in the show's first three minutes, a rate of lying that will be hard to maintain. But people will try their best. As House tells Wilson why he doesn't want to take the case, he pops a pill. An innocent viewer might wonder if House has a headache. You've got three overqualified doctors on your team getting bored, says Wilson, so why not use them? And soon we are traveling up Rebecca's delicately formed nostril and into her brain as if we're in *Fantastic Voyage.*

....

House is House and House is Hugh Laurie. For 131 episodes through season six we've watched open-mouthed as House elephants his way through the conventions of a doctor-patient relationship—in fact, any human relationship. In House's orbit is a group of characters, brilliantly drawn and marvelously inhabited by the standout cast. At Princeton-Plainsboro, they all have demanding jobs as members of House's diagnostic team, supervising the oncology department, or running the whole hospital. But their main occupation, their true purpose, is to interact with House. Working with this guy they deserve hardship pay. House is a misanthrope, the doctor who doesn't like patients, the relationship-averse addict with a bad leg, the man who has to solve the puzzle and get to the truth even if it means steamrollering people's feelings and lying, stealing, and cheating along the way—whatever it takes to get to the answer.

Shrinking violets don't last five minutes around House and none of the principals is that. His diagnostic team: the original three—the caring woman who is the moral center of the group; her (ex-)husband, the Aussie who isn't as much like House as he thinks he is; and the man of ambition who is much more like House than he admits, right down to the soles of his sneakers. House's second team: the philandering plastic surgeon; the beauty with a time bomb in her body; the man who set House the ultimate puzzle he can never solve. And the two people closest to House: his boss, his wrangler, redeemer, savior, friend, and off-on love interest, the person who gets to tell House what to do. Finally, House's best (and only) friend, the on-off roomie, the thrice-married (and counting) Man Who Loves Too Much, who in this misfit universe often stands by default as the voice of reason. To these people a great deal has happened in six years.

When the pilot aired, all that lay ahead of them. Resolving the case, Foreman exposes Wilson's lie that Rebecca is Wilson's cousin, which he deduced when he was illegally searching Rebecca's apartment. How did Foreman know? Because of the ham in

Rebecca's fridge. (Wilson is Jewish. If Rebecca were Wilson's cousin she wouldn't eat ham.) The ham springs a Eureka! from House—she has a tapeworm in her brain. It takes a save from Dr. Chase to prove to Rebecca the team is finally right, persuading her to accept treatment that is nothing more than a couple of pills taken daily for a month. The happy outcome seems neither here nor there to House. As far as he's concerned, his responsibility ended when he solved the case.

Rebecca's tapeworm is apprehended like the bad guy at the end of a police procedural. Week after week, *House*'s ultimate on-set authorities, creator, and show runner David Shore and co-runner Katie Jacobs provide a medical whodunit, a strange and elusive disease that House must track down. But it was clear from the pilot that there would be far more to *House* than that. We keep watching because we want to know what the writers are going to do with these great characters. At the end of the pilot, as House and Wilson watch a medical soap together, Wilson admits he lied about being related to Rebecca so House would take the case.

WILSON: "You've never lied to me?"

HOUSE: "I never lie."

WILSON: "Oh. Right."

House is joking. Everybody lies. Why do we lie? We lie because it's useful. Wilson's lie persuaded House to treat Rebecca. But the lie had another, unintended, consequence. If Wilson had browbeaten House into taking the case or bribed him rather than lying about being related to the patient, Foreman would never have thought the ham in Rebecca's fridge was out of place. Without the lie (and Foreman's breaking and entering), the patient would have died. It demonstrates the significance of something House offhandedly says to Foreman during a differential diagnosis session in episode one, something Foreman says doesn't mean anything. "Truth begins in lies," says House. "Think about it."

[H]OUSE
M.D.

THE START LINE

 **Creating the Show**

> "It's very easy to sit down at a typewriter and write
> completely contradictory character traits but it's
> another thing for an actor to come in and actually
> live them."

—DAVID SHORE

David Shore, the creator of *House*, is the first to acknowledge it takes a lot of people to develop a new show for television. In 2003, Katie Jacobs and Paul Attanasio, who together form Heel and Toe Films, approached Shore about starting a series with them for Universal Network Television, with whom they had a development deal. "I was a fan of his," says Katie Jacobs. "He said, 'Okay, I'll write a pilot for you and we'll figure out later what the idea is.'"

Shore had years of experience as executive producer and show runner on other people's series but he was more than ready to do his own thing. While Shore consulted on *Century City*, a series Jacobs and Attanasio's company was producing for Universal, he worked on creating the new show. The three would meet and discuss how they wanted to put together their pilot—the showcase episode producers make in the hope of securing a network deal. First essentials: What's the show going to be about?

Scripted dramas gravitate toward places where people find themselves in states of unresolved jeopardy—police stations, courtrooms, operating theaters. Here, either something very good can happen, or something very bad, and drama is implicit. With his own background in the law and years of work on similar shows, David Shore was certain he didn't want to work on anything with a legal setting. Paul Attanasio alighted on an idea inspired by the "Diagnosis" column written by Lisa Sanders in the *New York Times Magazine*. In the column doctors work their way through a patient's strange symptoms and come to a diagnosis. Paul and Katie knew from talking to the networks that they were looking for a procedural show, something like a traditional cop drama. This notion was like a cop show except that it was set in a hospital.

Shore didn't know. "I have to confess I was less convinced at the time," he says. "I had other ideas I would rather have done." But he went along with the medical theme. "I had grave doubts about it but the networks seemed very excited and I wasn't an idiot and I kept my grave doubts to myself." As Shore started working ("banging my head against a wall") a particular character took shape in his mind over the course of the next few months. As he put together an outline, Shore was concerned about the direction in which he was headed.

"I was very worried that it was much more of a character piece than a procedural piece. I was worried we had pulled a bait and switch on the network, we had sold a procedural and delivering a character thing."

—DAVID SHORE

There was a solution to the problem of what the network was going to think. "I will be forever grateful to Paul for the notion that we just don't show the network the outline," says Shore. "He says it's going to be a really good script, let's just not show them the outline, and we didn't." Having convinced the network that they were better off waiting to see the script, Shore then had to deliver on the promise.

Writing the pilot script took David Shore five months of hemming and hawing. After Paul and Katie and the studio weighed in with their few notes, the script was delivered, on a Friday right after New Year's of 2004. At ten o'clock Monday the network called to say they wanted to make the pilot.

To direct the pilot, Bryan Singer, experienced director of major movies like *The Usual Suspects* and the X-Men series, was hired. Singer remains an executive producer.

"There weren't a lot of changes to that pilot script, I am proud to say. I originally set it in Boston because it is a very academic place. One of the few notes Bryan Singer had when he signed on to direct was to ask to move it to Princeton, which was where he grew up. He liked the notion that it reeks of academia but is not a big urban center. . . . And it is something we hadn't seen before on TV, which is cool. Things like that do make a difference."

—DAVID SHORE

House's **nods to Sir Arthur Conan Doyle's unorthodox detective Sherlock Holmes** and his sidekick Dr. Watson are well-known. "House and Wilson very loosely are based on Holmes and Watson, inspired by them more than based on them," says David Shore. Holmes and Watson; House and Wilson. House's first patient is Rebecca Adler, a surname used by Doyle. House is shot by a man named Moriarty—Holmes was killed by Moriarty (and resurrected by Doyle). Holmes and Watson take rooms at 221B Baker Street; House's street address was 221B. Holmes takes cocaine, plays the violin, likes "sensational literature," and is a puzzle guy, like House. But of the original couple, it's Watson who had the bad leg.

Holmes can tell a lot from a quick glance. The first time Holmes meets Watson he deduces from his appearance that Watson has seen service with the British army in Afghanistan, then as now a military quagmire. He lives for the puzzle. In *The Sign of Four,* Holmes says, "A client is to me a mere unit, a factor in a problem."

"My mind rebels at stagnation. Give me problems, give me work, give me the most abstruse cryptogram, or the most intricate analysis,

and I am in my own proper atmosphere. I can dispel then with artificial stimulants. But I abhor the dull routine of existence. I crave for
mental exaltation. That is why I have chosen my own particular pro-
fessions, or rather created it, for I am the only one in the world."

—SHERLOCK HOLMES

Remind you of anyone?

For his Holmes, Doyle was inspired by Dr. Joseph Bell, under whom he
studied at Edinburgh Hospital. (In the episode "Joy to the World," House
receives a copy of Bell's *Manuals of the Operations of Surgery* as a Christmas gift. He throws it away.) Bell was Holmes in a hospital. He was a show-
man, fond of picking up on diagnostic and character clues from someone's
appearance: where and when they had served in the army, what their com-
plaint was. "Occasionally the results were very dramatic," said Doyle in his
Memories and Adventures, "though there were times when he blundered."

David Shore describes where he thinks the character of House
came from:

House a little bit is based on something going on in my own head,
an aspect of my personality. I can't claim to be as smart as him nor as
funny as him nor as anything as him but there was an inspiration
there. Usually his attitudes are my attitudes. Little experiences I had.

One of those experiences was especially formative. Shore hurt
his hip and made an appointment at the hospital for three weeks
hence. By the time the appointment rolled around the hip was
fine but Shore went anyway.

I went in and told the doctor where I used to have symptoms. That
may be the inspiration for the clinic stories. This was a teaching hos-
pital, so a whole series of doctors were examining me for nothing and
I remember thinking these people are being incredibly polite to me and
incredibly respectful and they shouldn't be—I am wasting their time. I

knew that as soon as they left the room they were bitching about me. I may have been wrong but in my mind. And frankly they should have been—I was wasting their time. And it occurred to me it would be interesting to see a character who didn't wait till they left the room. A guy who doesn't su er fools gladly.

QUESTION: "House says stuff doctors usually say when the patient is out of the room."

ROBERT SEAN LEONARD: "I've had doctors say they love that, that's one reason they love watching it. I've had some say they are offended. I don't care."

After FOX green-lit the script for the pilot and Bryan Singer was hired, the casting process could get under way. More decisions are made; more people are involved. Great ideas don't always turn into great scripts into great pilots into great shows. "You have to find the right director and it's very hard to make the right call," says Katie Jacobs. "It's very hard to make the right calls with the cast. It's very hard to make all the right calls."

Creating *House* took David Shore many months but its long-term success hinged on some moments of serendipity in finding the right actor for the leading role. The *House* casting team is casting directors Amy Lippens and Stephanie Laffin and casting associate Janelle Scuderi. All three worked on *Century City* and went on some interviews for jobs after it closed, all the while hoping *House* would get the go-ahead. They joined as a unit as soon as it did. The casting team is charged with finding suitable actors, who go through a selection process involving *House* producers and directors and in some cases, studio and network executives. Casting is like every other part of the process: The first time you do it is the most crucial. The right actor can bring a character unforgettably to life; a great group of actors means a pilot has a better chance of becoming a series.

Katie Jacobs has played a key role in casting decisions since the beginning. In television, casting proceeds in a very different manner from the movies, where Katie worked before changing

House co-show runner Katie Jacobs (right) on the set with Olivia Wilde

media. "It sounds crazy to say but it's true—Wilson was cast before House," says Jacobs. "It seems backwards but in the frenzy of casting pilot season you have to make your decision. Making a movie you would cast your lead first and then everything falls around [that]. You have to be so competitive when you are casting in pilot season, which is like hunting season. And Wilson was the first person we cast."

Robert Sean Leonard read for his role on the first day of the search for Wilson. Lisa Edelstein went into the studio right after him. Jennifer Morrison read the first day, too. Because she had other test options, Morrison was rushed for a network test even as other actors were reading for the role of Cameron in the office. Finding House himself took longer and Hugh Laurie wasn't cast until two weeks before shooting started on the pilot. What made the job more difficult was the fact that a lot of studios were looking for the same guy.

STEPHANIE LAFFIN: "It was the forty-year-old man pilot class: *Grey's* [*Anatomy*], *CSI New York*, *Medical Investigations*, *Desperate Housewives*, *Lost* . . ."

AMY LIPPENS: "We were all competing for the same actors at the same time."

JANELLE SCUDERI: "There are only this many people who can be the lead of a series. These twenty men."

Enter the story of the famous Hugh Laurie audition tape. At the time *House* was being cast, Hugh Laurie was in Namibia, in southern Africa, shooting the movie *The Flight of the Phoenix*. Laurie was on the show's radar. Amy Lippens had wanted to work with him on another project and the British casting director the team worked with mentioned him. Stephanie Laffin was living with her relatives, and her five-year-old cousin had *Stuart Little* (starring Hugh Laurie) on a loop. So Laurie was on a list, a long list, but the British-born actor faced a huge hurdle, one that should have disqualified him from the start. Director Bryan Singer was looking for an American actor to play House. Under tight shooting schedules, he didn't want an actor who had the added, and enormous, complication of tackling an accent. But it was decided Laurie should make an audition tape ("put himself on tape," in the lingo).

In Namibia, Hugh Laurie had another actor on the movie tape him at their hotel. They used the bathroom because the light was best there. Laurie read one scene for the part of Wilson and one for House. Laurie had put himself on tape before, but not like this.

"We had been in the desert all day and we were all sort of grimy and unshaven and I made some rather risky joke on the tape introducing myself and apologizing for my appearance because things hadn't been going well recently. I thought if they find that funny all to the good and if they don't, I probably shouldn't be doing it anyway. Fortunately they enjoyed that sufficiently."

—HUGH LAURIE

Back in Century City, weeks had passed since the original request for the Hugh Laurie tape. As far as finding House, Amy

Lippens said, "we were at our wits' end." People finally got to see Hugh Laurie reading for House (and Wilson). Janelle Scuderi remembers the moment. "So this tape shows up and I pop it in and it was like, 'Oh, this guy's good.'" It was the universal reaction, shared by David Shore.

> *Once we saw that tape . . . it was one of those great moments. That's a guy who thinks of this character exactly as I do. It has been such a pleasure because of that. It was an epiphany moment for myself when we saw that tape. You see something in your head and I guess he matched that but I guess I heard it my head and then I heard it out his mouth and then I saw it that way and said, "That's it."*

It was as if Hugh Laurie, remotely, from a bathroom in an African hotel, had validated all of Shore's hard work. "Prior to that moment I wondered if I had created something that couldn't exist in nature."

When it came to showing the tape to Bryan Singer, Katie Jacobs was well aware of the no-accent mandate. But to her, it wasn't about this person being Hugh Laurie or any actor, British, American, or otherwise—it was about him being, at once, House. "I want Bryan to get lost in the person that is House," Jacobs says. "You don't say, 'Now I'm putting on Hugh Laurie.'"

"What happened when I put the tape on for Bryan Singer and Bryan was looking at the TV and he literally came out from behind his desk and got closer to the screen. I was smart enough to put the tape in front of Bryan and smart enough to notice that and Bryan said, 'Who is this guy?'"

—KATIE JACOBS

Jacobs fessed up—he's English. She and Singer made a deal: They should keep looking but Hugh Laurie could be brought in for a meeting. That went against Jacobs's instincts. She can't imagine finding one person she loves for a part and then still be looking for someone else anyway. It's another difference between TV and the movies. Television networks expect to be able to make a choice; in movies, if the producer has more than one choice it's interpreted as a lack of vision.

In the interim before Laurie came to Los Angeles, no other actor had stood out and in the end he was the only candidate. That doesn't mean he was a slam dunk. The network was looking for someone younger. It had been a long time since he'd made the tape in Namibia and Hugh Laurie had mentally moved on.

"Months later my agent said, 'that medical show . . .' and I honestly didn't know what he was talking about. 'What medical show? I don't remember a medical show.' It was so much later that I had actually forgotten all about it."

—HUGH LAURIE

It was vitally important to Katie Jacobs that when he was meeting studio and network executives, Hugh Laurie should keep the unshaven and slightly rumpled look he had when putting himself on tape in Namibia. "I told the casting girls, he must not shave when he comes in," she says.

Representing Universal was Laura Lancaster, who recalls meeting Laurie:

He had on pretty much what he wears on the show—a blazer, T-shirt, jeans, some kind of bright tennis shoes and he had this little button on—a little punk button that said "sexy." The joke was, going into FOX everyone knew they were looking for someone "sexy"—it was very clever and funny and his sense of humor came across immediately.

"I remember meeting Hugh for the first time right on the lot outside the office. He had an umbrella instead of a cane. . . . He said how does it go in there, meaning in that room, and I said, 'With us it goes well.' I remember Gail Berman [of FOX] offering him a chair he could move and Hugh said, 'I take chairs where I find them.' And he sat down and blew everyone away."

—KATIE JACOBS

Actor tests take place in a sterile room with a dozen people watching someone read a scene. It's an artificial and awkward setup and the tryout bears little relation to what's being tried out for.

Laurie aced the test. "There wasn't one voice of dissent," says David Shore. "Everybody knew this was it."

All the network and studio executives and *House* brass knew that as character of House went, so went the show—he was that integral to its success. When Laurie came in to read, perhaps the only person that hadn't occurred to was Laurie himself. (Remember, *House* wasn't called *House* until shooting started.)

"At that point I hadn't read the whole thing. . . . I thought Wilson will be the central character and House will be working one day a week. Little did I know. I remember Bryan Singer . . . it seems ridiculous now . . . saying the show is actually really sort of about House and we all nodded. 'Yeah. I suppose it is.' It seems preposterous now. Things are never quite as evident at the time as they appear to be in retrospect."

—HUGH LAURIE

So *House* had its House. At this stage, Foreman and Chase had yet to be cast. Omar Epps read with Hugh Laurie and got the part. Jesse Spencer had put himself on tape in London, where he lived, and then paid his own ticket to Los Angeles for pilot season. The part of Chase was intended for an American, and someone older, but Spencer convinced everyone that the part belonged to a young Australian and that Chase should be a young Australian, too. The principals were in place.

The casting process had been an arduous one. "We would find an actor we liked and they would get halfway through the scenes and it wouldn't work," says Stephanie Laffin. "We had this one terrible session—'the Bad Session'—and I remember David walking out of the room—'These people are not the best doctors in the world.'"

JANELLE: "It was post-*O.C.* and it was hot FOX. If you weren't attractive, you're not on FOX. Even the random two-line costar on *The O.C.* had to be hot. Everyone had to be hot."

STEPHANIE: "Agents were telling me, 'This guy is really hot,' and I would say, 'This person is not attractive.' And they would come in and I would say, 'Look. I told you.'"

It's one thing to know who'd be great in the part, another to land the actor. Amy Lippens read the pilot and said, "I want Omar Epps." The idea came and went more than once. "Omar wasn't sure he even wanted to be in a series," says Amy. It's potentially a significant commitment: Auditioning actors, before they even test, have to sign that they are willing to play the part for seven years. Plenty of actors were willing to take the chance.

The casting staff jokes that Stephanie Laffin passed on a numbers of actors who have gone on to become movie stars or regulars on other shows. She has a list and isn't saying who's on it. But the success of the cast that was finally assembled means the job was well done. There's no one else who could have been Cameron or Foreman or Wilson or House. "You look at [Stephanie's] list and you say of course she passed on that person because there is no way that guy could be this guy," says Janelle Scuderi.

They had found their guy in Hugh Laurie. There was a lot of familiarity with the actor's comedic work in the United Kingdom, but less sense of his acting chops. Laura Lancaster's little brother was a fan of *Blackadder* and she watched boxed sets of the show over the holidays. "I knew his comedy work," says David Shore. "I knew he was hysterically funny. I had no idea that he had that kind of dramatic acting ability, not a clue. It wouldn't have occurred to me to ask him to do it."

One might wonder what would have happened had Hugh Laurie not been taped bearded and disheveled, inadvertently capturing House's look before the look had actually been established. Had he not been filming in Africa, Hugh Laurie would probably have been home in London and auditioned in a sport coat wearing a shirt and tie as he'd done before for American television. Perhaps that tape wouldn't have had had the same impact, as Hugh Laurie acknowledges. "It may not have caught Bryan Singer's eye or if it did catch Bryan Singer's eye, House might be a very different character. He might wear a suit and tie and be a whole different thing. And it might not be me."

"When you first start out it's like one of those swim races when there's a thousand entrants and everyone starts at the same line and you get where we're at now and it's a five-mile race and it's ten other swimmers and it's a different challenge."

—OMAR EPPS

A few current *House* staffers have been on the show from the beginning, signing up to make the pilot, which was filmed in Canada. Gerrit van der Meer and Marcy Kaplan were two key staff members to come over from *Century City*. Van der Meer went to Vancouver to set up the pilot. Kaplan remembers she had a decision to make between two potential projects. One was the "Untitled Attanasio/Shore," and the other was a pilot for Warner Bros., *Wanted*, which never went on to become a series. "It was a good choice," Kaplan says. "This was a much better script," says Gerrit. "That is a big factor—you want to work on a show that is great."

STEPHANIE: "It wasn't called *House* until day two of shooting."

JANELLE: "It was called 'Untitled Attanasio/Shore Project.'"

STEPHANIE: "We didn't know until Janelle pulled a call sheet out of the fax machine at our office in Century City. 'Oh, the name of the show is *House*.'"

The pilot was filmed in Vancouver and the show was picked up and went into series the summer of 2004. It's a curiosity that the show is made by NBC Universal and shown on FOX (rather than on NBC itself). As NBC Universal's Laura Lancaster explains, Universal, then an independent studio, had the original deal with Paul and Katie and with David Shore. In the spring of 2004, after the *House* pilot had been made and before series production started, NBC acquired Universal. Universal had taken the idea to all the networks. NBC had a show in development at the time called *Medical Investigations,* which had a somewhat similar premise and was the horse NBC decided to back.

House first appeared late in the 2004 fall season, airing after FOX finished with the World Series. The show was not an immediate hit. "At the time we were first on the air we followed Richard Branson—our ratings went up a hundred percent over his," says Katie Jacobs. "We had no lead-in." Katie Jacobs recalls it was a fight in the first season. *House* started airing in November and hadn't yet been given the boost of following ratings giant *American Idol* but she got a call from the network asking for a meeting. The network wanted a new character and other creative changes. "David and I attended this meeting and heard all of their ideas, agreed to some, didn't agree to others," says Katie.

David Shore went away for the holidays and the network called again. They had more ideas, of bringing in someone who could go "toe-to-toe" with House. "I thought we had successfully turned down the idea of a surgeon who can go 'toe-to-toe' with House," says Jacobs. But the network was firm—a new character there had to be, someone to threaten House's stability. David Shore figured out that someone should be Vogler, played by Chi McBride, a superrich hospital benefactor who engages in a fierce battle of wills with House.

But the shows that had already been made aired after *American Idol* and they were hits anyway without the new character. "I don't fault them for wanting to make the most out of what they are trying to do—this is their job," says Katie. She also acknowledges that McBride did a great job with Vogler. FOX was fixing something it turned out wasn't broken, though Vogler remains one of House's best adversaries.

Question: "Did you think then that the character had enough legs?"

Gerrit van der Meer: "In his case that is a peculiar choice of words."

There are so many factors out of the control of even the best casts and crews. Even though everyone who worked on *House* from the beginning knew it was good, that was no guarantee of success. Plenty of good shows have died on an executive's desk through no fault of their own. No one took success for granted, focusing on making the next show the best it could be. From the perspective of 131 episodes, nothing in retrospect seemed guaranteed as the show was being created. "When you are that point of it, you focus on the pilot and if you can get an order for twelve [shows] then you're happy," says Marcy Kaplan. "Then you think this looks like you can get an order for twelve. [And] maybe the back nine. I don't think that I was thinking maybe we could get ten years out of this. The pilot and maybe a few would be nice."

WHAT IF MICHAEL CAINE PLAYED HOUSE'S FATHER?

Writing *House*

> **QUESTION:** "You're thinking about it ten episodes ahead?"
>
> **DAVID SHORE:** "And in the present and on occasion twenty or thirty episodes ahead."

David Shore understands that many of the people watching *House* are doing so with less than undivided attention. "I'm sure people are watching making sandwiches . . . or coming back from the bathroom thirty seconds late," he says, but ideally he'd rather they didn't.

It's true that so much is going on in each episode, all delivered with a precise economy of language, that it's easy to miss a nuance in a scene or lose a thread in a story. And don't expect anything to be explained more than once. Tremendous hard work and skill go into getting the words down on the page. "We agonize over literally every word of the script," says Shore. "We may not come up with the ideal thing but that is the most important part for me—I consider that ninety percent of my job—working on the scripts."

"They are the most enjoyable scripts to read I have seen in thirty-odd years of doing this. I used to pick up scripts with a slightly heavy heart. 'This feels like homework' and it is homework but these are absolutely fantastic things to read. They always make me laugh out loud, they always surprise me, and there are moments when the hairs on the back of my neck stand up. It really is terrific stuff."

—HUGH LAURIE

David Shore manages a stable of twelve to fourteen full-time writers and their assistants. He has three number twos. One is executive producer Tommy Moran and the others are the duo of executive producers Garrett Lerner and Russel Friend, who have been a writing team since film school. Between them they split up the writers and alternate in supervising the writing of the scripts: Tommy for one and Russel and Garrett the next. Like many people who work on *House*, the three men have two jobs. Separate from their supervisory roles, they also write their own episodes, as does show runner David Shore.

Before anything as specific as an individual script can be contemplated, the writers have to devise medium-term story arcs for large chunks of the season ahead. (For information about what is happening any further in the future, you'd have to ask David Shore.) In order for scripts to be ready for production to begin in the summer, the writing process is more or less continuous from one season to the next. "It probably takes us ten months to film twenty-four episodes," says Russel Friend. "It takes us eleven months and three weeks to write them all."

The writers need at least a six-week jump on production, so well before the start of the season, there is a summit meeting of David Shore, Katie Jacobs, and writers and assistants to discuss the story arcs that will appear from the first episode. There are also meetings where medical stories are pitched and debated. These meetings will map out from six to twelve episodes ahead—no more than half a season at a time. They know that by the time they reach the midpoint, everything can and probably will have changed. Within the season the writers still have to run ahead in order to keep up. In October, four months into the production season, half a collective eye is trained four or five episodes into the future. "The episodes that need to be prepped in November seem very scary to us. We feel like we are already behind schedule. We just need to make it to Christmas," says Tommy Moran.

For the start of season six everyone knew the answer to the perennial, and central, question: What's up with House? At the end of season five he was seen entering Mayfield Psychiatric Hospital, so that's where he'd find himself in episode one, season six. Initially the plan was for House to remain in the hospital for six to eight episodes, triggering the elaborate and costly construction of the large Mayfield set on the FOX lot. But things change. The writing team realized they wanted to get House back to Princeton-Plainsboro at the end of the two-hour season opener. (House revealed he spent seven weeks in the institution in "Brave Heart," the sixth episode of the season and around the point in TV time it was speculated he was going to be released.)

"When you are doing a show like this you have to know what reaction you want from your audience at any given point. The second scene of act six, I want the audience to feel something and you have to know what that is. Even if it's ambiguity, you have to get the audience to feel ambiguity. I want them to be sixty percent sure House is thinking that. You are to some extent trying to be a puppet master."

—DAVID SHORE

The idea of placing House in a psychiatric hospital was hatched as season five was in progress and was dovetailed with a practical issue: what to do with Kutner. When Kal Penn announced his intention to leave the show, writers debated how to do it. Some ideas offered a pleasant way out for Kutner, such as winning the lottery. The odds against hitting a jackpot are astronomical; around House's diagnostic team they're exactly zero. When writer Leonard Dick suggested suicide, Tommy Moran told him it probably wasn't feasible to kill someone so soon after Amber's death. David Shore was exploring the notion of House ending the season in a mental hospital and although he initially resisted killing another character, Kutner's dying could help. Moran told Dick perhaps it would work. "We tried to look for other ways but kept coming back to this one," says Tommy Moran. "It seemed to fit in. And it ended up setting the ending."

The notion was that House's descent would be precipitated by Kutner's death and House's inability to get to the bottom of it. Just before the holidays in 2008, the writers retreated to a hotel for three days and locked themselves in a room to figure out the details of the arc from the discovery of Kutner's body in the bedroom of his apartment to House being led through the front door of Mayfield Hospital. There was a lot to figure out: House blaming himself for Amber's death, the idea of Amber returning as a hallucination, Cuddy detoxing House, and the seemingly romantic moment between them followed by the awful realization he was hallucinating that, too. "There were a lot of moving parts," says Russel Friend.

QUESTION: "Amber's bedroom has been dismantled so I reckon Amber is gone."

GARRETT: "I think Amber's gone."

RUSSEL: "I think Amber's gone. She's actually dead."

QUESTION: "That doesn't stop anyone . . ."

ALL: "That's true."

"Ignorance Is Bliss" was writer/supervising producer David Hoselton's seventh script in four years ("Lines in the Sand," in season three, was his first). It's the job of David Hoselton and the other writers to come up with story ideas for the individual episodes. It's David Shore's responsibility to fit the episode stories into the overall story arc. Tommy Moran is David Hoselton's executive producer. Hoselton's ideas, even as a three-sentence pitch, go to Tommy Moran. If Moran thinks the idea is viable, it goes to Shore. If Shore likes it, with or without tweaks from either of them, it comes back to Hoselton, who can prepare an outline.

"At the beginning of every season . . . we agree on what their medical stories will be, agree on what the arcs are. This is what David Shore brilliantly does all on his own: He matches up that medical story with where we are in the arc so it can have, in our very best cases, a thematic relevance to what is going on with our character. That he is solely and wholly responsible for and I am in awe of it."

—KATIE JACOBS

David Hoselton's outline might run anything from less than a page to ten to fifteen pages. Tommy Moran may have notes for Hoselton for the outline and they'll work on the piece together until it's ready to go to David Shore for his feedback. The outline may go back and forth three or four times before Hoselton can start the script. Needless to say, many ideas fall by the wayside. David Hoselton thought about a sick psychiatrist coming into Princeton-Plainsboro in season five but with House entering Mayfield Hospital himself, that story never got off the ground. Stories also move around. Before Hoselton started writing, "Ignorance Is Bliss" had a slot at the end of season five. It slipped into early season six and then to episode nine of that season to allow time for House to be reintegrated into the hospital.

The writing of the script will take a minimum of a month. If a writer knows she has to get a script to David Shore a couple of days before prepping the episode, eight or nine days before filming starts, that is probably how long the writing will take. Writers have a lot of balls to juggle in each episode. David Hoselton identifies three separate strands to the "A" story, the medical mystery at the heart of the episode. First, there has to be an interesting disease that can disguise itself and offer misleading diagnoses. Second, there should be a compelling patient. And third, how does the patient shed some light on or interact with House? And vice versa. The diagnosis needs to be resolved one way or the other, and usually the patient is cured of the original disease but there are often consequences.

The key point about the ending is not that it's anything as banal as being happy or sad; it's that it isn't obvious. In "Ignorance Is Bliss," the predictable road would be for the unhappy genius Sidas to come off the drugs he used to dull his intelligence and get back to being smart. His wife, much less brainy than he, would say, "We can make it work," and Sidas would say, "You're right, honey." Tidy, satisfying perhaps, but not credible. "It's okay to have a slightly unhappy ending as long as it makes people think a little bit," says David Hoselton. "Hopefully it's a little unsettling in a thought-provoking way."

Garrett Lerner admits that he spends a little time after each show online gauging fan reaction. He will ask his wife how she liked the show; he will ask his parents how they liked the show and he's curious to get a wider opinion. Not that what he reads could affect his work even if he wanted it to; the writers are so far ahead of what is airing that the story line fans are reacting to is fully established. It's not the case in Garrett's experience that people with a negative opinion are more likely to post: Some episodes are almost unanimously praised.

Climbing up on his high horse for a minute, Garrett laments the peevish industry that has grown up whose sole purpose is to reveal spoilers for popular TV programs. It happened with news that Cameron was going to leave Chase and Jennifer Morrison the series, if open-endedly. Even as the writers reunited the original diagnostic team, some viewers already knew the denouement. For Garrett, the tattling is highly unfortunate. "Someone who has access to the Internet who can go 'I found a script and I read an ending. Darth Vader is Luke's father! Bruce Willis is really dead!' All you've done is fucked up the viewing experience and ruined everything we have worked so hard to do. There's my soapbox."

As well as the A story there is a B story involving House and his team, and/or Wilson and/or Cuddy. The B story might be resolved to a certain extent. By "Ignorance Is Bliss," Chase is ready to boil over after the death of Dibala and the fallout that led to Cameron leaving him. A group of writers was sitting around and Peter Blake had the idea that right out of the blue, Chase should punch House. Then Tommy Moran added the delicious twist that Chase is doing it not because he's mad at House but to get people who won't stop asking him questions off his back. House can appreciate the pretzelated logic of his thinking. "I was thrilled it landed in my episode," says David Hoselton.

"House is a contrarian so he is able to look at the other side of everything. He's going to say something that you don't expect. But he's not saying it to be shocking or outrageous; he's saying it because he's got a unique perspective on the world. He can't be mean-spirited just for the sake of being a jerk. He's always making a point. That's the fun of the show but also the challenge of the writing, to find that unique take."

—DAVID HOSELTON

Hoselton also had the first House-Cuddy kiss in one of his stories. Of course, House and Cuddy are still engaged in their peculiar tarantella many moons later. A writer may not know where the main characters are being left off in the previous episode until very close to the time they have to write their scenes. "You find out. Okay, I got this," says Hoselton. "This is something I have to deal with." In "Ignorance Is Bliss," House is trying to find out where Cuddy and Lucas are spending Thanksgiving. House gets Cuddy's address, or an address, and he's rebuffed. The question for the next writer is, now what are they going to do? The larger story, House's relationship with Cuddy, isn't resolved here for sure. Of course, perhaps it never will be.

Every writer plans his stories differently. David Hoselton writes out the gist of his story on index cards fixed to a notice board. He uses one index card per scene with the cards arranged in columns according to the acts, numbered one through six. There are ten cards in act one, five in act two, and so on. The stories are color-coded: the medical story in one color, the House/Cuddy angle another, and so on. In this way Hoselton can see he's not running scenes from the same story back-to-back. Between finishing the outline and starting the script the cards help him see if the story is flowing.

Writing for *House* is both a solitary and a collaborative endeavor. In getting the script down on paper the writer is faced with the lonely prospect of the blank page and their computer screen or typewriter. ("You know this episode is shooting in eight weeks and nothing helps like a deadline," says David Hoselton.) Once there is a draft, the process of feedback starts and the script makes its way from the writing side across to production. Part of a writer's job is to help with other writers' scripts. The head writers (Tommy or Russel and Garrett) will edit and rewrite and then the script will go to David Shore and be rewritten again.

The last pass takes place with the episode writer, with either Tommy or Garrett and Russel and with David Shore. Here the final polish is applied. The continuity of a character's voice is best maintained if the creator of the series has the last look at each script. Most of the writers have been around long enough for someone to notice if something Wilson says in episode 112 contradicts episode three. Russel Friend mentions that Ira Hurvitz, the script supervisor, has an incredible memory for continuity issues like that, while he himself does not. "Everyone remembers bits and pieces," says Tommy Moran. "It's a team effort."

Writers acknowledge the value of the assistance they receive from their colleagues, especially with honing the original idea. "We talk to each other constantly," says David Foster. "You go and sit on [someone's] couch and say, 'I'm thinking of doing this; what do you think?' There is a lot of that in getting the story off the ground." David Hoselton credits David Shore with promoting the collegiality, saying he's very generous with help and insight and won't put his credit on every episode as some head writers do. And the attitude trickles down. "I know it's Hollywood [but] it really does seem to be ego-free," Hoselton says. Garrett Lerner says he and Russel are collaborating the way they have worked with each

Hugh Laurie with script supervisor Ira Hurvitz

other since film school more than fifteen years ago. "We're not possessive about anything or take ownership over everything or get precious about anything. It's about making it better."

"The first script I ever wrote, I turned it in and the show runner, who was David Shore, was very complimentary and I thought, Man, I did a great job! Then I saw the script again and I thought there is nothing that I wrote in that script. People who work in television are used to being rewritten and there are a lot of changes, even when we start filming."

—TOMMY MORAN

The writer takes full part in the rewriting process, whereas on other shows, the script might go away and as far as the writer is concerned, it never comes back. On other shows the story is "broken" in the writers' room with all the writers collectively deciding what happens in each scene and where the act breaks are going to be. An individual writer might then add the dialogue. A lot of sitcoms are written start to finish by a team of writers in a room with one of their names picked out of a hat for the credit. On *House*, a writer has more independence but with substantial support. "This show I think has the best of both worlds," says Tommy Moran.

....

David Shore is keen to fit as much story as possible into each forty-four minutes of television. Every scene, every line, is an opportunity to advance the plot and the characters. There are only so many lines available in an episode. "I am attracted to elegance in writing," says Shore. "I like everything to be as fundamental as it can be. I don't like anyone repeating themselves. . . . I hate the line of dialogue, 'What?' You see that on most shows and I will cross that out almost every time and replace it with 'Thirteen gives him a look' or something like that." "Shore doesn't allow you to have any waste dialogue," says David Hoselton. "There's no, 'What did you say?' You're not allowed to explain anything twice or to really expand on things. It forces you to distill everything down."

Garrett Lerner explains that a writer's initial impulse, when faced with a mountain of research on a medical condition and reams of jargon, might be to include a lot of the information in the script. With experience he realized he could take most of the medical story and say, "Don't need that; don't need that; don't need that." It leaves more room for what viewers are watching the show to see: the characters interacting with each other. "All of the actors are intelligent," says David Hoselton. "Our audience is intelligent. By the time you get to season seven there is a lot of shorthand between the characters. We know how House is going to enter a room. A lot is communicated with a look." "I am dealing with smart people here," says David Shore. "And I don't want to talk down to my audience."

More often than not, a scene is written long and then cut. David Shore jokes that on the first show for which he was head writer, the preferred method of cutting a scene was to remove the first line and the last line and then the first two words of every line and the last two. To David Hoselton, it's at the outline stage that a lot of unnecessary scenes are taken out. Then David Shore will tighten it further. Can you make these two scenes one? If there is going to be a joke, it has to mean something.

The ability of the actors to impart meaning without saying anything is invaluable in conserving screen time. It's important that *House* has directors who are familiar with the writers and the cast and who can pick up on the moment. The nonverbal approach may improve the scene. Says David Shore, "So many times we have had this great punch line, a poignant, pithy, statement about life or something and then we find the scene is better with a look from Wilson. House knows exactly what Wilson said with that look and the audience knows as well and we cross out the dialogue. It's all about getting to that point. You need great actors and you need to have earned that but you need to get to that point with the script as well."

> "I play the violin; David wrote the symphony. I can tell you how it feels to play somebody."
>
> —ROBERT SEAN LEONARD

"We have been on other shows and sometimes you get the dailies and it's like, 'Oh man, what happened?' On this show [the actors] always elevate the material, which makes our job great. It is amazing what they do with the material. You couldn't ask for more."

—RUSSEL FRIEND

Katie Jacobs, together with production designer Jeremy Cassells and construction coordinator Stephen Howard, works on the visual side of the show to create stages on which the writers can manipulate their characters. Take House and Wilson's shared apartment.

The script said Wilson was moving but the only information provided was that it was to "an upscale loft." Jeremy Cassells and Katie Jacobs discussed the apartment and spaces where House and Wilson can run into each other or spend time together. Jeremy also envisaged a library—the two men are successful doctors and they have a lot of medical literature. A library would give them somewhere more sophisticated to hang out than the couch in the living room.

"I go to the writers and David Shore and say, 'How many bedrooms, how many bathrooms, who has a better bathroom, whose apartment is this?' We try to create story opportunities. I think it has to be two bathrooms and maybe House only has a stall and Wilson has a tub so you can see what the scene is out of that. Waking up one morning and groggily find House in his tub."

—KATIE JACOBS

The apartment was given its own backstory. A man bought the apartment, knocked down some walls, and flipped the place. Originally Cuddy was going to buy the apartment with Lucas but Wilson snuck in and bought it to share with House (the move that Lucas exacts his revenge for in "Moving the Chains"—the opossum, the loosened handrail, the sprinklers). To begin with, the space was quite bare and vanilla so the odd couple could give it their own stamp. Katie's idea was to have House's and Wilson's bedrooms sharing a hallway. "I want Wilson to be able to say, 'Good night, House,' and House 'Good night, Wilson,' and now they can." Then Steve Howard and his crew built the place. Let the fun begin.

Immediately (in "The Down Low"), Wilson flirts with their sexy new neighbor Nora and discovers she assumes he and House are gay. "We're not gay," says Wilson. "Seriously?" says Nora. House, wearing a lavender shirt and showing interest in musicals and Nora's shoes, tells her they are closeted. House's diabolical plan is to jump Nora and the two are discussing a "sleep-over" at dinner in an intimate restaurant when Wilson interrupts them.

WILSON: "I love this man. And I am not wasting another moment of my life denying that. [*offering ring*] Gregory House, Will you marry me?"

HOUSE: "Wow. This is unexpected."

"She has given it a lot of thought, which helps us narratively. The idea she had was that Wilson will have the master bedroom with the fancy bathroom and the fancy tub and House doesn't have a tub; he is in the kid's room with a shower. That's really funny and we are going to use that . . ."

—RUSSEL FRIEND

In the season-six opener, *Broken*, the design and writing departments had to work together particularly closely because the set and the scripts were being put together almost at the same time. Does anything need to be added to the set so the story can be told? What's the set going to look like so we can write the story? For the writers it was jarring to be moved to a new location with almost a whole new cast of characters. With only a notion of the story, the two-parter was cast. When the writers were "breaking" the story on the whiteboards in the writers' room, they started calling House's psychiatrist "Andre" because they were picturing Andre Braugher in the role. He was the consensus first choice and that's who Katie Jacobs delivered.

"[Katie] came and said, 'I found this great actor for Alvie [Lin-Manuel Miranda],' and we watched his tape and he was great and we built his character around his actual persona, the fact that he sings and raps and all that stuff. We built that in after he was cast."

—RUSSEL FRIEND

"I am in such awe of [the writers]. They're great. It's a really nice relationship. I have never been on a show where there is such a lovely vibe between the writers and actors and producers. It's very warm and open. I'll be in the office and see they have on the computer pictures of some bizarro medical procedure and I know they are working on something that weeks from now will turn into a script."

—PETER JACOBSON

....

After shooting is completed on his latest episode, David Hoselton will open the window and take a breath for the first time in a long time. Then he'll be ready to move on to the next story. He has an idea that he'll put on paper and he'll look to get back in the writing rotation. He jumped back in at episode twenty ("The Choice").

David Hoselton went to law school with David Shore at the University of Toronto. Together they edited the law school newsletter, which was called *The Law School Newsletter*, when they started and *Heresay* very soon after. Hoselton never practiced law; twenty-five years ago he moved to Los Angeles with another law school friend looking for work as a screenwriter. He wrote scripts for hire, then *First Knight* with Sean Connery, and worked on movies at Pixar and Disney before moving to *House*. Hoselton enjoys the team aspect of TV. Writing screenplays can be a solitary job, which means when it isn't going well, it's a long, lonely haul. He doesn't have any desire to go back to that world. "There's so much fantastic TV now," he says. "*Dexter* and *Mad Men* and *Lost*. They're just really great little works of art."

Epilogue: House and Michael Caine

In "Birthmarks," written by Doris Egan and David Foster, the patient of the week is a Chinese woman whose parents tried to kill her as a baby with pins pushed through her fontanel. "We're all screwed up by our parents," says House. "She's got documentation." Eli Attie got the idea from a news story. It's a good example of the medical story playing off and illuminating the second story in the episode, in this case the death of House's father and House and Wilson's road trip to attend the funeral. At the ceremony, House leans in to his father's casket, apparently to whisper a poignant, or at least somewhat poignant, farewell but in fact it's to snip off a piece of his dead father's ear to run a DNA test.

"It honestly came out of this notion of having Michael Caine playing House's father. This was my own personal fantasy, my own stupid idea. Unfortunately I had that notion after we had cast House's father but I got to thinking, how could Michael Caine be House's father? Maybe Michael Caine could be his father if we say the father we have seen isn't his real father. That maybe House has had this theory his whole life that when his dad was off serving somewhere, his mom had an affair. Since he hates his dad, all along he has this fantasy. 'My dad's not my dad and I have known that since I was twelve, one of my first deductions.'"

—RUSSEL FRIEND

Planted seeds can take a long time to sprout. Speculation about House's father finds a payoff thirty-five episodes after the question is raised, in "Private Lives." Wilson catches House reading *Step by Step: Sermons for Everyday Life*, actual sermons written by a Unitarian minister. Understandably, Wilson is perplexed as to why the avowed atheist House would be seeking spiritual advice in this way but when he sees the author photo on the book's jacket (House had concealed his copy with a jacket from Henry James's *The Golden Bowl*), Wilson figures it out. House admits the author, a friend of the family, is his biological father. On reading the book, House decides he can no more make a connection with this man than he could with his putative father.

. . . .

With 131-plus episodes, David Shore's characters have a lot of established story. Still, a lot is unsaid, and even more remains unwritten. Or, more accurately, nearly written or merely speculated.

Which of the characters did and did not have a good childhood? Cameron, perhaps. Did Foreman's parents drive him toward juvie? Was Chase pampered?

RUSSEL: "But [Chase's] dad was distant."

TOMMY: "I don't remember what we did to Chase's dad."

RUSSEL: "He died, didn't he?"

TOMMY: "It's like studying for finals: Once I do it, it's out of my brain and I'm on to the next one. At lunch today I was trying to remember what we had just done in episode ten, which was a week ago and hasn't even been filmed yet. Now we're working on episode thirteen. We keep having to look forward.

"It's not just the episodes we have done; it's all the episodes we have thought about doing. I was talking to David [Shore] yesterday about an idea. I can't remember what idea it was and I was sure we had done that. Didn't we do that? And he was like 'no I think we talked about doing that but we never did it.' In my head I can see the scenes."

RUSSEL: "It was Wilson's brother."

TOMMY: "The whole idea that Wilson's brother comes back and gets out of the hospital."

GARRETT: "He went and visited him but he didn't pick him up. In fact you never saw Wilson's brother."

RUSSEL: "We were trying to remember that too . . ."

TOMMY: "He was helping out and he was doing real well and at the end he kind of relapses and leaves."

GARRETT: "It was all just a notion."

TOMMY: "I thought we did that . . ."

RUSSEL: "I think Peter [Blake] wrote a whole outline. We had a whole thing on it. It's a good story. We should do it."

GARRETT: "Sometimes you look through an old folder on your computer and you think, Oh God, did we never do this? Thank God because we need something now."

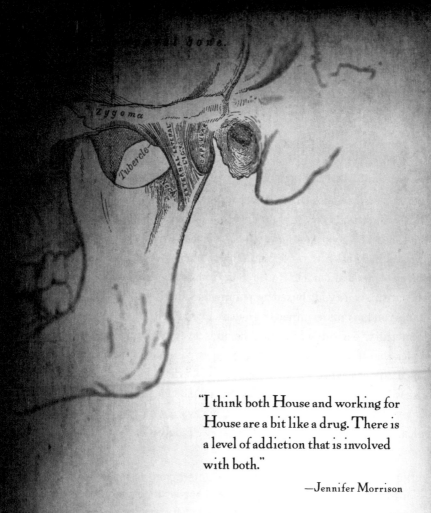

"I think both House and working for House are a bit like a drug. There is a level of addiction that is involved with both."

—Jennifer Morrison

CAMERON

Jennifer Morrison

As far as House is concerned, Allison Cameron starts out as one of his little puzzles. In the pilot, worried that House doesn't respect her, Cameron asks her boss which of her qualifications got her the job, only to have her worst fears confirmed: She was hired because of her looks. House admits she was a good candidate but he's curious why she wanted to work her "stunning little ass off" rather than marry rich. "Gorgeous women like you do not go to medical school," House says, "unless they are as damaged as they are beautiful. Were you abused by a family member?"

Cameron isn't undermined by House's intrusiveness but she is still raw—in "Maternity," early in season one, she finds it very difficult to tell the parents how sick their baby is and then it's almost impossible for her to say the baby has died. "It's easier to die than to watch someone die," she says, like she knows. House wonders if Cameron's reaction means she lost a baby herself, and he asks her. "You can be a real bastard," she says. By digging into Cameron's medical records, House rules out the theory ("Fidelity").

> "Her overwhelming losses leave her determined to make her life mean something. Although her ethical battles may seem extreme at times, for Cameron they are comforting. If she is 'doing the right thing' at her own expense, perhaps she can establish her purpose in this life."
>
> —JENNIFER MORRISON

Despite this shabby treatment, Cameron is prepared to give House the benefit of the doubt over his drug use, telling Foreman he's not an addict, that he's in pain. Cameron has fallen for House and fallen hard. House has two chances with her and blows both. First he asks her to a monster truck rally ("Sports Medicine"), which isn't a real date. House professes to be mystified by Cameron's interest. In "Role Model," he asks Cameron why she likes him. "I am not warm and fuzzy and you are basically a stuffed animal made by Grandma," he says. Cameron's first, self-protective, instinct is to leave the hospital but she comes back, provided House goes out with her, "and not just a meal between two colleagues. A date." ("Kids")

> "Cameron is attracted to talent, and House is a brilliant diagnostician. Even though he is sarcastic and almost mean at times, his talent and determination to save lives outweighs anything else."
>
> —JENNIFER MORRISON

House dresses up for the date (he wears a tie!); he buys a corsage; he listens to Wilson's dating advice. At the restaurant, Cameron tells House he's mean to her because he likes her and if he starts being nice it means he's getting in touch with his feelings. Cameron says she has one chance: She wants to know how House feels about her. By now House has abandoned Wilson's playbook and rather than attempting to make a connection, he looks to answer the puzzle. He says Cameron thinks she can fix anything—that's why she married a man who was dying of cancer and she's looking for a new charity case. He's twice her age, he says, not great looking, charming or nice. "What I am is what you need," House says. "I'm damaged." ("Love Hurts")

> "It could never work out for House and Cameron because if we were all in love and happy, there would be no show."
>
> —JENNIFER MORRISON

Soon, Stacy shows up at PPTH and it's clear when they discuss their mutual interest in House that Cameron has moved on. In "The Honeymoon," she tells House, "I thought you were too screwed up to love anyone. I was wrong. You just couldn't love me. That's good. I'm happy for you."

Ask David Shore to describe Allison Cameron in a word and he says, "humanity." Cameron is the anti-House, the positive to his negative. Consistently, she shows compassion and care to patients (*caring* is a word House throws back at her like an insult). In "One Day, One Room," Cameron sits with a lonely, depressed homeless man as he dies regretting the meaninglessness of his life, then she tenderly washes his body. Meanwhile, House, who would no doubt agree about the man's pointless existence, is trying to avoid talking to, and possibly comforting, a rape survivor. House is about the puzzle, Cameron about the people.

Examples abound of Cameron's essential considerateness: She wishes House a happy birthday ("The Socratic Method"); she wants to know why Chase doesn't talk to his father ("Cursed"); and she tries to engineer a meeting between House and his parents ("Daddy's Boy"). She also has the most acutely attuned moral compass. When Vogler is on the warpath insisting House fire someone, Cameron suggests he cuts everyone's pay instead ("Heavy"), and when she finds that Jeff the professional cyclist has been cheating, she calls the newspaper to blow the whistle ("Spin"). In "Skin Deep," against House's wishes Cameron tells Cuddy a fifteen-year-old model's father slept with her even though House didn't want her to. She's always doing the right thing.

Cameron works to escape House's labels. When House sees a spark between Cameron and Sebastian, the TB doctor ("TB or Not TB"), he thinks she's attracted to the fact Sebastian is prepared to die for his cause. But soon she's jumping Chase and before long suggesting their friends-with-benefits arrangement. It might be surprising to see Cameron being so bold. In "Spin," she tells Wilson she fell in love with her husband's best friend as the husband was dying in the hospital although she didn't sleep with him.

There's a toughness developing in Cameron. Kalvin, the HIV-positive patient who spits up blood over Cameron in "Hunting," tells her to get angry but she stands her ground. Then, in "Euphoria," after Foreman stabs Cameron with an infected needle she agrees to act as his medical proxy but won't immediately accept his apology. "We're gonna get you better first and then, if you still wanna apologize, I'll be around." House is rubbing off on Cameron: She drugs George, the morbidly obese patient in "Que Sera, Sera," to prevent him for leaving PPTH before he can be treated. Detective Tritter asks Cameron why she's sticking by House ("Finding Judas"). She's changed, Tritter contends, and we can see she has. Ten years ago she turned herself in during a calculus test and now she's mad at Wilson for ratting out House.

"Cameron grows over the course of the six years she is at Princeton-Plainsboro. I think it would be impossible to work for someone like House and not be greatly impacted by his decisions and methods of accomplishing things his way."

—JENNIFER MORRISON

On Valentine's Day, Cameron propositions Chase, who says, "What if I'm offended?"

"Then you're not the man I'm looking for," says Cameron ("Insensitive"). It's a Housean arrangement, at first. Chase breaks the rules by asking for more, so Cameron shuts him down. "It was fun. That's it. And now it's over" ("Airborne"). Cameron's now okay with looking after number one. When she thinks House may be planning to quit PPTH ("Half-Wit"), she writes her own letter of recommendation—she's concerned about having a job. By the end of season three, when the team breaks up and she's leaving, she tells Foreman, Chase, and House she'll miss them but she's not broken up. She's going to be fine.

When Cameron comes back to PPTH to run the ER, she's a different woman, and it's not just the new blond hair. She's engaged to Chase and she's happy working away from House. House berates her for taking an apparently less important job. "I can do good here," says Cameron. "Get it out of my system." In "Living the Dream," Cameron shows she's over House when he asks if she wants to come back and work for her again.

CAMERON: "I miss the job. I miss running around playing private investigator. I miss the puzzles."

HOUSE: "Seriously, I'll fire Thirteen. Or Kutner if you think Thirteen is hot."

CAMERON: "I don't miss you."

Cameron has matured enough that when Cuddy goes home to be with her baby, Cameron is the one she asks to stand in for her ("Painless"). A good proportion of Cuddy's job is corralling House (maybe half) and House immediately tries to manipulate her. Cameron quits: She's done playing games with House.

With Chase, Cameron has trouble committing. Chase complains that she kicks him out in the morning, he doesn't have a drawer for his stuff, and he's a visitor at her place. "I can't keep chasing you forever," Chase tells her ("The Itch"). Later, when she finds a ring ("Saviors"), Cameron at first doesn't want Chase to propose, thinking he's reacting to Kutner's death. Even when she changes her mind about marrying Chase, she wants him to give her some of his sperm in case they break up, an arrangement she had with her first

Cameron and Chase, married

husband ("Under My Skin"). Cameron tells Chase she has doubts, that it's naïve not to (Chase says he doesn't). In "Both Sides Now," House tells Cameron to destroy her husband's sperm and Cameron tells Chase that's what she's doing but Chase says it's okay, the doubts have been allayed.

Of course, Chase and Cameron's happiness is short-lived. After Dibala's death, Cameron knows there's something wrong. She thinks Chase is having an affair and has to know. "I love you no matter what," she says in "Known Unknowns." "Dibala," says Chase. "I killed him." Cameron can forgive Chase but he has killed her love as surely as Chase killed Dibala. When Chase decides to stay, Cameron has to leave. As she tells House, Cameron confirms House's original diagnosis of her feelings for him. "I was an idiot. Tried to be like you, tried to understand you, because I thought I could heal you."

CAMERON: "I loved you. And I loved Chase. I'm sorry for you both. For what you've become because there's no way back for either of you."

Cameron offers House her hand and he won't shake it, echoing what happened the first time she left PPTH. And again, she kisses him and leaves. House has precipitated the crisis in Chase and Cameron's marriage and engineered the re-formation of a team. Taub, Thirteen, and Chase have come back. As for Cameron, House tells Wilson, "She's broken up with Chase and she's leaving the hospital. Still, three out of four ain't bad."

Given a choice of which doctor to lose, it's doubtful House would choose Cameron. In the beginning, House wanted to know what Cameron's vulnerability was. In the end, if this is the end, he finds out that it's the same quality that gives Cameron her great strength.

QUESTION: "Cameron's look: vests, brighter colors . . ."

CATHY CRANDALL: "There was an arc for Cameron. They were all fellows and they didn't make so much money so we gave her much less expensive clothes. When she got the job in the ER we started to give her more expensive clothing because she was running the place."

QUESTION: "So the clothes got better?"

CRANDALL: "We did try to tell that story. The shapes of clothing didn't change. She still wore little puff-sleeved blouses and vests and pants."

Jennifer Morrison on . . . House

QUESTION: "What do you think Cameron sees in House?"

"Cameron is drawn to a project. She sees a glimmer of vulnerability and compassion in House's eyes despite his rough exterior. Against her better judgment, she will always find herself attracted to him."

QUESTION: "Cameron has left her job more than once. How hard is it for her to give it up?"

"When you become accustomed to being a part of curing the most rare conditions and saving the most unsavable lives, I think both the job and the man behind the job are bound to be seductive."

QUESTION: "I asked Hugh Laurie, Robert Sean Leonard, and Lisa Edelstein if they thought their characters will still be friends in twenty years' time. Will Cameron look up House if she's in the same town as him in 2030?"

"I don't think she would have to look House up if they were in the same town in 2030. I think he would look her up before she even knew he was in town. Despite the strong romantic attraction between them, there is also a paternal connection between them. It seems like his team members become his children in some metaphorical way. I think that bond and his insatiable curiosity would lead him to look her up."

Jennifer Morrison on . . . Cameron

QUESTION: "Does Cameron care too much for her own good?"

"Cameron finds a sense of identity in her quest to be a good person. David Shore and I spoke a lot about how Cameron has a history heavily impacted by loss . . . The real woman that David based Cameron on lost three siblings in a fire at a young age and then lost her husband to cancer within the first year of marriage. I have always considered all of this to be a part of Cameron's past."

QUESTION: "She shows a lot of toughness after Foreman denies that they are friends by not accepting his apology. She's never a pushover. Is it fun to play a complex character like that?"

"I have always appreciated that Cameron is not predictable. In real life, no one is completely predictable, either. We all do things that seem out of character or surprising at times. David Shore does a beautiful job of infusing all of the characters with this element of surprise. I greatly appreciate being able to play a woman on television that grows and changes and is filled with unexpected complexities. It is exciting and challenging, and it has made me a better actor."

QUESTION: "How much do you think Cameron changes over the course of the series?"

"Cameron comes from a compassionate and ethical background. As she spends more and more time around House, she learns when to bend the rules to help someone and when to stand up for the ethics in which she has always believed. Along with that, she grows accustomed to House's sarcasm and his rough way of relating to others and she grows thicker skin. In the end, she is better at seeing the big picture."

QUESTION: "[*House* medical adviser] Bobbin Bergstrom told me someone came up to you on the street and said, 'Are you the person who plays the nurse on *House*?' Do you remember that? What does it say about our perception of doctors?"

"I believe that nursing is one of the most selfless and noble jobs on earth, and I have the utmost respect for nurses. It is not about someone thinking I was playing a nurse; it is that some people really do assume that women are not doctors. I wear a lab coat, say the same medical words, and perform all of the same doctor-like procedures that Jesse Spencer does on the show, and sometimes people would come up to us when we were together and say to him, 'You're that doctor on *House*,' and say to me, 'Oh, and you play the nurse on that show.' It's like anything I guess; it takes time for people's perceptions to change. It really hasn't been that many years since the workplace began welcoming women as equals to men. Slowly but surely, we will get there."

QUESTION: "How easy or hard do you find the medical terminology?"

"The medical terminology was difficult. It never seemed to stop being difficult unless it was words that came up often."

QUESTION: "How did you hear about the part of Cameron?"

"I was just sent the material like any other pilot. It was called the 'Untitled Paul Attanasio/David Shore Project.' I never imagined I would even be considered. I was twenty-four at the time and the role was listed as thirty-two-year-old doctor. There was an episode where Cameron is working on her CV and it listed Cameron as graduating medical school the same year I graduated from junior high. I guess that is the magic of TV . . ."

QUESTION: "Now you have been immortalized as Captain Kirk's mom [in *Star Trek*]. How does that feel?"

"I don't think I can really comprehend it, but it is very cool. I just feel very blessed and lucky to have been involved with that film. The entire experience was beyond amazing."

QUESTION: "You made *Warrior*—was that a big change from *House*?"

"Yes, *Warrior* is a drastic change from *House*. I play the wife of a UFC fighter. I really enjoy the challenge of new things. I feel very lucky that I was able to fit films in my hiatus time every year. It gave me an opportunity to continue growing as an actor. I feel like the more work I did outside of *House*, the more I could give to Cameron and the show. *Warrior* and *Star Trek* both stretched me to find different parts of myself that I had never had to portray on screen before.

"And I had a totally new challenge, playing the role of Kate Keller in *The Miracle Worker* on Broadway. I've been dreaming of Broadway since I was about five years old. It is truly a dream come true."

QUESTION: "You are a fan favorite on the most-watched TV show in the world. Does that make you proud?"

"Being a fan favorite on the most-watched TV show in the world is such an unbelievable honor! I am constantly blown away by and humbled by the Cameron and Hameron [a House-Cameron hook-up] fans. I have had the most amazing job for six years because of those fans, and I will continue to have opportunities to keep doing what I love because of those fans. I am proud to be in that position, but mostly I am thankful and overwhelmed. The support that the fans have poured out for me, and my character, is a beautiful gift. It warms my heart and gives me hope that what I do brings joy to others. I wish I could personally hug and thank every fan."

EIGHT-DAY WEEKS

 **Making the Show, Part 1**

> **QUESTION:** "Delivering the episode to the network for broadcast, does it ever get down to the wire?"
>
> **GERRIT VAN DER MEER:** "Every show."

Katie Jacobs is standing in her office brandishing a yellow piece of letter-sized paper. It's a memo from FOX, the network that airs *House,* the show for which Jacobs is co-show runner and executive producer. Bigwigs at FOX have long since re-upped *House* for another season. Well before the season starts, they send the producers at *House* this memo which outlines the schedule for the forthcoming season.

"Everything is dictated by our air dates," says Jacobs. "'This is when we want you to be on the air.' The air dates are the boss. Sometimes you get a repeat but the dates don't move. You go from there. So you have to figure out something that's not just ready but that's great."

With unyielding regularity the *House* team has been ready, filling that network slot twenty-two to twenty-four times a season for six years (one writers' strike notwithstanding)—a total of 131 times. Being ready is hard but being great is harder. That responsibility collectively falls on the shoulders of upwards of 150 people who work, like Katie Jacobs, on the FOX lot in Century City in Los Angeles (there are more *House* people scattered in other locations around L.A.). *House* creator and show runner David Shore is here on the lot, as are producing director Greg Yaitanes and David Foster, who is the real doctor who works on the show. All the writers, producers, department heads—production design, makeup, visual effects, construction, set decoration, props, casting, publicity—the assistant directors, camera operators, focus pullers, editors, grips, craft services, production assistants (PAs), and interns populate a warren of offices and four vast soundstages. It's a measure of the show's success that *House* takes up more space on the lot than any other series.

Everyone's focus is on making those stone-set air dates. The network doesn't accept doctor's notes, even from *House*. Episodes are made one after another in a steady flow beginning when production picks up in the summer for the fall schedule. Viewed episode by episode, the series has a basic rhythm described in eight- or nine-day sections corresponding to the filming of one show. (Each day of filming on set follows its own jerky stop-go cadence. Long hours of prep are cut with intense periods of action from the morning crew call to the final wrap, which might be sixteen hours later.) First, from the longer perspective.

Shooting an episode of *House* generally takes eight days. There's often a day of overlap at the end when one unit finishes up an episode and another starts filming the next one the same day. Occasionally a ninth day is required on a tricky shoot but if every episode went nine days the math wouldn't work and the production would run out of shooting days at the end of the season. While one episode is shooting (the "A" episode); the next is being prepped (episode "B"). Some of the crew works on one episode start to finish as it goes from B to A to the director's cut, the film that is sent for editing. For a time, producing director Greg Yaitanes was behind the camera on every other episode. One assistant director preps while the other films; the prop masters rotate in the same way.

Other staffers operate on a different personal schedule. According to the regulations laid down by their guild, a director gets fifteen days to work on an episode. When they're not shooting, they are prepping with an assistant director. *House* has three editors who each take primary responsibility for eight episodes in a full twenty-four-episode season. Longer-term projects don't fit into the eight/nine day cycle. A new set, like the apartment that House and Wilson moved into in season six, takes longer to design and build, though not as long as you might imagine.

Nothing can happen without a script. It's more accurate to say almost nothing, because it's not always the case that the script comes first—casting and set design and construction might have to begin before the writers have fleshed out the parts being cast or written action for the set being built. The writer might be working alone on her script for two months before intense rounds of edits and revisions begin. Earlier even than this, the writing team and key producers will have mapped out story arcs running up to half a season ahead. The script returns to David Shore for polish before it is distributed to department heads. Usually the first inkling anyone gets of what they have to prepare for the next episode is when they receive the script. They'll get the B script on the first day of filming the A, meaning they have about a week to get ready before filming starts over again.

Department heads like costume designer Cathy Crandall and the prop masters Tyler Patton and Mike Casey break down the initial script to identify what they're going to have to provide for that episode. In Cathy's case, each new character will have to be given a look and found the appropriate number of outfits depending on the number of scripted days they have in an episode. Anything that an actor holds on-screen is a prop so Tyler and Mike figure out what they're going to have to pull together. Often a script won't include a lot of descriptive details of characters or locations.

The director holds a concept meeting with department heads where whatever is penciled in between the lines of the script can be more fully described according to the director's vision of how the action is going to unfold. Meanwhile, the script can still be amended. Various drafts—a director's draft, a limited draft, a production draft–follow until the final production version is ready. The production draft usually includes feedback from the concept meeting and a final production meeting cements the departmental assignments just before shooting starts.

Publicity manager Geoffrey Colo supervises the clearance process. The script goes out to a clearance company that generates a report marking red flags: names that might represent a conflict or permissions that are needed. A copy of the report goes to the lawyer at Universal and broadcast standards at the network. Broadcast standards may ask for something to be toned down: "Make sure there's no nudity in the porn scene"; "instead of this say that." "There is a recurring phrase in the report," says Gerrit van der Meer. "'Please do this in your usual tasteful manner.'" The legal department may ask for a name to be changed. There are laws protecting public figures in fictional shows. You can mention public figures as long as it's not derogatory or misrepresenting. There's also a pharmacology adviser who says the drugs are okay to use.

Occasionally, something written in the script seems unlikely to survive the standards review. In "Autopsy," a nine-year-old girl asks Chase to kiss her because she thinks she's dying and this may be her only chance. "I read that script and thought okay, show's over," says Marcy Kaplan. "David Shore really pushes the envelope and he's spot-on."

It's the same process for the other departments. After breaking down the script, special effects makeup head Dalia Dokter will know if she'll need any prosthetics and which lab she's going to outsource to. Tyler Patton and Mike Casey attend a separate prop meeting a couple of days after the concept meeting with key colleagues: medical advisers, set dressing, video playback, visual effects. After that meeting Tyler and Mike have their marching orders. If the script calls for "a bag," they'll know what kind of bag and what color. If the script says, "sandwich," they'll know if an actor is going to take a real bite and if they have any dietary restrictions. If someone picks up a defibrillator, the prop masters will be ready with one that works if that's what's required.

By the time shooting starts, the script has been broken up. The order the scenes are being shot in is laid out in a shooting schedule that includes summaries of which departments are needed that particular day. One-liners, brief descriptions of the scenes, are also available so everyone knows what is happening on which day before they get the call sheet that finely details how the day is going to proceed, minute by minute and line by line. Tyler and Mike have a board in their office where they make lists of what they need day by day. The principals' personal items don't make it on the list. Stuff like reading glasses, sunglasses, watches, cell phones, House's canes—they're readily available all the time.

"We keep notes: Robert Sean Leonard is left-handed, which is a good thing to remember. Large exam gloves—size-eight surgical gloves—and he wears his own watch. If he forgets it we have a close match."

—TYLER PATTON

House has two first assistant directors. When Robert Scott is working on the set running the shoot, Kevin Williams is prepping the next episode. When the episode is done, they will switch off. Kevin works closely with his director, in the case of the episode he is prepping right now, Lesli Glatter. She drops by Kevin's office to say she's finished casting for the day and reports they've found someone for a key role in their episode, younger perhaps than they'd anticipated but a great fit. Kevin says the location department has found some houses for them to look at tomorrow.

To create the shooting schedule, Kevin deconstructs the script into scene-sized chunks and puts it back together in the best shooting order he can devise at a rate of about six pages of script per shooting day. It's a very sophisticated jigsaw puzzle. Utilizing a computer program made by Entertainment Partners, called Movie Magic, Kevin adds information for each scene: which principals

The two first assistant directors: Kevin Williams (left) and Robert Scott

are involved, whether background actors are needed, which cameras on what set together with special effects, wardrobe, makeup, prop requirements—in short, everything.

Kevin outlines some of the criteria he needs to balance when deciding the shooting order. If there is a daytime exterior scene it makes sense to schedule that earlier in the week. Crew call times (the times they have to be on the set), which are dictated by union-regulated rest periods, tend to get later as the week goes on. If you shot a nighttime exterior at the beginning of the week, call times would be impossibly late. If sets have to be built, the scenes affected may be moved to the end of the week to allow more time for construction. It saves time if the crew doesn't have to move all the equipment from hospital room to hospital room after each scene, a lot of time if it avoids switching stages. But bunching scenes out of sequence because they're shot near each other might not please actors who'd rather shoot scenes in script order to assist their preparation. While choreographing the week, the assistant director (AD) has to try to keep everyone happy.

"I have the best job in show business," says Kevin Williams.

Kevin Williams has painted sets and moved furniture in his time and he worked ten years in Miami before moving to L.A. When *Miami Vice* came to town he worked as an extra and a stand-in for Philip Michael Thomas and doing PA work, all the while showing round his résumé. By the fourth season he was a PA for the show and worked enough days (six hundred) to qualify for the Directors Guild so he could work as the second second AD. After Miami, Kevin worked all over the country and got his taste of L.A. as a second AD on the *X-Files* ("a three-ring circus") and *Seven Days* on the UPN before Gerrit van der Meer hired him for *Gideon's Crossing*. He was working on *Crossing Jordan* when Gerrit called him again. *House* was a hit show—"How could I refuse?" said Kevin.

In this process, everything is geared toward giving the director the best possible conditions for him to realize his vision of every scene in the script. The director will figure out how much "coverage" he needs, which dictates how many times the scene will need to be shot with the camera (or cameras) trained on a different actor or actors each time. A light, funny scene might need only two shots. Intense, pivotal scenes require a lot of coverage. Perhaps they can be bookended with quieter scenes to allow enough time for the bigger part of the story. Action shots bring their own dynamic, with stunt coordinators on set supervising the fight. Directors have their preferences. "Some directors are comfortable with packing a lot of heavy material all in one day; a lot would rather have one big bang per day," says Kevin.

The more an AD works with a director, the better he knows his style. The longer a director has worked with a particular cast and crew, the more comfortable in turn he will be. He might be able to send less "coverage" to the editing department (that is, fewer takes) because he will be more confident he has it with what he has shot. That decision will be made in the planning stage when the director looks at the scene and says, "I want this shot and this shot," and so on. After working with a director a number of times, Kevin Williams can predict how they'll say they are going to cover the scene to get what they need on film.

As the number and type of shots are being worked out, Kevin must liaise with the crew to make sure what the director wants is feasible and whether they're going to need particular equipment on a particular day. For a walk-and-talk (when the camera, facing backward, follows characters talking while walking along, down a corridor, say), the director might want to use a Steadicam, a counterbalanced camera rig that allows for smooth shooting even if the operator is walking backward. The AD would let the camera people know to rent a Steadicam that day and that the operator needs to be ready for the rehearsal. The *House* Steadicam operator Rob Carlson is the B camera operator. A cameraman is paid more to operate the Steadicam. Once he's bumped up to the higher rate, he's on that rate the full day, so it's an expense that needs to be taken into consideration.

Kevin is careful to maintain good relations with the writers. If he can get a heads-up on something unusual they might be cooking up he can possibly get an invaluable head start. For example, if there's a minor in the cast, especially if the patient of the week is a kid in peril, special provision has to be made. Kids can only work a certain number of hours a day and need a teacher or welfare worker on set. Regulations for babies are more protective still; they can only work twenty minutes of two two-hour periods a day. If the baby is being shown asleep, a doll might be used or an animatronic baby might work if she only has to move an arm or blink. But that requires two puppeteers to manipulate the model off-camera, which might be more trouble than it's worth. Animals are even more difficult. It takes years to train dogs to do what you want them to do and he only has eight days, says Kevin from bitter personal experience.

Setting up a Steadicam shot. Director
Greg Yaitanes is in the foreground;
director of photography Gale Tattersall
is at right.

The biggest scheduling wild card is the teaser, the piece that opens the episode setting up that week's medical mystery. They're often filmed in locations away from Princeton-Plainsboro (that is, away from the FOX lot). The quality is very high: the rooftop police chase at the beginning of "Brave Heart" is every bit as good as any similar movie scene. Writers will try to keep departments informed if they're planning an especially ambitious teaser. Some ideas simply aren't feasible. There might not be time within the schedule to pull it off or it the setup is too expensive.

The ranking producers on scheduling and money issues are unit production manager Gerrit van der Meer and producer Marcy Kaplan. Gerrit and Marcy do everything they can to make it happen, whether it's building an Antarctic research station on set, rolling over a city bus in Princeton or a Humvee in the Middle East, crashing a crane in Trenton, or creating an African refugee camp—but to do it on budget. Gerrit must decide when it becomes counterproductive to tire everyone out and add an extra day's shooting. Then you might run into problems of actor availability. Scheduling double-up days with two camera units is tough because you have to make sure actors aren't being asked to be on two different stages at the same time. Sometimes ideas have to change. In "Wilson," in season six, Wilson was originally going to go sailing with his friend Tucker but the scene ended up as a much cheaper turkey hunt in the woods.

"David Foster came in and said, 'I'm changing it from sailing to hunting. Are there any elements in it that are problematic for you guys?' And we say, 'No, we love hunting. That's better than sailing.'"

—MIKE CASEY

The series as a whole has two budgets: the "amort" budget (amortized budget) and the "pattern" budget. The amort budget is capital costs that aren't episode-specific, such as the major construction projects that happen between seasons. The pattern budget is what is planned for each specific episode and the amort budget divided by the number of episodes shows up here as a line item. Gerrit and Marcy are very aware that if something planned for episode three is going to cost a couple hundred thousand dollars more than was budgeted, then episode eighteen, now just a gleam in David Shore's eye, better be more straightforward. So get it done, but watch the bottom line. "My goal," says Marcy, referring to the series budget, "is to come in within a dime."

House is made by NBC/Universal. Until December 2009, the show was subject to the financial regulations of NBC's then-parent company, GE, one of the biggest corporations in America. The show is periodically audited and everything the show has created or purchased—anything they've spent money on—is theoretically an asset that might need to be produced for an auditor. At the end of every season the accounting department generates a list of assets for every other department, stuff that all has to be tracked down. This means that no one ever throws anything away. (Within reason—sets are usually too large to break down and store.) The show also has to be ready to do an insert—reshoot a scene if a problem crops up in postproduction (after filming), and also to pick up seamlessly if an old character returns or the writers start revisiting the past, but still, the majority of single-use items are kept anyway.

Tyler Patton and Mike Casey store every prop they've ever used, most of it in towering mountains of clear plastic boxes at the back of one of the stages. Amid the plastic bodies and fax machines and fake porn movies is a box labeled "Vintage Douche" and "Clear Plastic Frogs." In the first season House threw a frog at someone and the prop guys found a selection of frogs to choose from (there's never just one of any prop). They keep it just in case. "We get audited and they come with a random list of things," says Mike. " 'Where's the vintage douche?' 'Where's the two-thousand-dollar frog?' " Television was different from other GE businesses.

"We're not spending like drunken sailors," says James Wallace, a PA. One of the jobs of the production office is to keep an eye on what everything costs. The office maintains the lists of departmental assets and copies of all purchase orders generated by the show. If you want to know how much was spent catering a shoot three years ago, ask the production office. They spend money, too. Production coordinator Meg Schave is looking into implementing a new NBC policy phasing out the use of Styrofoam plates and cups to save landfill space, which means asking vendors for biodegradable cutlery. From a potato-based fork to a multimillion-dollar construction project, there is a great deal that needs to be corralled. "It is a very big thing to make a TV show," says Elisabeth James Rhee, production supervisor. "It's huge. There's a lot that goes into it, all the different departments. We do try to find ways to be cost-effective."

QUESTION: "You guys have to be able to answer any conceivable request?"

JAMES WALLACE: "On 'House's Head' there's a scene where Cuddy is doing a striptease in front of House and they had to bring a girl [to rehearse]. We had to facilitate an ideal environment for her so we went out and bought a stripper pole, one that can extend. It came with a nice DVD illustrating how to use the pole."

ELISABETH JAMES RHEE: "The grips installed the stripper pole in one of our patient rooms so that rehearsals could take place—Lisa had to practice and there was another stripper in the episode.

". . . [After shooting] the grips called and said, 'Do you want us to leave the stripper pole in the patient room or are we done with it?' "

MEG SCHAVE: "And what do you do with it because it's an asset and you have to keep it somewhere?"

QUESTION: "Where is it now?"

MEG: "It's in the back room."

Production assistant Dan Horstman describes the production office as the nerve center of the show. They keep records of everything: all the call sheets and versions of scripts and shooting schedules, what film stock was used for what scenes, and how much was left over after a shoot. They make sure pertinent information reaches the departments; that memos about meetings go out and that there's food and drink available at the meeting; that everyone who needs a script gets one when they need it and the same with call sheets and location information. It's obviously vital that everyone who is needed on a location shoot knows where they have to be. They also have to have everything they need to facilitate shooting when they get there.

One of Elisabeth James Rhee's jobs is to arrange travel for an actor from out of town. Actors are hers until they touch down, at which point they become the responsibility of the second AD who makes their schedule. If there's bad weather on the East Coast on Sunday and Hugh Laurie needs to get to L.A. from New York to shoot Monday, Elisabeth needs to find a solution (when this happened, she had him driven to Philadelphia to fly back from there).

As if his character, Detective Tritter, hadn't suffered enough indignities, David Morse was stuck on a plane that didn't take off for hours on a trip west booked at the last minute. He needed a script and Elisabeth complicatedly arranged to get one to him on a scheduled stop in Salt Lake City, which involved a special delivery of a package to an en-route passenger (for security reasons, scripts can't be e-mailed). But Morse never made it to Utah and was rerouted through Cincinnati, where he stayed the night. He flew in the next morning, exhausted and a little beat-up.

For today's location, Elisabeth hired a generator operator for the day and made sure they knew where they had to be. How did she know they needed a generator operator? On a technical visit to the scripted location found by the location scout, the set lighting department figured out how much lighting they needed and that the power they were going to need wasn't available on site. The transportation department, which has workers who are in the right job category to operate generators, didn't have anyone available, meaning Elisabeth needed an outside contractor. In ways like this do lines on a script become lines on a shooting schedule become actual job assignments.

"They said, 'We're going to reshoot scene twenty-one-A from episode four.' It's on the one-liner schedule and I say, 'Gosh, I don't remember that scene,' so I look at the schedule and I look at the breakdown and there isn't a twenty-one-A. Which will happen because new pages of script come out after we're shooting. So I say, 'Okay, I'll look at the page.' There are different colors representing every stage of script changes but there's still no 21A. I go to the production office and say, 'We're doing scene twenty-one-A from episode four and I can't find it.' Everyone looks and they can't find it, either. So I say, 'Let's call the writers,' so they call the writers and they say, 'Oh, yeah, we haven't written that yet.'"

—MIKE CASEY

If someone is confronted with a curveball they can't hit, they'll bring it to the production office. Says PA Lee Perez Gonzalez, "Anyone has a problem they come to us, any department. Even if we can't fix it they come to us." "If they can't use their printer," says Meg Schave, "if they don't have any coffee, if they need a banana." Adds Dan Horstman, "Those are all real-world examples."

More intractable production problems will reach Gerrit van der Meer and Marcy Kaplan. Which is just how they want it. Because their task is to look at the big picture, they want to know what the issue is even if someone is going about the job of fixing it. Gerrit and Marcy know what the knock-on effects of one department's problem is going to be on everyone else. "And give me the opportunity to let me help," says Marcy. "If I don't know, you've made that decision for me."

"They say I didn't want to tell you because it would have cost money," says Marcy. "Well, it would have cost a thousand dollars yesterday and now it's going to cost twenty thousand dollars."

The episode you just watched Monday night, one of the slots on Katie Jacob's yellow piece of paper, probably filmed six to eight weeks ago. The entire process is a great example of the law that states that the task expands to fit the time available. Like Tyler and Mike, Gerrit and Marcy have schedules pinned to the wall marking production landmarks. In their case, blue dots represent script delivery; green dots are when the director starts; shooting dates are in red and everything in yellow is postproduction. Sixteen days are allocated to edit the episode and ten days for the sound mix, the layback (adding the audio to the video), and color correction. The producers have to see it, the studio has to see it, the network has to see it. Many of these dates are arbitrary, Gerrit admits. "It usually takes much longer."

The editors of *House* are Amy Fleming, Dorian Harris, and Chris Brookshire. They start working on their episode as soon as they see it in the form of "dailies" of the previous day's filming. The look and sound of the show that is crafted in postproduction is part of another chapter. In the big scheme of things, they are working at the end of the schedule. While the air date is rigid, the overall schedule has some give in it here and there, but not much in postproduction. "They start shooting in June [and] we are running with them and the goal is to never have them get so far ahead of us that we are constantly trying to catch up," says Chris Brookshire. "The schedule will sometimes get compressed and we are the last battalion that takes care of the show so we have to work faster toward the end of the year."

When the picture element of the show is locked, the music added and the sound mixed, the show is delivered from the postproduction office to the network in the form of a high-definition tape. The network then transmits it to the stations around the country. When FOX moved *House* from Tuesday to Monday it meant the show had to be delivered on the Friday rather than the Monday. When it gets pretty close to the wire, as happens on occasion, that change can be significant.

Once the last episode of the season has been delivered, most of *House* goes on hiatus. There is a two-week break around the holidays as well. Long seasons have meant very short gaps in between and some departments are always working—a hiatus is a perfect time to design and build sets when there's no filming taking place, for example. The production office remains open, boxing up material from the last season, preparing for the next. It's important that records are meticulously kept. Meg Schave used to work on *Everybody Loves Raymond*. At the end of shooting the last season the show was over and the production office closed. The following year, the show was nominated for a number of Emmys and there was no one in the office to make the calls. "So if they needed something you have to go back to the files, to look up who was the photographer on that day . . . If you don't have clear records then it's impossible to find that information," says Meg. "You never know when they'll need to find that frog."

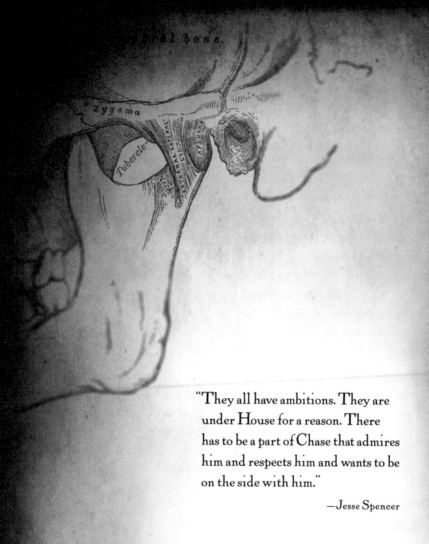

"They all have ambitions. They are under House for a reason. There has to be a part of Chase that admires him and respects him and wants to be on the side with him."

—Jesse Spencer

CHASE

Jesse Spencer

While House saw something in Foreman and Cameron, he hired Robert Chase because Chase's father, a prominent doctor, made a phone call on his son's behalf. Early-season Chase is eager to please his boss, whose qualities he admires. "I like the guy," Chase says. "He says what he wants. Does what he wants" ("Sports Medicine"). If Chase is pleased to get the opportunity to work for House, he doesn't show any gratitude when his father, Rowan, turns up at Princeton-Plainsboro ("Cursed"). Chase tries as hard to avoid his dad as House does when his parents visit. Chase tells House his father abandoned his alcoholic mother and him years ago, when Chase was fifteen. But he doesn't hate his dad.

> "I loved him until I figured out that it hurts a lot less to just not care. You don't expect him to turn up to your football match, no disappointments. You don't expect a call on your birthday, don't expect to see him for months, no disappointments. You want us to go make up—sink a few beers together, nice family hug? I've given him enough hugs. He's given me enough disappointments."
>
> —CHASE

House deduces Rowan is visiting to see Wilson because he has cancer. Chase and his father share an awkward moment together and the father says he'll see Chase next time he's through. But the father knows there won't be a next time. In "The Mistake," Chase learns his dad has died and, preoccupied, he botches a routine patient interview. The patient dies and Chase tries to punish himself by exaggerating the scale of his negligence. But House won't let Chase be a martyr and he stays on the team with a reprimand.

> QUESTION: "Chase seems to have a bead on what House is thinking. Foreman is often horrified; Cameron, too. Everyone a lot more than you."

JESSE SPENCER: "I made that a bit of a choice myself. A lot of the time the Chase character wasn't fully explained so I made the conscious decision that if nothing was written, I would like to be the guy that maybe agrees with House. We're all working for him for a reason. . . . Parts of us go along with what he wants. At the end of the day, all these characters are not so self-sacrificing."

With the death of his father, Chase is more independent. Part of this is necessity. He takes a second job in the neonatal intensive care unit because his father had cut him out of his will—Chase is not a rich kid anymore ("Forever")—gone are the days when Chase can go snowboarding in ritzy Gstaad as he did in season one ("Control"). When Vogler is looking for someone to rat on House, Chase obliges, but later, he won't do the same for Tritter ("Finding Judas"). Detective Tritter, who knows the history with Vogler, makes it look as though Chase has turned by leaving only his bank account unfrozen but he remains loyal, even if House thinks Chase has sold him out again and punches him. Chase stood up to House, too, refusing to write him a prescription for Vicodin. He is left with a reputation—in "Family," House calls him "a sneaky bastard."

"I've always thought there was something similar about the characters [of Chase and Thirteen]. Chase has at least since season four this kind of stubborn, very independent, for lack of a better term, an 'oh screw it' attitude toward House and there's something that Thirteen would really respect about that."

—OLIVIA WILDE

There's obviously deep conflict in Chase—he has a very human side, too. In "Autopsy" he obliges the nine-year-old cancer patient by kissing her—she thinks this might be her only chance to be kissed.

Chase was clearly romantically interested in Allison Cameron from the beginning. He asks her out in episode three, "Occam's Razor," but Cameron cuts him off before he can finish his sentence. It's a no. In "Hunting," Cameron jumps Chase when she's high ("don't turn into a good guy on me now," she says.) Later, in "Insensitive," Cameron suggests to Chase they make an arrangement to have sex: they're busy, it's convenient. And she's not likely to fall in love with him. Chase is happy to go along even if he thinks, as he tells Foreman, that Cameron is only sleeping with him to make House jealous ("Fetal Position"). But Chase tells Cameron he wants more from the relationship and as soon as she does (in "Airborne"), she breaks it off.

Chase is persistent. He buys flowers and every Tuesday, he reminds Cameron he has feelings for her. In time, Cameron realizes she does reciprocate those feelings. (Much later, in "Private Lives," Chase is worried that Cameron was only taken with his looks all along. Chase goes speed dating with House and Wilson and predictably racks up handfuls of contacts despite his best Forrest Gump impression. Are people really that shallow? In the face of the evidence, Thirteen assures Chase that Cameron's feelings were genuine.) As House is taken away to the hospital at the end of season five, Cameron has gotten over her considerable doubts and she marries Chase.

QUESTION: "I was surprised you got married."

JESSE SPENCER: "Yeah, so were we. But then it provides a good contrast to House losing his mind and going into the hospital."

QUESTION: "It also means you have further to fall."

SPENCER: "Right."

Perhaps self-sufficient Chase will be able to get along without House. At the end of season three, House fires Chase. "Because you've been here the longest, you've learned all you can or you haven't learned anything at all. Either way, it's time for a change" ("Human Error"). All Chase says is "Fine." "Getting this job was the best thing that ever happened to me," he says. "Everything about it. And losing it? Well, I think it's gonna be good, too." When House is looking for replacements for his first team, House thinks Chase has found a job at a branch of the Mayo Clinic in Arizona and is with Cameron. But Chase, trained as a cardiologist and an "intensivist," is back to PPTH and working as a surgeon, apparently contentedly, until Foreman asks him and Cameron to come back and help him after he fires Thirteen and Taub quits in season six during the time when House has no license.

> "I don't think Chase is particularly naïve about House. He is more naïve about himself."
>
> —DAVID SHORE

But Chase can't get away from House. Cameron believes House created the environment that enabled Chase to (depending on your viewpoint) cause to die/kill/murder the tyrant Dibala before he could go back to his country and unleash a genocide on hundreds of thousands of his people ("The Tyrant"). Ultimately, Chase is not like House, and Dibala's death proves that. "I've crossed some line," he tells his co-conspirator Foreman. "I'm having trouble getting back to the other side" ("Instant Karma"). Foreman has already asked Chase, "You really think you can kill another human being without any consequences to yourself?" And Chase knows he can't. In "Damned if You Do," Chase says he left seminary school when he lost his faith. After Dibala, he turns back to the church for help and goes to confession but the priest won't absolve Chase unless he turns himself in. "I killed a man," Chase says to the priest. "But it was the right thing to do" ("Brave Heart"). As his marriage is disintegrating in front of him, Chase tells Cameron that even if it destroyed him, he'd kill Dibala all over again.

> "Even when you lose your faith there is an awareness of spirituality and that has an impact on his life. I go to confession . . . it's always lingering. Nothing is ever black and white . . . it's all gray areas. That's what I like to see when I watch the show—those things raised and not necessarily answered but showing the impact that it has on the characters."
>
> —JESSE SPENCER

After stewing on it, Chase admits to his wife that he switched Dibala's test results so the dictator would be given the wrong treatment and die. Initially Chase agrees to leave Princeton-Plainsboro with Cameron to make a new start. House thinks Chase and Cameron's marriage won't survive Dibala and he hastens its demise by planting the idea in Chase's head that Cameron doesn't hold him responsible. It works. When Chase realizes Cameron blames House more than she does him, Chase decides he has to assert ownership over his decision to kill Dibala. As House predicts, and according to his plan, Chase wants to come back to work for House to prove he is not a puppet, to show he is his own man. Cameron believes Chase's decision proves the reverse.

> "This is what House is saying to Chase and Cameron—this will come out and it might as well come out now and not later."
>
> —DAVID SHORE

Did House turn Chase into a murderer? Cameron certainly thinks so and she tells House, as she leaves the hospital and her husband, "You ruined him so he can't even see right from wrong. Can't even see the sanctity of a human life anymore" ("Teamwork"). When Cameron returns to PPTH to get Chase to sign their divorce papers ("Lockdown"), Chase is fixated on the idea that Cameron never loved him. At first, she says she doesn't know if she did—but that isn't true. Cameron lays the blame on herself, saying it was she who's screwed up—first, marrying a dying man and then pushing Chase out of her life. The parting is amicable to say the least: Cameron says she'll miss having Chase hold her in a dance, so he plays Elvis Costello's "Alison" for her and they dance, kiss, and make love. Chase seems to feel vindicated: The break-up wasn't his fault. So House won.

Perhaps Chase would have been well served remembering something he said of House to Foreman way back in episode three. "He thinks outside the box," he says. "Is that so evil?"

KATIE JACOBS: "Chase was written as an American character. An older guy than Jesse. I heard him read and I liked his natural essence and I don't want him to work against that."

CATHY CRANDALL (COSTUME DESIGNER): "He's a little preppy. Australian but he has East Coast sensibility in his preppy. He's more *Esquire*— Foreman more *GQ*. I want him always to look young like he doesn't really care but he knows he's handsome. He knows he can look good. I want to keep him hip and young always."

Jesse Spencer on . . . the Philosophy

QUESTION: "The philosophy of the show can be dark. How does it fit with your own viewpoint?"

"The show is different from a lot of TV. It's part of the show's success, staying true to the show's core values. Sometimes it can be quite cynical and it's definitely not an idealistic point of view. I like it. It makes the moments of hope or surprise when House is proved wrong, or something happens where he has to rethink his view of the world, it makes those moments stand out even more. It's the contrast. We do give that lighter side of House a moment to shine."

QUESTION: "It can be funny."

"There is humor within the darkness. Even the darkness, House will turn it into a joke or mock the way that humans react to certain situations. It has to be done with humor; otherwise it would just be too depressing."

Jesse Spencer on . . . House

QUESTION: "There is no filter with House."

"We wish we could be like that. He doesn't live by the same rules and conventions."

QUESTION: "When he says 'everybody lies' . . ."

". . . there has been a lot of lying."

QUESTION: "You get to punch out Dr. House [in 'Ignorance Is Bliss']. How long have you wanted to do that?"

"It wraps up nicely because he's punched me before ["Finding Judas"]. He was detoxing and I run and try to stop an operation. I realize it's erythropoietic protoporphyria—I won't forget that one—and he turns around and smacks me on the nose. It's nice I end up smacking him.

I think it's surprising because the audience thinks, Why doesn't anyone stand up to him? They think it's never going to happen."

QUESTION: "You tell him, 'I just want people to leave me alone.'"

"There are contrasting roads in dealing with a situation. Do you take the American way and sit down and talk about it in psychotherapy or do you just get on with your life?"

QUESTION: "Is that an Aussie way of doing things, just put your head down?"

"Yeah totally. It fits in with the Australian viewpoint. Americans love psychotherapy."

Jesse Spencer on . . . Jesse Spencer

QUESTION: "In one episode you're accused of being English and Foreman says, 'You have the queen on the money; you're English.' Were you offended by that?"

"No. They always make me English because they don't know. That English stuff does offend some Australians. It's like calling English Americans. English sometimes get called Australians over here. I get English myself. Chase was originally American but . . . then we thought, Why not make him Australian? We thought that was a more interesting choice."

QUESTION: "You paid your own way to come to L.A.?"

"Yes. I nearly didn't audition for the role. [Chase] was a thirty-seven-year-old American guy and I was twenty-four and I didn't think they would change it but in America, they do. Just go in and audition and if they like you, they will change it. The writing was different from anything I had seen."

QUESTION: "You have medical professionals in your family."

"My dad is a GP. My oldest brother is an ophthalmologist, the second oldest is an orthopedic surgeon, then there is me, then my younger sister who is slightly House-ish in the way that she is supersmart and can't deal with patients. She's going to be an anesthesiologist. And I play a doctor on TV. It's not that weird [I play a doctor] because in the States, if you work in film, at some point you are going to play a doctor or a cop or both. It's going to happen."

QUESTION: "Did you have any thoughts about doing that yourself?"

"I got into university but I never went. I had intentions of doing medicine but I didn't really want to. I decided I would be doing it because it's what my family did. I knew what the life looked like."

QUESTION: "Music is important to you."

"I have a violin [on the set] and a practice amp. Violin, guitar, a bit of piano. I play with Hugh in this charity band [Band from TV]. This is outside stuff, nothing to do with acting. We play casinos, we played Atlantis in the Bahamas. They pay us and we give it to charity."

QUESTION: "You're pretty good?"

"Yes and no. To someone who can't play, I'm good. To someone who can play, I'm terrible.

"I stopped playing for eight years when I was in the U.K. I was trying to get a career going and focused on acting. I should have kept it up but I didn't. Trying to get it back is tough. I've been playing again about two years. Your fingers move much slower than they used to."

Jesse Spencer on . . . Chase

QUESTION: "Chase has done some ruthless things—feeding Vogler information . . ."

"That's right; He's a snitch."

QUESTION: "How do you justify that behavior?"

"He knows he's going to get away with it."

QUESTION: "Do you think House respects Chase?"

"He would never say face-to-face but you know he has this team around because they are good at their job. Though he has tried to fire me a few times."

QUESTION: "That was very powerful stuff with your dad . . ."

"It was sad to watch. Relationships are never perfect and they create great intrigues out of things that people don't know."

QUESTION: "Chase would not back down . . ."

"No. It was pretty full-on."

QUESTION: "It comes up that you were at seminary. Is it a diversion to make you think of Chase as a choirboy?"

"We investigate the similarities between science and religion. What is faith? What does faith mean? Are people blinded by faith or are their eyes opened by faith?"

QUESTION: "Is Chase on House's side on this question?"

"This kid did have faith and he lost it somewhere along the way and decided that science was better suited for how he was perceiving the world around him."

QUESTION: "With Dibala, you made a decision."

"Is it better to get rid of someone who is going to commit genocide? Is that okay? Is that the right thing to do? It's murder but not directly. It was kind of ambiguous. We weren't one hundred percent sure what he had. There was still a guess in there. I'm guessing that I'm killing him. It's a fudging which leads to his death. Then you have to live with it even if you think it is the right thing."

QUESTION: "But you have taken an oath . . ."

"Right, I have broken the Hippocratic oath to do no harm. Even though Chase believes he did the right thing, guilt that you have deliberately taken someone's life is something you can't get away from. And you will never get away from."

QUESTION: "Which is why Cameron left you."

"The marriage is already on the rocks because she knows something's wrong and she ends up blaming House instead of blaming me. That is the ultimate insult, saying it was House that did it and not Chase when Chase believes he made the decision on his own. He hasn't been infected by any House virus that made him do this. House doesn't do that stuff—House is about solving the case. He doesn't really care if Dibala lives or dies. He wants to solve puzzles. She leaves because she believes he is polluted by House."

QUESTION: "You had just got married."

"You knew it was coming. You thought, Well, how long is this going to last? No one gets happily married and rides off into the sunset. He realizes he can't run away from whatever is going to happen. So he decided not to run away. He has to be on the team. He has to be as close to his enemy and that hospital as he can. He has to stay."

QUESTION: "Do you enjoy the roller coaster?"

"Yeah, it's great. I hope we do a good job because it's such good writing and we have to make it work and make it believable."

QUESTION: "You can remember the medical terms?"

"I remember the first. Progressive multifocal leukoencephalopathy. And they cut it from the pilot."

4

FOURTEEN-HOUR DAYS

 **Making the Show, Part II**

> "I love the collaborative nature of TV, the sense of
> teamwork. There's a great scene in *Apollo 13* where
> Ed Harris dumps all this stuff on the table. 'This is
> what they have to get them down.' I feel like that
> with the episode of TV. We have seven days to
> prep it, eight days to execute it, and we've got this
> script, these actors, this director. How do we do it?
> How do we do it best? How do we do it together?
> And we pull it off."
>
> **—GREG YAITANES, DIRECTOR**

The call time of a shooting day on the *House* set is determined by
union-mandated turnaround times from the end of one day's
filming to the start of the next. The minimum is for camera union
members who get eleven hours, so if shooting has wrapped at 7:30
P.M., there can be a crew call at 6:30 A.M. the next morning. Actors
get twelve hours off during the week and have a fifty-four-hour
minimum turnaround at the weekend. Whatever time shooting
starts, the decision to call it quits at the end of each day, ten,
twelve, fourteen hours later, belongs to the director. For part of
season six half the time that director was Greg Yaitanes.

Greg Yaitanes has two full-time jobs—as the directing producer
he directed every other episode from "Simple Explanation" through

Director Greg Yaitanes (left) with first AD Robert Scott

"Ignorance Is Bliss" and he fit his producing responsibilities in editing and pre- and post-production around that. Yaitanes likes to keep in touch with the show's fan base via Twitter. He's been a fan since the service started—he's friends with one of the founders—and he likes the instantaneous feedback. He's encouraged his colleagues to join in so *House* has a major presence in the Twitter community. Yaitanes tweets on his iPhone between shot setups on the set. He's always in motion; every minute he's not directing, he's producing. "The constant sense of multitasking keeps my mind sharp," he says. "It's like doing a hundred crossword puzzles." Yaitanes works from 4:00 or 5:00 A.M. for sixteen, seventeen, eighteen hours a day, gets back home, and crashes hard. Weekends he spends as much time with his wife and young family as he can.

Consistently late crew calls caused by long shoots keep other people away from their families. Even though he works fourteen-plus-hour days, Yaitanes has made changes to try to ensure not everyone else has to. He wants to make best use of the time that the "first team" of actors, especially Hugh Laurie who is in almost every scene, spends on set. Yaitanes sets the pace of the shoot and he's known for working very quickly.

Production designer Jeremy Cassells, construction coordinator Stephen Howard, and Yaitanes got together to motorize walls on heavily trafficked sets so they move up and down, allowing the crews to get in and out of a set more quickly. "He moves pretty fast," says Jeremy Cassells of Yaitanes, "and isn't one to wait." The wall between House's outer and inner office moves, as does the wall behind the coffee maker in the outer office. They are built with a track in each side of the wall and a carriage system, precisely made to within a sixteenth of an inch, according to Steve Howard.

From his position at the heart of the action, Yaitanes feels uniquely well attuned to the needs of the crew and the actors alike. Under the creative umbrella provided by Katie Jacobs on the visual side and in partnership with lead producers Gerrit van der Meer and Marcy Kaplan, Yaitanes works to make sure the day-to-day running of the shoot is as efficient as possible. He also preps his fellow directors and works to give them the safest creative environment he can so they can make their best possible *House* movie.

As a producer, Greg Yaitanes will know the concept of a story long before he, as director, receives the script seven days before shooting starts. Looking at the script for the first time, the director is looking for a way into the story. Yaitanes encourages each director to go with what speaks to them personally. Directors' styles are as varied as the writers'. For "Epic Fail," Yaitanes wanted to maintain the motion and fluidity of the video game sequence from the teaser through the rest of the episode. He shot single-camera rather than using two or three cameras per sequence to replicate the first-person feel of a video game. It was very different from how Katie Jacobs shot the two-part opener to the season and different from David Straiton's take on "The Tyrant," which matched with its heavy-toned intensity the subject matter of the story.

"Epic Fail" marked House's return to Princeton-Plainsboro after his stay at Mayfield Psychiatric Hospital and was the first appearance of most of the cast since the end of the previous season. Yaitanes explains how that affected his directing. "I went in very close and wide with the lensing for very intimate close-ups [and] very sculpted faces because I felt we haven't seen everyone in so long. I wanted a real physical intimacy with everybody on camera."

....

All the work that has gone into scheduling and prepping the day's work has to be followed through if shooting is going to start smoothly on Monday morning. The key second assistant director, Vince Duque, always works on set. He checks that everything is in place and flows information on the set's state of readiness back and forth to the first AD and the director. As the crew stands by to set up the first scene, the actors will come onto the set for their private rehearsal. Together with the director and writer the actors will work out the blocking and talk through how they are going to play the scene. To help them focus, the set is cleared until they're ready. *House* is a closed set, meaning only crew is allowed on set. Publicity manager Geoffrey Colo was a PA on *Dr. Quinn, Medicine Woman*, which filmed at Paramount Hills in a public park. An unwelcome part of his job was keeping curious onlookers away.

House actors get endless requests for everything from print media and on-camera interviews to hosting benefits. All requests get filtered before they reach *House* publicity manager Geoffrey Colo, whose job it is to facilitate the ones that get approved. Once the actor has agreed, Geoffrey works with the ADs to find time in the schedule. *House* is unusual in having its own head of publicity on staff; the actors also have their own publicists for red-carpet events and media not specifically related to *House*. The network also organizes its own publicity, including the big "FOX Gallery Shoot" every season, where publicity stills and "wraparounds" for commercial breaks are shot ("*House* will be right back"). These shoots have become more elaborate in an attempt to get away from the familiar hospital setting. Hugh Laurie was photographed with two snakes to mimic the caduceus medical symbol. It was actually one snake wrangled in place and mirrored. The snake was itself a veteran of the Indiana Jones film series.

Laurie had a big hand directing a gallery shoot of a broken-down RV with the cast in various characteristic poses. Cameron is in a taffeta gown fixing the engine; Taub is shaving in the side mirror; Cuddy on the roof tanning; Chase cooking burgers on the barbie; Foreman sitting on step pumping iron; Wilson is chipping golf balls and Thirteen is in full Lara Croft, Tomb Raider getup with a crossbow. They're all in back. House is in front, staring at the camera wearing a hat saying "I'm in Charge."

House is the seventh drama Geoffrey Colo has worked on. Of the actors, he says, "These people are by far the easiest to work with. They have no ego; they're very down-to-earth, very inviting, very positive." Geoffrey says everybody gets it and no one is trying to undermine anyone or undercut anyone. "I will say that the majority of other shows I worked on, there was that going on."

When the actors are done with prepping the scene, the lighting and camera crews can get ready for the shoot. The first team of actors is joined by their second teams of stand-ins, who literally stand in the places the actors will occupy so they can be lit and the focus pullers can adjust the lens on the camera to the correct setting. Once the stand-ins have noted the actors' blocking and movements in a "marking" rehearsal, the first team is sent away. Setting up the shot might take from twenty to forty-five minutes. As the stand-ins move around, director of photography Gale Tattersall selects the lights and bounces for each part of the scene.

House has five stand-ins. Patrick Price is Hugh Laurie's stand-in and doubles for Jesse Spencer. Cuddy and Thirteen share a double. There is a second Taub and another Foreman and Wilson. If anyone else is needed to stand in they will be brought in from among the background actors. Stand-ins are a similar height and skin tone to the first-teamer they are doubling so they shoot and light the same. The twenty or thirty minutes they spend on set while the shot is set up is time the first team can rest or rehearse or go over their lines. The schedule for the first team is punishing enough. Without stand-ins it would be unbearable.

Heavy equipment

Patrick Price appears in *House* as Nurse Jeffrey Sparkman. He has also appeared as parts of Hugh Laurie, for occasional shots over his shoulder or of an arm or an insert of a hand injecting a syringe. Patrick worked with Hugh Laurie on *Stuart Little* and joined *House* for the pilot. "I knew from the beginning," he says. "I just had this vibe. I knew it was an incredible show, I just knew."

Patrick has been around *House* from crew call to wrap-up for practically every day of shooting and sees standing in as a wonderful training ground for acting. If he works on a commercial he urges other actors to take stand-in work if they can get it. By now he's intimately familiar with how Hugh Laurie moves and works with his cane. He can replicate the walk to show the camera how Laurie might teeter in and out of the frame on a walk-and-talk. "I watch him like a hawk," Patrick says. "I can be him in my sleep."

The director is set up in what's called "video village," an area set aside in a room next door to where shooting takes place. Here the monitors showing what the cameras are seeing are arrayed.

Patrick Price, Hugh Laurie's stand-in, lying down on the job.

Ira Hurvitz, the script supervisor, sits next to the director, with the writer of the episode on the other side. On high movie chairs at the back of the room might be producers, or actors who aren't in this scene and are kicking back. Makeup and hair people are here ready for touch-ups. If there's a prop needed in the scene, Eddie Grisco, assistant property master, has it ready. Headphones with the audio feed are available should anyone want to listen in.

Robert Scott, first AD, is bouncing on the balls of his feet anxious to get the shot started. From the set the director of photography (DP) warns the AD that he is almost ready by calling out "five minutes" or "less than five" and that's a signal to the AD that the actors should be ready. This is the moment for the makeup splashes. Background action—extras walking back and forth or interacting with the cast—is choreographed by a second second AD, John Nolan, who will also have his people in position, ready to take their predetermined routes back and forth across the set when shooting starts.

There are red lights placed outside doors leading onto the set and when those are illuminated, no one can come in the door. The sound mixer has control of a bell up in the rafters of the stage, which he'll set off as a signal for everyone on set to be quiet. By ringing the bell the sound mixer is letting the stage know he's ready to roll. An AD will remind everyone "cell phones off." The set is clear of crew; everyone is quiet; the director's focus is on the monitor. The AD calls "rolling" which means the sound mixer rolls the sound. Before sound went digital the clapping of the slate in front of the camera accompanied by "scene six, take one" was used to synchronize the sound with the picture. Now the "smart slate" is hooked into the sound mixer's board. When the clapper comes down the time code readout is frozen and synced. If there are extras, the AD will shout "Background!" so they are moving when the actors start and not wandering all at once into the shot. Then the director is read to call, "Action!"

The actors make their way through the take as the director watches on his monitor. The take may last only a few seconds; this take might focus on one actor reacting to a second actor talking. For the next, they run though the same dialogue with the camera shooting the other actor. The cameras swoop according to the pre-arranged dance, closing in or pulling out. Quickly the scene is done and Greg Yaitanes calls "cut" and hops out from behind his monitor. He might say, "Nice," or "Very good," and walk over to the actors and give a note on their performance. The lighting might need adjusting. Either the take is done or they'll go again till they get it. Take three, it's done, and Yaitanes can say, "That was awesome. That was great."

ROBERT SEAN LEONARD: "We have a read-through of the show every week and you're supposed to read these ahead of time and make sure you know these pronunciations. I'll say, 'Well with this discharge it's got to be . . . 'I can't say this. Okay, next line.' I just don't bother. Whenever anyone bungles it, I say, 'If you say it like that the day we're shooting, I'll give you anything.' Because that's a show I'd watch, the doctor says 'Maybe he has por-pro-por-por-porphia?' I'd say, 'Jennifer, please God say it that way when we shoot it.'"

PETER JACOBSON: "There is coming to terms with the terms themselves. I think I am pretty facile verbally, so I don't have trouble pronouncing but it takes some time because if I'm not going to sound like I know what I am talking about, then forget the whole thing. One of then I just couldn't get *pancytopenia* and I was saying 'pancy-to-penia' (not pan-cy-to-penia) and the writer said, 'You make it sound like a silly kids' game; please get this right.' That was embarrassing."

QUESTION: "What is pancytopenia?"

PETER JACOBSON: "Literally, when they say, 'Cut. Wrap that scene,' it is out of my head. It is a more dispersed occurrence of cytopenia. Whatever that is."

Everyone on the *House* set is quick to sing the praises of director of photography Gale Tattersall and the look of the show. "He is the rare breed of DP that can move incredibly fast and deliver you beautiful images," says Greg Yaitanes. "He shoots every episode, which is not something a lot of shows do anymore," says Katie Jacobs. "He amazes me in terms of his work ethic and the quality of the look of our show . . . I put the look of our show up against any other show."

Tattersall himself will barely admit he does anything at all. When pressed Gale will say, "My job is to interpret what the director's looking for in the imagery and suggest shots and take control of the visual side of the show, doing the lighting with the grip crew, the electric crew, and the camera crew and put the right interpretation on a scene whether it be a moody scene or a gloomy scene or a joyful scene." What's notable about television for Gale, who has a background in commercials and movies, is the speed at which everything's done. You'd better have a clear plan or you'll be run over in the stampede.

Tattersall denies the show has one distinctive look; each episode is handled differently. He loves the constant, and constantly changing, striving for perfection. He cites the episode with the suicide of Kutner ("Simple Explanation") as one that was visually completely different with a gloomy and desaturated look that matched the gravity of the subject matter.

English-born Gale Tattersall directed and shot commercials at the same time as fellow Brits Alan Parker and Ridley Scott, future feature directors. He worked frequently in the United States and after he shot *Wild Orchid* with Mickey Rourke and Carrie Otis in Brazil he took over on short notice as DP of the first Addams Family movie. He moved his family out to L.A. from England and, professionally, never went back.

California may have great weather, but to an expert like Tattersall, it has terrible light. In the early days, film was so slow, the movie industry needed a place with long hours of sunshine so they came to Southern California. They used natural light and graduated painting up the sides of studio walls so it wasn't too "hot" at the top. Then, as Gale says, some idiot decided to put roofs on the studios and use lighting. The light itself outside the studio is harsh, causing long shadows and black eye sockets because there are no clouds. His favorite light? "Up near the Arctic Circle in February when the sun never gets above eleven degrees and it's coming through haze. It lasts for five hours just like that. Here [in L.A.] magic hour is like magic minute, just at sunset. Then it goes pitch black and is all over in a second."

Greg Yaitanes mentions the exceptional work Tattersall put into the teaser on "House Divided," which was set in a gym and featuring deaf high schoolers wrestling. Given the usual week's notice with a script, Tattersall found a way to let Yaitanes film around the wrestlers in a 360-degree arc by building a track into the floor. The gym used for filming had a high glass roof and Tattersall designed a lighting rig suspended from a huge crane 180 feet above the ground that brought a single shaft of light straight down onto the floor. The lights were so powerful that a translucent opal was spread over the roof to diffuse the light, which was then reflected up into the kids' eyes with bounce boards.

"'Frozen' was one of my first episodes. I worked closely with Gale, and the idea was to have a claustrophobic set and we had a circular dome that had lights I thought would be like a sundial and the sun is so low it comes banging through the windows. . . . Gale is a great DP. He loves the shafts of light, the smoke. There is certainly a look that Gale has created and he has done a great job."

—JEREMY CASSELLS, PRODUCTION DESIGNER

One director to another: Greg Yaitanes and Katie Jacobs

Tattersall was confident his idea would work and it would have been "major egg on face" if it hadn't. "I can only ever be as good as our crew," he says and mentions Monty Woodard, gaffer (chief lighting technician); Shawn Whelan, key grip; and Tony Gaudioz, camera operator, who also shoots the B unit. Then he talks about the "amazing, talented" directors: Katie Jacobs; David Straiton, Greg Yaitanes. "I'm very, very fortunate." The producers show that night's episode on a big screen during crew lunch on

Mondays and fifty people turn up to watch and applaud. "It really is a family," Gale says. Because the crew spends more time with the family at work than with their real family it's very important that they respect and like each other.

Unfortunately, Gale Tattersall has no control over the way in which many people experience his work on television. Everyone's TV is set up differently and a lot of us watch with all the lights on, perhaps with a light reflected right in the screen. Gale has thought of doing a film with a lamp superimposed on the screen and wonders how many viewers would notice. Statistics show that a lot of viewers change channel if they think a show is too dark so when he's trying to create mood and darkness, it's a balancing act. "Once it goes to the network it's out of our hands," he says. "I'm sure there's a guy in some gloomy box somewhere that has a big knob that says DARK and LIGHT on it. We have no control at all."

....

It's important to set a quick tempo from the beginning of the shooting day. It's part of the AD's job to make sure time isn't wasted. If a rehearsal stretches on, he might suggest that the actors huddle to the side and discuss the scene so the lighting guys can start. And an AD can say to a director who's asked to redo a take, "Are you sure?" but they intervene to this extent at their peril. A novice director might be redoing too many takes and the AD could say, "Don't we have this?" or "Don't you think we can move on?" "If by going again we are making it better then everybody is on board with that," says AD Kevin Williams. "[Not] if you're going again just because you're nervous or you think you don't have it."

Gerrit van der Meer tells a story. Peter Medak was directing "The Socratic Method" and he was putting together a "gag," a trick where the patient projectile-vomits blood. It took a long time to rig the hose to the woman's face and to get the flow quantity right. It was 2:30 A.M. when the shot was ready, thirteen and a half hours after filming started. Gerrit watches the shot on the monitor and it goes off like a horror film. "It was perfect and [the director] calls 'cut' and he turns right to me and says, 'Another one?'" and I said, 'No, that's it.'"

On any show, if Number One, the lead actor, says he or she wants another take, then it's more than likely there will be one. The director himself may see tiny flaws in a shot and ask for another take. Greg Yaitanes had two actors redo one walk-and-talk four or five times. On takes using a Steadicam, much can go wrong. "You're just tweaking," says Yaitanes. "You try to direct by bumping the sides. I try to give a pretty wide road for everyone to travel down and then I just try to nudge the boundaries of it so you know where you want to work." An actor's timing might be slightly off. "There were just slight intentions and inflections in the performance I just wanted to adjust. Everybody knows their characters well and I talk to them ahead of time. Most often they land where I need them to. [It's a] pretty phenomenal cast."

Having another takes provides the opportunity to make other subtle changes. Lighting can be adjusted. Perhaps the background was too busy ("thin it out") or not busy enough.

> "Filming has never been fun for me. There are a lot of actors who adore it; I've never liked it. Twelve-, fourteen-hour days, who needs that? In the theater, you rehearse eleven to five for three weeks then you're done. [During the run] you're at the theater at seven-thirty and you're home in time for *Letterman*. Are you kidding me? Theater's the best; it just doesn't pay anything."
>
> —ROBERT SEAN LEONARD

"There's an expression, *Gone with the Wind* in the morning and *Dukes of Hazzard* in the afternoon. In the morning, we've got twelve hours and all the time in the world. Then after lunch as it's cranking down and we have to be done by a certain time, that last scene gets shortchanged because everyone lollygagged earlier in the day. '*Dukes of Hazzard*' is just get it done, just get it done."

—KEVIN WILLIAMS

The more takes there are of one scene the more difficult it can become to maintain continuity. The actors' lines and actions need to be replicated. The background actors have to make sure they cross the screen exactly the same way each time. A mistimed cross can mean it appears the same person is crossing the screen left-to-right twice in a row. In addition to marking down scenes and takes in a formidable binder, script supervisor Ira Hurvitz watches the continuity to make sure an actor performs the same physical function at the same point in the action.

On occasion, an actor will say a line slightly differently from how it is written. The phrasing he uses might be more comfortable or familiar to him. The script supervisor will check with the writer to make sure the meaning the writer intended is maintained. By no means every show allows the writer on the set; *House* does. Nuances on the page can turn out quite differently on the set and actors can find other meanings the writer didn't anticipate. "I want to be a resource," says David Hoselton. "Hopefully no one knows the story of this particular script better than me. So if anyone has any questions–'Why am I saying that?' [I am here]." Filming "Ignorance is Bliss," Hoselton chimes in to say that it's a big admission for the genius Sidas to admit his cough syrup abuse to his wife. The inference is that it needs more emphasis.

"We didn't want to miss the moment," says Yaitanes. "What I love about having the writer on set is that we have another set of eyes. . . . David felt maybe I was being too subtle with it and we want to make sure the audience understands that moment. Sometimes we have to push it a little step more." Another set of eyes is provided by Hugh Laurie who is constantly involved in the filming process. "Hugh is like a second director on set," says Greg Yaitanes. "He is a great collaborator. You'd be crazy not to want to listen to his ideas."

For "Lockdown," the sixteenth episode of season six, Hugh Laurie worked both sides of the camera when he directed the episode. Katie Jacobs told the *New York Times* she'd been trying to persuade the leader of the show to direct for years. Laurie said he'd been fascinated by the directing process and the diverse set

"Hugh is like a second director on set."

of skills it demanded. Having him direct was like the flight attendant looking for someone to fly the jetliner in *Airplane.* "I'm not saying I would push people out of the way, if there were anyone else more qualified. But if no one else wanted to, I would love to try that."

"Hugh is a real perfectionist. He is a real hard worker. He doesn't ever take a day off. Sometimes the writer will be on the set and say, 'That's okay,' and Hugh will be like, 'No, no they missed this thing.' He is a disciplined hard worker, which helps with all those little moments because he won't let anything slide by."

—TOMMY MORAN

With some takes, the director will finish the shot and say, "still rolling, still rolling," (meaning the sound) because he wants to make just one small fix. Rather than taking the time to say "cut," at which point people rush onto the set to make their adjustments or touch up hair and makeup, it might be easier to keep rolling, ask for the scene to be quickly reset so background will match, and shoot it again. It's all about getting to the point where Greg Yaitanes can say, "Cut. It's nice. Print it." The phrase "print it" is slightly redundant at this point in technology but it lends a sense of finality. (Someone may also say "check the gate," meaning open up the camera to make sure there isn't a hair in there, which does happen, but infrequently.)

Every spare flat surface on the stages and in the *House* offices is laden with snacks—breakfast cereal, energy bars, fresh fruit, chips, nuts of every variety. Cast and crew can enjoy hot breakfast, lunch, and dinner set up at stations on each stage. On a separate truck there is a fully loaded pantry where crew can come and go and make a sandwich or a cup of coffee. The phrase "enough food to feed an army" comes to mind. It's all managed by husband-and-wife craft services team Susan and Brian Bourg. Unless there are two units filming, Brian and Susan set it all up themselves, providing for a regular crew of 125 plus background actors. "Sometimes we run out of food and it could get nasty," says Susan, "but then we run up to the [FOX] commissary and get something over," says Brian.

Union regulations say that six hours after work starts, there has to be a catered meal, but producers Gerrit van der Meer and Marcy Kaplan decided to provide a cooked breakfast, which isn't mandatory. "People spend so much time here so you're making it as comfortable and convenient as possible," says Gerrit. "If you provide junk all day then people will eat junk all day," says Marcy. "We've gone a different route and provide real food. Yes it is more costly but it makes people happier."

The hot breakfast is a choice of the staples: eggs, potatoes, French toast, oatmeal. The big meal is lunch (today, corned beef and cabbage) and the menu rotates every three weeks or so. "Chicken and beef . . . and fish and chips. Which Hugh Laurie loves," says Susan. There's always a vegetarian alternative. ("Lisa [Edelstein] is very health conscious.") Susan says Hugh Laurie goes out of his way to help move the trash up the hill from the truck. Susan would tell Brian to be on the lookout for him so he wouldn't be bothered with hauling garbage cans:

"One day I was getting ready to go through the door and he showed up and I couldn't stop him and I said, 'Why is it every time we're going to do the trash you're here?' and he looked at his watch and said, 'Well, I've been standing here thirty minutes waiting for you—where the hell have you been?' He's a great guy."

—SUSAN BOURG

Brian Bourg has worked all his career in the business doing commercials and industrial films. Brian and Susan were about to relocate to Phoenix when they heard there was nonunion work available in craft services–"permit" jobs that lead to the essential union accreditation. Then Susan was called in to help work on *House*. Susan was left on her own and she called in Brian. "Marcy [Kaplan] interviewed us and trusted that we could do it," says Brian. The Bourgs don't do the cooking; the hot food is trucked onto the set and unloaded onto carts and transferred to electric chafing dishes for the various stations. Actors or directors may cater a meal themselves and the Bourgs arrange for restaurants like Panda Express, Versailles, and In-N-Out Burger to bring food in. "They love Panda Express," says Brian.

Susan Bourg has another story. Every breakfast without fail and like clock-work, the Bourgs serve what they call cheesy eggs. When Hugh Laurie won the Screen Actors Guild Award, he mentioned them in his acceptance speech, "I want to thank Brian and Susan Bourg for the best cheesy eggs this side of the Rio Grande."

QUESTION: "What is the recipe?"

SUSAN BOURG: "We don't make 'em! Then we have changed vendors and it caused an uproar. They don't like the new cheesy eggs."

"It's hard as a married couple to work together," says Susan. "I was a stay-at-home mom and he was very successful. If anyone had told me I would be doing this at fifty-nine years old . . . but we do love our job." Susan and Brian have been married thirty years. Says Brian, "I do love my wife more than I have ever loved her before."

....

As the crew starts to set up the next scene, for many people on set it's a case of hurry up and wait. Background actors assemble outside the front door of the hospital lobby in front of the backdrop. They sit, read the paper, check messages, or visit the craft services table. Signs on trash cans by the lobby entrance remind everyone this is not a real trash can—it's part of the set. The actors may repair to their trailer or sit in video village reading a magazine. In a corner someone is catching up on a nap.

Craft services' Brian Bourg makes another snack run.

At lunch, people make themselves scarce, going to the food setup in another stage, the FOX commissary, their office, or their trailer.

Other crew members complete their very specialized tasks. June Park, the camera loader, takes the film that has been shot and carefully slots the footage into a crate before it goes to the lab for processing. Once it is delivered to the lab it becomes postproduction's responsibility. All the film is meticulously labeled and logged in a daily inventory that details what film has been shot and what has been wasted or recycled and Meg Schave in the production office has to balance that particular checkbook. June loads the fresh film in the camera magazine for the next take.

The set is an arena in which the director is definitely in charge. There's an atmosphere of great industry but no tension, which is not to say a screw-up isn't going to be allowed to slide. Everyone

Background actors waiting for the call on the hospital grounds

does their job with efficiency and precision; collectively the cast and crew push through each eighth of a page of script at the highest possible tempo. Cast and crew have known each other a long time and they can joke around with each other. Today, the director is in on an outtake played by Olivia Wilde. A patient complains about how long it was taking for the team to find out what was wrong with her. I'm sick, you said it was this, you said it was that, and Wilde cuts her off: "Am I the only one here who watches this show? That's what we do." Moments like this help everybody stay loose and provide fodder for the gag reel at the wrap party.

Although ADs make a point of reminding everyone to switch off their cell phones before a take, every now and then one will ring right at the wrong moment. It can be funny if, as Kevin Williams recalls, a camera assistant's phone with a joke ringtone goes off right next to the actors. "But it breaks the rhythm and actors react adversely. Once in a blue moon it has been the actor's cell phone and it's even happened that it has been the director's cell phone."

QUESTION: "Has it ever been your cell phone?"

KEVIN WILLIAMS: "It did happen once. Not a good feeling."

Patrick Price says there is a "no names on set" policy when a phone goes off. No one wants to know who it is; just don't do it again. But it does happen again. "Right in the middle of the scene, bing! And it's kind of jarring. You think, Don't let it be a scene with Hugh, and 99 percent of the time it is."

For Greg Yaitanes the priority is not to do it his way but to do it the best way it can be done. He doesn't want to constrain the actors with a strict style. "My motto is you go where you want. I'll make cool shots wherever you find yourself." He's worked to build an environment that's supportive of the process and everyone in it: Gale, the ADs, the whole crew. He's conscious every time he directs an episode that everyone has to go again the next week at the same level of intensity. He knows he can't work the set fourteen hours a day, "because then it leaves nothing for the next guy. . . . I need everybody to be able to do their best work until March." Through choice, Yaitanes exempts himself from the stricture about long hours. "For everybody on set to do their best work I've got to go that extra mile and this show makes that commitment a pleasure. This show doesn't make it seem like I'm working; it's just the hours that it takes. I do not practice what I preach but that is what this show deserves."

With variations, the producer-director job exists on other shows and Yaitanes had been offered them many times. He was happy to direct for *House* and he won an Emmy for his work on "House's Head." When the previous producer-director left to make a pilot, he was offered the creative partnership he was looking for and took the job. Fifteen years ago, if asked, he'd have thought he'd be making feature films at this stage of his career. He feels fortunate to have gotten into TV when it wasn't as good as it is today. As a result, he had the opportunity to rise up through the ranks. Though he resists the notion that this is a golden age of scripted drama (you have to wait to identify such a thing after it's passed). Yaitanes would be reluctant to leave now that he's made a significant personal contribution.

"About three years ago I came to the conclusion that I am completely okay not directing a movie. The movies that I get offered are not of the quality of an episode of *House*. Or as exciting as *Lost* or an intriguing as *24*. They don't hold up." Asked about his personal favorite episodes, Yaitanes cites his first as director, "Damned if You Do," "House's Head," "Unfaithful," for which David Hoselton won the Humanitas Award, and the last six episodes of season five, starting with "Locked In," which was his first episode as producer. "It was a great arc of six episodes. If you look at those episodes not one of them is the same." Meaning visually, in terms of the acting, the stories, "House Divided," which won the sound Emmy, the finale. . . . "If this wasn't an amazing experience to be here," says Yaitanes, "I would be somewhere else."

The collective hard work and skill put in by the cast and crew results in great work at whatever level you care to look. Series; episode; scene; shot. It's hard to imagine removing any of the people involved and maintaining the same quality. Kevin Williams talks about one shot that was particularly memorable. Chase has had his fateful hand in the death of the dictator Dibala and Foreman knows. Chase's job, his marriage, even his freedom are in peril. Is Foreman going to help him? Laid on top of the drama are the ethical issues: Is it okay to take one life to save others? And where does a soul in crisis turn to help when they have been let down before?

Foreman asks Chase, do you think you can do this and there not be any consequences to yourself? Says Williams: "We had three cameras, one getting Chase's profile, an extreme close-up shot of him with his hair hanging down in his face, silhouetted and half-lit: half of it was in the dark. You can just barely make it out as he says, 'No.' He knew there would be consequences. The depth of the emotion he was feeling that was conveyed with that one-word answer and that tight shot on his face as he was sitting there, devastated. That was great and you say to the director, 'You aced that.' He said we had it.

"So much goes into that the lighting the set, in settling the set down and make the atmosphere conducive so Jesse could get to that place . . . guys standing around having a soda on the set, just scoot that away for a moment. Let him get there and do his thing and when he's done then the party can start. . . . Cut. Print. We got it. Then what time are we getting to the bar? There's a time for everything."

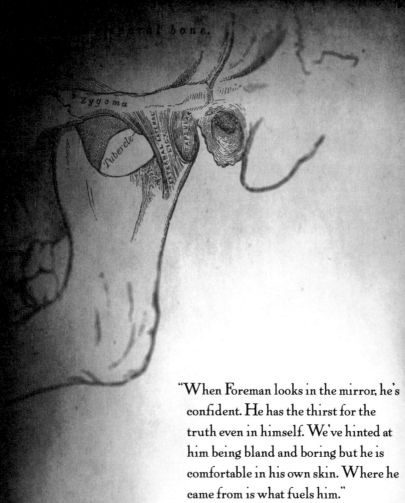

"When Foreman looks in the mirror, he's
confident. He has the thirst for the
truth even in himself. We've hinted at
him being bland and boring but he is
comfortable in his own skin. Where he
came from is what fuels him."

—Omar Epps

FOREMAN

Omar Epps

All the doctors in House's diagnostic teams have left at one time or another and been drawn back—only Cameron has made it out alive. Eric Foreman was the most reluctant to return. Of the team members, Foreman has always been the first to criticize House and his methods. He knows House is capable of stealing Wilson's scrip pad. "House is a junkie" ("Son of a Coma Guy"). He resists any suggestion he's at all similar to his boss. "Yeah, I'm just like him," he says in "Poison." "Except for the angry, bitter, pompous cripple part." The mother of the teen whom House and Foreman have treated sees little difference. "You're just as pompous and superior as he is," she tells Foreman. The boy asks his mom of House and Foreman, "Who are those guys?" She says, "Oh, they're the arrogant jerks that saved your life." As Foreman and House get in a hospital elevator they look down and see they're wearing the same sneakers.

> "House is all about the puzzle. Foreman has that same drive for the puzzle; he just has a different route to get there."
>
> —OMAR EPPS

From the pilot it's established that Foreman was in court at sixteen for housebreaking and that House hired him for his "street smarts." What House doesn't seem to know is that Foreman was once on academic probation for fixing a lab test. Taub catches Foreman trying to remove the record from his file in "Lockdown" (Foreman justifies his act by saying he had to beat the elite kids). Taub doctors the record on Foreman's behalf but not before Taub and Foreman discover House has already redacted his own file.

Detective Tritter knows Foreman has a brother in jail and tries to coerce Foreman into rolling on House to get accelerated parole for his brother ("Finding Judas"). Foreman has seized his second chance and is constantly working to prove he is worthy of it. In "House Training," Foreman can't connect with a woman, Lupe, who has wasted her own opportunities. The team, Foreman included, makes bad decisions with her treatment, her immune system is destroyed, and she is powerless to fight an infection. Foreman stays with Lupe, telling her he stole cars and robbed houses but got another chance and entered a whole other world.

> **FOREMAN:** "There's some part of me I can't get rid of [. . .] always thinks, if I'm not the smartest, if I'm not the first, everywhere I go they'll figure out I'm not supposed to be here. They'll send me back."
>
> **LUPE:** "You know that's not going to happen. You're out."
>
> **FOREMAN:** "I'll never be out of there."

House believes there is nothing to forgive for her death; mistakes are going to happen. At the time, Foreman's parents are visiting. Foreman hasn't been home in eight years and his mom is sick. When Foreman tells his mom what happened, she absolves him but it's clear she doesn't know who her own son is.

In "Histories," Foreman is initially hostile to a homeless patient but comes to comfort her as she dies. He knows her husband and son died when she crashed their car. She's delirious and Foreman tells her he is her husband and he forgives her. Foreman has no sympathy for LL Cool J's death row inmate ("Acceptance") but when it's found that his murderous rages were caused by a tumor, Foreman's prepared to testify in his defense. (House insists he does that on his own time.) Again, the distance Foreman tries to put between himself and his background is narrowed by the fact that in the end, he cares.

> "There's the great episode when LL Cool J is the prisoner and he tried to have the black connection with Foreman and Foreman is not that guy. You lace up your boots, you put in hard work, you get good results. He's not going to play in the confines of race or status or economics."
>
> —OMAR EPPS

Driven by the need to prove himself, Foreman is the most ambitious of any of House's doctors. In "Detox" he complains he trained fourteen years (he's a neurologist by trade) and House has him digging up a dead cat. He's taken charge of the team more than once: when House was suspended in season two for lying to the transplant committee and when House lost his license after his stay in the Mayfield Hospital in season six. Although Cuddy liked the tight ship Foreman ran the first time, House completely failed to respect Foreman's authority. "A person who has the guts to break a bad rule, they're a hero," says Foreman. "House doesn't break rules, he ignores them. He's not Rosa Parks, he's an anarchist" ("Deception"). Foreman shows the extent of his single-mindedness when to prevent his relationship with Thirteen affecting his running of the department, he fires his girlfriend ("Epic Fail").

Foreman did have his shot at running a department—it just wasn't at PPTH. After the death of Lupe, Foreman has a crisis of confidence until his Hail Mary saves two brothers who have been put through a harrowing diagnostic ordeal. He quits.

> FOREMAN: "I hate that I can listen to a kid screaming in pain and not even take a moment to question whether I'm doing the right thing. I hate that in order to be like you, as a doctor, I have to be like you as a human being. I don't want to turn into you."
>
> HOUSE: "You're not. You've been like me since you were eight years old."
>
> FOREMAN: "You'll save more people than I will. But I'll settle for killing less. Consider this my two weeks' notice." ("Family")

Cuddy tells Foreman there are worse things to turn into than House. "It's not worth it," says Foreman ("Resignation"). "I don't wanna be you," he tells House. "You're miserable."

Foreman takes a job at New York Mercy. Now he's the boss: his own team, his own whiteboard ("97 Seconds"). Immediately putting into practice what he has learned at PPTH, however, he breaks a rule to save a life. Except here he's told he confused saving a life with doing the right thing and gets fired. Now he's unemployable and has to come back to Cuddy to ask for a job. He wants a raise, an office, an assistant; she'll give him his old position. "You're gonna be miserable," says House. "I already am miserable," Foreman replies. He just can't get away.

"Foreman has made that comment, if we allowed every doctor to act like House then the morgue would be overflowing in no time. He made so many excellent points about House."

—DAVID SHORE

Foreman has certainly succeeded in leaving his delinquent past behind. When House has Lucas snoop around the team ("Lucky Thirteen"), Lucas says Foreman hasn't done anything remotely interesting since he was seventeen. When asked, Chase agrees that Foreman is boring, although he does have a tattoo. So he's a worker. As for relationships, on Foreman's online profile page, he has three friends ("Epic Fail"). Foreman thinks the Romany kid in "Needle in a Haystack" must want to make his own way without the cloying attention of his family, but the boy points out that Cameron, Chase, and Foreman are all alone. Cameron and Chase find each other; what does Foreman have?

A good test of any character's suitability for human interaction is to have them face off with Cameron. In "Sleeping Dogs Lie," Foreman writes a journal article on a case Cameron was working on. Cameron is horrified—that's not what people do. House of course is not surprised—that's exactly what people do. Cameron comes to terms with her disappointment and tells Foreman she should have handled it better and she doesn't want it to get in the way of their friendship. I like you well enough, says Foreman, but we're colleagues and not friends and I don't have anything to apologize for.

"When Foreman was dying and he stabs Cameron with some of his blood, that was intense. Once again, if you create the monster, when the monster disconnects from the outlet it's plugged into and walks on its own, you can't control its movements."

—OMAR EPPS

Soon, Foreman is stuck in a clean room with a pain-racked cop ("Euphoria, Part I"). To make Cameron go back to the cop's house to find the source of their illness, Foreman stabs her with a dirty syringe. Foreman survives and reaches out to Cameron. "I'm sorry, Allison. I shouldn't have stolen your article. I shouldn't have exposed you. You were a friend. I need to know that we're okay." But Cameron doesn't immediately accept the apology. Perhaps it takes Foreman a while to warm to someone. In season six, he saves Chase's bacon over Dibala and asks Chase if he wants to go for a drink after Cameron leaves ("Ignorance is Bliss"). But at the end of season three, he'd told Chase: "I don't like you. Never have. Never will" ("Resignation").

Distant with his parents, remote with his colleagues, Foreman may seem destined for lonely bachelorhood. He did have a relationship with a drug company rep in season one ("Sports Medicine"). When he meets Thirteen, at first he's content to join House in his jokes about her going "both ways." But he falls for Thirteen—for sure, she isn't boring. Within weeks, Foreman is confronted with an ethical problem when he administers Thirteen's drug trial. Foreman shouldn't even have someone he knows on the trial in the first place. He breaks into Thirteen's apartment to find out if she is keeping to the protocol ("Let Them Eat Cake"). Then he manipulates treatment sessions so Thirteen sees Janice, a patient who is responding well to the drug ("Painless"). When Foreman finds that Thirteen is on the placebo, he wants to switch her to the actual drug, which he can't do without ruining his career, surely the most important thing Foreman has in his life.

Are the one to three extra years with Thirteen the drug might offer worth his career? House asks Foreman. Jeopardizing his reputation and career would seem out of character for Foreman. "Unless you love her," says House. "If you love her, you do stupid things" ("Big Baby"). And Foreman switches the meds anyway. Thirteen realizes what Foreman has done and stops taking the drug but they have given her a brain tumor. Finally, Foreman torpedoes the trial and manages to hold on to his license and to Thirteen ("The Greater Good"). Foreman was reckless—he'd only known Thirteen a short time. House isn't prepared to have Fourteen on his team: Foreman plus Thirteen. "Separately they're great doctors," he tells Kutner. "Together they're morons." They both look for new jobs in the wake of the drug trial and House fires them both and only rehires Foreman when it looks as though he is no longer with Thirteen ("Unfaithful").

"Once you get to season six, it wasn't about Foreman trying to take over from House. As Cuddy says, the department of diagnostics only existed when House was here. . . . Foreman's retort was you kept us all on salary. If you didn't want us to be here we would be gone and have moved on with our lives. Let's reopen the department and forge ahead. I think that is where Foreman is coming from. I think the audience took it as he's trying to replace House and you can never replace House."

—OMAR EPPS

But Fourteen survives, until Foreman's ambition trumps his heart. Cuddy gives the department to Foreman when House is without his license after his spell in Mayfield but Foreman is distracted with Thirteen on the team. They make each other miserable at work when Foreman is boss but he wants her in his life. Foreman takes action ("Epic Fail").

THIRTEEN: "You're breaking up with me?"

FOREMAN: "No. The other night when I thought I was done, you were there. I need you. I don't want to lose you."

THIRTEEN: "Why are you . . . You're firing me?"

FOREMAN: "I'm sorry."

QUESTION: "Foreman is polite. When he fired Thirteen you basically did it with a cock of your head."

OMAR EPPS: "It's a style. He has a lot of heart."

Foreman isn't prepared to leave his job as head of the team, which Thirteen implies she would have done in his position. (Even House, in "No Remorse," says what Foreman did was "moronic.") Foreman loses out both ways: Thirteen is gone and House comes back and reassumes control whether he's technically in charge or not. When House decides he wants Taub and Thirteen back, Thirteen resists until Foreman says he doesn't have a problem with her working on the team ("Teamwork"). But you wouldn't know it. Finally, in "No

Remorse," Foreman apologizes to Thirteen for firing her, admitting he did it for himself. "I screwed everything up," he says. "I hope that we can still work together." This time, perhaps he means it. His ambition squashed, Foreman might be able to take care of his heart.

Inevitably, Foreman's past catches up with him. In "Moving the Chains," House gives Foreman's brother Marcus (Orlando Jones), recently released from jail, a job. House is trying to get more leverage on Foreman, who assumes his brother will inevitably relapse back into crime. Beyond revealing some trivial bedwetting stories, Marcus is little use to House. When Marcus breaks his brother's confidence, telling House their mother died and Foreman didn't give a eulogy at the funeral, House breaks Marcus's confidence and reveals he knows about the men's mother. Marcus and Eric are drawn together by House's deceit and Eric takes his brother in, a development Wilson, for one, believes House was engineering all along.

Whatever their relationship, Foreman needs the challenge of House as a negative and positive force in his life. When Foreman was near death ("Euphoria, Part II"), Foreman's dad, Rodney, talked to House, discussing what might happen if Foreman went into a coma. When Rodney tells House, "Eric says you're the best doctor he's ever worked with," it seems like he's articulating the thing that is most important to his son in the world.

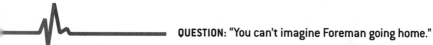

QUESTION: "You can't imagine Foreman going home."

OLIVIA WILDE: "He sleeps in a cot in the office. In a fantastic suit."

QUESTION: "He is always well turned out."

OLIVIA WILDE: "That's because Omar Epps is always well turned out. Straight out of the pages of *GQ* at all times. He's always immaculate. His wife is always teasing him about it."

CATHY CRANDALL (COSTUME DESIGNER): "His clothes are so beautiful. But he's a beautiful man. I mean, God, he would look great in anything. He's in great shape and takes great care of himself and he's fastidious. It translates over to Foreman. His look is so neat and put together. Foreman has really good taste is clothing. Mostly Paul Smith. Some Hugo Boss."

Omar Epps on . . . Foreman

QUESTION: "Your character is always immaculately turned out."

"Pretty good gear, huh?"

QUESTION: "Do you ever wear anything other than a suit?"

"Only if there's a scene in his apartment will he wear sweats or something. Foreman's pretty stiff. Tightly wound."

QUESTION: "Foreman is an ambitious guy . . ."

"Definitely. He's been in an interesting place the last couple of years. Chase and Cameron left and he left and was running his own department at a different hospital and did a Housean thing and got fired. He ends up back at the hospital begrudgingly. Once the new team comes on there's definitely the hierarchy. I've been here and I'm kind of in charge. House is everyone's boss but I'm the leader of the team and you have these other two doctors saying, 'but there is no leader of the team.'"

QUESTION: "You've been here for six years . . ."

"I know a couple of doctors and they say, 'Well, how long are they going to be fellows?' They're actually choosing to work under House and they're going to become the best in their fields by these apprenticeships. Foreman's main concern is, is he becoming a better doctor?"

QUESTION: "When you fired Thirteen, what were you thinking?"

"Surely, somewhere in the world someone felt vindicated by Foreman's choice."

QUESTION: "They tried to get Foreman a girlfriend before, the drug rep."

"Who was using Foreman. Of course."

QUESTION: "Do you think about where Foreman is going to go?"

"Yes, definitely. I talk to David Shore sometimes. The really interesting thing is that they don't know. Everything is so tightly done you would think they've got this whole season written but they really don't.

"I definitely want Foreman to keep evolving as a character because that keeps me refreshed. Where is he headed? Does he want to stay in this hospital and work in his own department? Does he want a private practice? Does he want a family?"

QUESTION: What about Thirteen?"

"Thirteen has another so many years left on her life and if she were to have a child it would have a fifty percent chance of having Huntington's. I could have thoughts and say left and they go right. Maybe Foreman will run away from that but they'd say, 'No, he loves her so much he wants to give her a child.'"

"I think what is so interesting about their relationship for the audience is that it has given them a chance to see Foreman in his personal life as well as Thirteen. There's something so fun about seeing Foreman in his pajamas eating cereal at the breakfast table. His character has never been seen that way. That vulnerability is fun and interesting and surprising."

—OLIVIA WILDE

QUESTION: "What about Foreman and the drug trial?"

"Telling her was about respect and trust and an element of fearlessness knowing she trusts him."

QUESTION: "Would Foreman give his whole career for the chance of two or three years with Thirteen?"

"That all hinges on someone finding out. One of the underbellies of the show is the dysfunctional family atmosphere. House is the father and is very protective. Chase has done some crazy stuff, Foreman has . . . Cuddy has been aware of it all and is sort of the Mother

Goose. Wilson is like House's conscience but at the same time he is an enabler. In the trial, Foreman wanted to be the honorable one. I'll go tell them and House is like, 'what are you doing? They're going to take your license' and he had to bring him back to reality."

QUESTION: "We have to address your terrible behavior with Cameron. You stole her article . . ."

"That was all fueled by ambition and self-righteousness. That was interesting because Foreman justified that by the idea that Cameron wasn't going to use it."

Omar Epps on . . . House

QUESTION: "Do Foreman and House think on the same wavelength?"

"They definitely have the same drive. . . . He ribs Foreman about his adolescence; he had gone astray a little in his teenage years. Obviously he is a talented doctor and he can think outside of the box and he is willing to take risks. Maybe House knew that and Foreman didn't."

QUESTION: "He's going to find things in your background . . ."

"That comes back to the puzzle. House is just obsessed with knowing. Okay, I'm going to hire you but I'm going to go through every chapter of your life and know every detail about you and then we're on an equal footing. He was an addict and he was very open about that. Everyone knows my stuff so I should know everyone else's."

QUESTION: "The difference is that Foreman is going to be more concerned about the person?"

"Definitely. With House, a guy comes in, he's all messed up, we cured him, we figured it out, get him out of here. Foreman is, we cured him we figured it out, but if we just send him out of here he's just going to go back to doing it so maybe let's get him some counseling.

"That's one of the main things about House, the character. It's just the truth. Whether you like it or not, there is an attempt at consistently being true even if he has to lie and play and game. It all comes back to the truth of the matter and I think people respect that and they admire that and it's something that, as human beings, we all want to have that quality."

QUESTION: "Is there any such thing as absolute truth?"

"Yes. It doesn't need any reason to be justified; it just is what it is. And that's separate from facts. No, the truth is the truth. If people are religious or believe in a higher power or they don't, they still have the truth within themselves. When you look in the mirror, you know what is and you know what ain't. That's the daily battle. That's what we deal with every day."

QUESTION: "Foreman has a bit more of a filter than House . . ."

"With House, people get to live vicariously—I would love to say that to my boss. I would love to say that to my friend. In real life, there is a time and a place for things and he lives in that small space where his timing is off. He says certain things to the patients and Foreman is like, 'Come on!'"

QUESTION: "Foreman tries to keep House on the rails when Kutner dies."

"He has to rein him in. The thing with Kutner was that House didn't see it coming. And that's the thing that all the other characters are trying to say—look, shit happens. House is saying no, there's a reason for everything, there's a science in everything. Before he did it to the parents he did it to Thirteen and Taub and they fought him off. 'Hey this is not our fault. No one could have known,' and House has a hard time accepting that. He just goes into his natural state of trying to find a reason and he projects that onto the parents. That was intense to film."

QUESTION: "House says some terrible racial stuff to Foreman."

"That doesn't bother Foreman as he knows House. Last season, House was making meatballs with Wilson and Wilson said are you going to make a balls joke? You can see it coming. But it's still funny.

Those guys hold a mirror up to our own bigotry and hypocrisy. He is playing what is going to be in certain people's subconscious. Foreman has a thick skin.

"That goes back to that family aspect, You can say and share certain things with your family members no matter how dysfunctional it might be that you can't share with other people outside of that circle. Our characters dwell in that world."

QUESTION: "He's looking out for you?"

"Definitely. We are looking out for him, too. At the end of the day it is about saving lives."

QUESTION: "Although you have all killed people."

"Well, you can't win 'em all."

Omar Epps on . . . Omar Epps

QUESTION: "You went to La Guardia High School [the 'Fame' school in New York City]."

"Yes, come a long way."

QUESTION: "What's it like in L.A.?"

"I moved out here thirteen, fourteen years ago. I moved out here for the business. The first few years I never paid attention to my surroundings. I was out here to try to work. Now that I have my family and my kids, I pay more attention. I love L.A. but I miss home. The quality of life here is amazing.

"I want to feel at home wherever I'm at. I miss certain things and when I visit I soak it in but this is where I am at and where I am living so this is where it has to be."

QUESTION: "You have played some intense scenes, close shots of you in incredible pain."

"A lot of it comes down to the people you work with, the crew, the cast, all of those things play into your performance. When all those things are gelling, it doesn't make it easy but it gives you the platform to go where you need to go. I feel supported so I can be vulnerable and go to those places."

QUESTION: "You've been doing this a long time. Do you seek a fresh challenge with the acting?"

"Yes, certainly with this show that's been one of the greatest rewards, feeling I have grown so much as an artist. Our writing is, I think, some of the best on TV and it's a constant challenge. It's different. . . . When you first start out there's no expectation, meaning there's no support, the network is like, whatever. Once you get the numbers, and you get the formula and the machine rolling, now the bar is set. We set our own bar. You know the nature of business is to outdo what you just did. The thing that we had fun with from day one is we all believe in the first script; we all responded to it for the right reasons. Creatively it is the same as it was on day one."

QUESTION: "It's the most watched show in the world. Does that affect your work?"

"Not at all. We're humbled and we're flattered . . . One thing about audiences, they are very fickle, so you can't rest on your laurels.

"We have a rabid fan base. When we first came on the air, we had six million viewers but those people were in love with our show and those same people are watching now and the word of mouth is ridiculous. People come up to me all the time and say, 'My mom is really into the show, I finally watched and I loved it' . . . or she'll say, 'This is my kids' favorite show and they kept bugging me to watch it and I finally watched it and love it.' To me that's incredible. All things in TV are sold to a specific demo [demographic] and we seem to hit the whole thing, which to me is amazing."

5

CITY OF ACTORS

 **The Casting Process**

"Sometimes the best orange is the best orange or
the best John Wayne is the best John Wayne."

—AMY LIPPENS, CASTING DIRECTOR

House's three casting professionals—Amy Lippens, Stephanie
Laffin, and Janelle Scuderi—are responsible for finding actors to
play everyone who has a speaking role in the series. The three
have been with *House* since the beginning and have seen thousands of actors for hundreds of roles. Between them, the casting
team knows untold numbers of actors. They watch almost everything on television as well as films, plays, and workshops. They
will often keep an actor in mind hoping a suitable part will come
up. Or someone will read for one role and get called in for another
a year later. Janelle Scuderi had a picture of Dave Matthews on her
wall—his name kept coming around and he was finally cast (in
"Half-Wit"). Stephanie Laffin brought a crumpled and torn-up
photograph of Zeljko Ivanek with her from office to office and
he too finally was cast, as the desperate hostage taker in "Last
Resort."

The casting team's reach is far and wide. They have people in

New York who can put an actor on tape; they know who is hot in West End theater in London. They think of hundreds of possibles for some roles. "That's all we do," says Amy Lippens. "Think of wonderful actors and where to place them." Every week the script throws up multiple opportunities and often the face that fits is a familiar one. There are kids whom Amy Lippens cast in movies when they were twelve who are now getting parts in *House.* "We work with certain people multiple times over the years," says Amy. "Or other people we wanted to work with for years and finally do. . . . This is a career, not a job, for us so we have been in the business a long time. Actors are open to us their whole career until they retire. We're just judicious about how we cast each season."

. . . .

Same as everyone else, the casting team gets a script eight days before shooting starts. (And they are thankful they do. They all know of shows where scripts are late and casting is done from a few pages or none at all.) They may get a heads-up about some exceptional circumstance but everything is subject to change until they see the actual pages. Once the team has the script they will determine how many actors are needed and what special considerations will have to be taken into account. Do they need to find children? They've had to ask actors if they can fire a gun or find someone who isn't sensitive to latex and can wear a lot of prosthetics or who isn't allergic to cats or dogs or doesn't mind having maggots crawling over their body.

The script often is not specific about a character other than for her age. Parts have gone from being a man in the script to a woman actor, or an ethnic to a nonethnic actor. The same is true on other series: The character of Dr. Ben Gideon in Katie Jacobs's *Gideon's Crossing* was inspired by Jerome Groopman and played by *House* alum-to-be Andre Braugher. The part as written is always an opportunity to find someone great, not a narrow definition that someone has to be squeezed into a square peg or round hole.

"We work fast and have to set the tone because a lot of departments are waiting for us to get the talent so they can do their jobs. And the editors are the ones at the end who are making it all happen so it can get on the air."

—AMY LIPPENS

After the script is picked apart, conversations start, with Katie, with the writer, and with the director. Changes will be made that affect the casting team's work—a character getting a little younger, a little older. As the requirements get slightly more specific the team draws up a list of potential players. For a larger role that will audition in front of the director and producers, they want to call in eight actors at the most for one session. (Only series regulars have to test in front of studio and network executives.) If there's a list of twelve to fifteen it might self-select nearer to eight because some actors aren't available. Last cuts are made and a session set up.

Perhaps surprisingly, for a smaller role, a nurse with one line, more actors are seen, about fifteen per role. The actors up for these kinds of roles generally have less experience and need more coaching. There is a *House* standard that must be maintained. "We need people to be on the level of every actor who has ever been on the show," says Amy Lippens. "We have a very high level of acting. Even if you have one line you have to have the chops to play that role."

The acting pool is enormous, from people for whom this is a second career and late starters to seasoned theater players to actors who have had their own shows and leads in movies. "We run the whole gamut," says Amy. There's so much acting talent in Los Angeles because this is where most of the television work is. A few series film on the East Coast and *House* has hired people out of New York, such as Cynthia Nixon in "Deception." "There is a flavor of the East Coast and Chicago actors we do miss sometimes. People who are wonderful character faces," says Amy Lippens.

Relatively few actors are actually *from* Los Angeles. Foreigners apart, on *House*, Jennifer Morrison is from Chicago, where Peter Jacobson was born. Jacobson lives in New York, where Omar

Epps was born, along with Robert Sean Leonard, who was born in New Jersey, which is where Boston-born Lisa Edelstein was raised. And Amy, Stephanie, and Janelle: from Baltimore, Boston, and Connecticut, respectively.

Hugh Laurie is far from the only British actor plying his trade in Hollywood. Laurie blazed a recent trail. *FlashForward* had a red telephone booth full of Brits: Joseph Fiennes, Sonya Walger, Jack Davenport, and Dominic Monaghan (also of *Lost*). Throw in Tim Roth on *Lie to Me*. There have been almost as many if not more Aussies on recent shows: Anna Torv and John Noble, two of the three leads on *Fringe*, Simon Baker (*The Mentalist*); Julian McMahon on *Nip/Tuck;* Anthony LaPaglia and Poppy Montgomery were on *Without a Trace,* as was Marianne Jean-Baptiste, who is British. And so on. Not all these actors play characters with American accents and it's not a given that any actor from the British Commonwealth can pull it off. "Absolutely not," says Janelle. "You should hear the bad ones."

Fact is, television, movies, and theater are all international businesses and plenty of American actors work in Europe. The team likes to cast what's on the page: If the script calls for a Japanese person, find a Japanese actor; a British character a British actor. Stephanie Laffin has a list of British actors she'd love to work with and mentions Gina McKee and Henry Cavill. Getting work authorization for nonresidents is problematic and takes at least six weeks, which was okay for Franka Potente, who was cast in "Broken" in the summer hiatus but not for somebody operating under the usual eight-day schedule. So actors generally need a green card or to be a citizen to be in contention for a part.

The casting team is universal in its praise of Hugh Laurie's accent. For Stephanie Laffin the only ones who can compete are Mark Rylance (*Boeing-Boeing* on Broadway) and Damian Lewis (*Life*). "When someone says that person does a really good American accent I say, 'Let me check this with you. Is it as good as Hugh's?' There's usually a very pregnant pause and they go, 'Well, not really.'"

Amy Lippens thinks it's just one more thing to admire in Laurie. "We read many, many other British actors and they did not come close. . . . He has a flawless American accent. He also has to play a very complicated character who has to walk with a cane. And the vocabulary! It is a difficult role. And being British just added a whole other dimension. And he is still brilliant."

In finding actors the team has records of previous auditions to draw on and notes from their long hours of TV and movie watching. They constantly check and recheck actor availability. Television used to run like school from September through the spring but nowadays new programming runs all year and actors can be hired at any time. Agents pitch their clients constantly: by letter, postcard, e-mail, phone, when they see someone from the show down at the yogurt place. "I love it when agents pitch," says Stephanie." "'They played a priest on another show.' That makes me crazy. I had no idea they could only play a priest." Amy Lippens says of relying on agents, "Would that make our job easier? Yes. Would that make us feel we were doing the best job we can? No."

Katie Jacobs is the source of a lot of casting ideas. "Katie never forgets an actor," says Janelle Scuderi. She'll file a face away and figure out where they might fit later on. Casting for "Three Stories" in the first season, Jacobs asked who the actor was she liked who read for Chase; he should read for this role. Thus did Andrew Keegan become the med student who talks back to House in the amphitheater scenes.

"For Mos Def's episode we made a list of people. Russ and G [Russel Friend and Garrett Lerner] wanted someone you would be okay more with hearing speak than seeing speak so it had to be someone with a distinctive voice. We ended up with the perfect fit, with a guy who spends his life telling stories through his music and became a movie star."

—STEPHANIE LAFFIN

The offices where the casting takes places are some of the oldest, and smallest, on the lot and auditions take place in pretty close quarters. What might be imagined as tense and competitive situations can be anything but. A recent audition of older men got so loud in the waiting room they had to be quieted down. They'd been going to auditions together for thirty years and when they see each other it's like a reunion. "Actors are all different," says Amy. "Some like to talk; others go outside to be alone and quiet."

The call is made; the actors gather and come into the audition room where they read. The team reviews the films they take of the audition because the camera can catch subtleties that might elude the naked eye. Sometimes a decision is made there and then or it can take a day or so. Time is of the essence. If the producers or the team feels they don't have it, they'll start the process again and keep going until the last second. They can go back to the well time after time because, as Stephanie Laffin likes to say, L.A. is a city of actors.

....

Casting directors develop an eye and a look, a feel for an actor. They rarely ask their colleagues on other shows for help unless they are looking for something very specific, an actor who speaks Mandarin or a hard-of-hearing teenager. It's important to develop the personality of a show and ensure it doesn't look like anything else on TV. "We work really hard to make it look different," says Stephanie Laffin. It's important that viewers don't see the same actor on show after show. Says Amy Lippens, "We try to be fresh and have a distinctive look and acting voice of our show."

So what are they looking for in an actor? They need to be believable, whether they are a doctor and patient or an air force pilot. They might need to be able to say "alveolar rhabdomyosarcoma." They need to display confidence in their read and be able to work with the other cast members. So far so good. They also have to play someone who's living in New Jersey, where a tan is less available in December by natural means than it is in Los Angeles. What is being sought is intangible, which is where the skill of the casting team comes in. "It's the person who is right for the job," says Janelle. "They might have no credits or be James Earl Jones." It's always important not to be obvious. If an actor always plays the wealthy man or the working class or the crime victim then they probably won't be cast like that on *House*. Although, as Amy says, once in a while you will do that because the best orange is the best orange.

Just because an actor is a famous name doesn't mean he's getting a role. Some shows routinely write parts with specific actors in mind but not on *House*. Of course, if an actor is famous it doesn't mean he's not getting a role, either. James Earl Jones was cast as the dictator Dibala under the strictures of the usual eight-day schedule. Jones was in New York while other actors read for the part in Century City. Some actors are of sufficient standing that they don't have to read but the process takes place just the same.

"Stunt casting" is when a show uses somebody famous for a role simply because they are famous. When a show is getting off the ground the network often asks producers for big names to attract the idly curious viewer. "The first season they say, 'You have to stunt cast,'" says Katie Jacobs. "The funny thing is it is really hard to stunt cast when no one knows who you are. It's really easy to stunt cast now when you don't need it."

The story of how Peter Jacobson did, and nearly didn't, become Taub is instructive. Before Taub existed, Jacobson was offered a role on *House* as a guest star, as a lawyer for Vogler in a court scene with House in season one. Jacobson didn't have to audition; the part was his and his agent said he should do it. But ten days after filming he was due to fly to Australia for a three-month shoot on the series *The Starter Wife*. At the last second, the thought of all the travel involved was too much and through his agent, Jacobson turned down the part. If he'd taken the first role (for two scenes), Jacobson would never have been considered for Taub. ("Hey, that plastic surgeon, wasn't he a lawyer three years ago?")

Katie Jacobs had worked with Peter Jacobson on an episode of her series *Gideon's Crossing* in 2001 and Jacobson's was the first name Jacobs thought of for Taub. The casting team was told Jacobson was in New York. They would have pursued him there and put him on tape but Stephanie Laffin saw the actor sitting having lunch in a restaurant in Venice. "What's he doing here?" she thought. "It was definitely meant to be." (Jacobson and his wife were "randomly" in L.A.) Jacobson found out that the role might be a recurring one which was definitely attractive. His wife saw the sides—the lines for the audition—and she had an immediate and visceral response. "That is totally you." When Jacobson so much as hesitated this, the second time around with *House*, his wife said, "are you out of you mind?" And Taub was cast.

Curveballs take different forms for each department. In casting they can come in trying to cast without a fleshed-out character to work from. Katie Jacobs cast many of the roles for the two-hour episode "Broken," which she also directed, before the script was written. She cast Andre Braugher, who she knew from *Gideon's Crossing*, and Lin-Manuel Miranda, whom she'd seen on Broadway in his musical *In the Heights*. Franka Potente (*Run Lola, Run* and the *Bourne* movies) had expressed an interest in the show, met Katie at the end of season five, and was cast in "Broken" soon after.

To these and other actors Jacobs made a pitch: "'We're doing something different. I think you'll be great as House's roommate, [for example], do you want to come and play?'" Jacobs says. "And they all said 'yes' without seeing a script. The writers worked with them in mind." If Jacobs had waited till the script was ready to begin casting they never would have made their air date.

Alternatively, an unusually heavy workload might drop out of the sky. "We left at the end of season three and I remember Katie saying in passing, 'We're going to add some new blood next season,'" says Stephanie Laffin. "And I was like, 'Okay, see ya, have a nice summer.' And Amy got a call: 'We're going to be adding some people . . .'" Forty people. "But we didn't get any added time," says Amy. House's cattle call to replace his first diagnostic team was cast over a two-episode period. There were forty applicants but not forty speaking parts: House dismissed a whole row who didn't have time to get a word in. Still, there were more than twenty speaking parts, including three that would go on to become regulars, which required five actors to have studio and network tests—those for Taub, Kutner, Thirteen, Big Love, and Amber.

"We just jumped in," says Amy Lippens. "You have a beginning, a middle, and an end in TV casting and you have a very short period of time and that's the bad thing. We care about doing our best work and we have to do our best work in eight days as if we had two months."

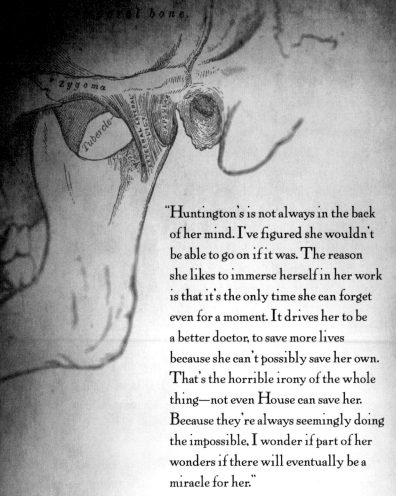

"Huntington's is not always in the back of her mind. I've figured she wouldn't be able to go on if it was. The reason she likes to immerse herself in her work is that it's the only time she can forget even for a moment. It drives her to be a better doctor, to save more lives because she can't possibly save her own. That's the horrible irony of the whole thing—not even House can save her. Because they're always seemingly doing the impossible, I wonder if part of her wonders if there will eventually be a miracle for her."

—Olivia Wilde

THIRTEEN

Olivia Wilde

No one at PPTH is concerned much with first names—even Chase called his wife "Cameron." When the forty applicants show up in "The Right Stuff" to replace Eric, Allison, and Robert, House uses his own endearments. He calls applicant number Thirteen "Kitty Carlisle," a seventy-year-old reference to when the socialite was a Broadway actress. Thirteen makes the right call that the patient is a pilot. She doesn't tell him her name, so Thirteen it is. Being called by her number is better for Thirteen than being called "Cutthroat Bitch" (Amber, who might have been "Twenty-four"), or "Overly Excited Former Foster Kid" (Kutner, number Six), and is certainly better than anything House calls Cole: the Dark Religious Nut, or Big Love.

Despite her number-only status, Thirteen arouses House's curiosity as Cameron did before her. Right away, Thirteen's carelessness causes a patient's death when she fails to make sure he takes the pills prescribed him to kill his *Strongyloides* parasite ("97 Seconds"). This would seem like a reason to fire someone (House is firing candidates who mistake Buddy Ebsen for Neville Chamberlain) but Thirteen stays.

> "I was so honored that they were immediately trusting me with this strong story line I thought, Wow, they're really letting me have some fun. If I can kill someone right away they must like me. Just don't have a character kill a dog, which will mean everyone hates you."
>
> —OLIVIA WILDE

With his sixth sense, House knows there's something up with Thirteen. Wilson calls out House for his attitude to women like Thirteen, Cameron, and Amber. "You hire beautiful girls, enslave them, force them to be around you because you don't know how to have an actual relationship. If they're qualified, keep them. If not, fire them and ask them out," but House only follows this advice with Dr. Terzi from the CIA. Instead, he drugs Thirteen with caffeinated coffee, which is enough to give her the shakes ("You Don't Want to Know"). House knows there is a history because he found an obit for Thirteen's mother, who died after a long illness. Parkinson's? No, Huntington's. Even House says, "I'm sorry."

> "It's good for dramatic purposes because it is a dreadful disease with no hope of treatment at this point in time. In the conception of a character, the idea of a disease where there is a horrible thing in your future and do you find out whether it's going to happen? It's an interesting dilemma."
>
> —DAVID FOSTER

Huntington's disease is a pitiless condition that affects both mind and body. Someone with Huntington's gradually loses control of their movements until they can't talk or eat. They might remain alert but also become depressed and suicidal. There's a fifty percent chance a child of someone who has the disease will contract it themselves at some point in their lives and then it will take ten to twenty years to run its course. Huntington's used to be called "St. Vitus's Dance"—sufferers were thought to be possessed and for years it was called Huntington's "chorea," chorea referring to the uncontrollable movements, a word also originally meaning dance. At first, Thirteen hasn't been tested: she doesn't know if she's going to develop the disease.

> **THIRTEEN:** "Not knowing makes me do things I think I'm scared to do. Take flying lessons, climb Kilimanjaro, work for you."
>
> **HOUSE:** "Yeah, 'cause if you knew, you couldn't do any of those things."

Obviously this knowledge is something House won't be able to leave alone. He outs Thirteen and makes it clear he'd want to know. When Amber is injured in the bus crash, Thirteen can't do her job. She didn't like Amber but the thought of a young woman dying before her time is too much. "Deal with it: Get back in there or pack up your stuff," House says. Thirteen deals by taking the test for Huntington's after Amber dies. The test is positive. In "Dying Changes Everything," Thirteen tells a patient she figures she has a dozen years. "I don't wanna be just tightening bolts and following instructions. I want something to be different because of me." House is characteristically deflating. "Almost dying changes nothing," he tells Thirteen. "Dying changes everything."

DAVID SHORE: "I liked the notion that it was a gigantic question mark hanging over her head. The notion that someone would possibly have an extremely shortened life but has chosen not to know."

QUESTION: "Which is something that House is not going to be able to keep away from."

SHORE: "Exactly. Had she known one way or the other it would have defeated the purpose at the beginning."

In "Lucky Thirteen," Thirteen believes her disease is progressing fast and she joylessly goes about living it up. When the woman she picks up in a bar seizes, Thirteen brings her to PPTH and admits she doesn't know her name. "Empty transient sex," says House. "I've been waiting for you to spiral out of control ever since you got your Huntington's diagnosis. But this is more than I dared hope for." When Thirteen misses a diagnostic session to get an IV for her hangover, House fires her. But Thirteen sticks around, helping find out what's wrong with the girl, Spencer, even though she only met Thirteen so she could get treated by House. Thirteen can empathize with Spencer when it looks as though she has an incurable disease, too. House has a eureka moment when he sees Thirteen has chapped lips, brought on by Spencer's Sjogren's syndrome. "Another life saved by girl-on-girl action," says House.

Thirteen's risk-taking behavior escalates. House hires Thirteen back, saying she's going to spiral down till she crashes but until then, she's useful. She's with another pickup at the end of "Lucky Thirteen." Then, in "Last Resort," she agrees to test the drugs House prescribes hostage-taker Jason (Zeljko Ivanek). "This is a level of risk taking beyond girl-on-girl action," says House. House tells Thirteen she wants to die but she doesn't have the nerve to do it herself. She says, "I don't want to die." Thirteen enrolls in a drug trial Foreman is administering for Huntington's patients. This idea is loaded with ethical and personal minefields from the start. Thirteen feels bad that Foreman got her in the trial. Then meeting a patient named Janice reminds Thirteen of seeing her mother being taken to hospital when Thirteen was a child named Remy. She tells Foreman her mother used to yell at her. "I wanted her to die," she says and she never said good-bye.

Thirteen is ambivalent about being on the trial when it seems like Foreman is manipulating it and with it, her. When Foreman switches her to the real drug it seems as if there is real hope for Thirteen. She even talks about having kids one day ("Big Baby"). But Foreman has gone a step too far and the real drug makes Thirteen sick; she develops a brain tumor and goes blind. Foreman scrambles to save Thirteen, his career, and his job at PPTH.

> "She has swung the other direction from her death wish she showed in the hostage episode when she was throwing herself in front of the gun. It was Foreman who encouraged her to choose life, to try to be healthy, but his guilt during the drug trial is worsened by the fact that he's pulled her to the other side of the spectrum of hope . . . The trial was a fluke and there is no happy ending."
>
> —OLIVIA WILDE

The drug trial fails to help Thirteen but the spiral has been halted. She's content to be a member of the team at PPTH and to be with Foreman. She admits she misses other women, and other men:

THIRTEEN: "Monogamy is like saying you're never going to have any other ice cream flavor besides Rocky Road."

FOREMAN: "So you're saying if you don't have pink bubble gum for a while that one day you're gonna chase down the ice-cream truck?"

THIRTEEN: "No. Rocky Road is great. It's a very delicious and complicated flavor . . ." ("The Softer Side")

QUESTION: "What about her 'Monogamy is like Rocky Road' line?"

OLIVIA WILDE: "She's a realist. She knows Foreman has a more traditional sense of relationships so she likes making him admit the reality of it. I love the Truffaut quote when he was discussing *Jules and Jim*—monogamy doesn't work but everything else is worse. And that's really Thirteen's position—it's not realistic but companionship is valuable. I think she will find a way to be healthy but still exploring."

Foreman decides he can't be the boss, have Thirteen on the team, and have a relationship with her at the same time so he fires her, and loses the relationship, too. Foreman won't admit he's made the wrong choice, even if he magnanimously climbs down later to say he can work with Thirteen on the team. Thirteen is prepared to move on to another job until House returns and entices her and Taub back. When House is wooing Thirteen, he shows up at her gym, where she's doing crunches, strengthening her core to ward off onset of her disease, House says. She's prepared to spend the time with House as that time bomb in her body ticks on.

THIRTEEN'S LOOK

"She is superhip. She is bisexual so she prefers to dress a little bit an-drogynous. Still, supersexy, superfeminine, and masculine at the same time, if that's possible."

—CATHY CRANDALL

QUESTION: "Does she have a color palette?"

CATHY CRANDALL: "She does. She wears a lot of gray and black and navy and aubergine and a sort of dusty blue and dusty teal. Very sort of grayed-out coloring. It all looks good with her skin color and with her eyes."

Olivia Wilde on . . . Thirteen and Foreman

QUESTION: "The question was, would Foreman throw away his whole career for the chance to have another couple of years with Thirteen?"

"At that point they had only known each other a short period of time . . . It's what he loves doing, staving off the inevitable. There's nothing we want to do more than to do that for the people we love."

QUESTION: "Do Thirteen and Foreman have a future?"

"Thirteen will try to make it work with Foreman. If that's not realistic then finding a way to stay healthy but to still enjoy her romantic life and perhaps pursue relationships with other people."

QUESTION: "She needs to date someone outside the office . . ."

"I think so but they spend too much time at work. One thing that concerns me is that she only had relationships with women when she was down and out and it somehow implies it's a side effect of being depressed and out of control. I definitely don't think that's true and I don't think that was their intention but that's the way it seemed. I think it's important once she's with a man and is healthy she explore her bisexuality and perhaps try a healthy relationship with a woman again so it's clear it's not just when she's depressed and sick."

Olivia Wilde on . . . Huntington's

"It's probably a fascinating disease for our writers because there is something very mysterious about it. . . . They have found ways to test yourself early like Thirteen did and many people have chosen to do that and many not and I'm fascinated by the difference in the quality of life of those two groups."

QUESTION: "What would you do?"

"I would want to know. Existentialists through the centuries have said once you face death, once you come to terms with it, you live your life in a different way and you live your life more fully."

QUESTION: "Your character has done that."

"I think that's inevitable. I think I probably would. It would have to be love to stop you from doing that."

QUESTION: "But you can't stave off the inevitable. You're a time bomb."

"Not only did I see my mother die of Huntington's, so I know exactly what's in store, but I then went on to study exactly how the body works and how it breaks down so there's no mystery involved at all."

QUESTION: "Do you have any symptoms?"

"She has some nerve damage but it would be a few years before she started seeing major symptoms. The character we had who had full-blown Huntington's illustrating what was in store for Thirteen was important for the audience because most people don't know what Huntington's is. Talking about it in a grave way that Thirteen is going to develop these symptoms and not knowing how horrible they really are, it was hard for the audience to have any emotional attachment to them. But once we met Janice it was, 'Oh, no, this can't happen to Thirteen.' We hope she stays healthy. I think she will find a healthy way to have fun."

Olivia Wilde on . . . Thirteen

"*House* is probably the hardest-working show in the business and I knew that coming into it. It was interesting coming in a few seasons in because you hear things in the outside world about what it's like on the set."

QUESTION: "Did you watch *House* before you worked on it?"

"I was never a big TV watcher but I was aware of it and I knew it had great roles for women. I was doing a play in New York and my agent said they might add a female doctor to *House* and if you were so lucky to get that role, you'd be crazy to turn it down and I said, 'I'm not doing TV again.' He said 'No, this is different. Where else are you going to have consistently brilliant writing like this?' And he was right. It was good advice."

QUESTION: "What was the season-four selection process like?"

"We didn't know what was going to happen week to week. There was a group of us who knew we would be here for a handful of episodes. We didn't know how it would happen. I certainly didn't expect as much work, as much involvement as I got immediately."

QUESTION: "You originally auditioned to be Amber."

"I auditioned for the role of Amber and Annie Dudek originally auditioned for Thirteen. I really wanted to play Amber. I thought she was hilarious and I thought it was be so fun to play someone that conniving . . . [When] they said Thirteen, I said, 'I don't know, she's a mystery.' They said, 'She has some interesting things she's covering up,' and I said, 'But Amber.' Annie was doing the same thing with Thirteen. They were so right because my interpretation of Amber was not as brilliant as Annie's and in the end I am so happy it worked out the way it did."

QUESTION: "How do you find learning the medical terms?"

"I think the medical terminology is a lot like learning Shakespeare because you can't paraphrase, you have to know it. You have to find the beauty in it and you have to find your understanding of it. I remember getting the audition sides and at the time it seemed very complicated but the most complicated word was *intestine* but it felt like, 'Oh God, how am I going to remember small intestine? Large intestine?' and in the middle of the audition I lost it and just screamed, 'Fuck!' I remember being horrified and Katie Jacobs looked at me and said, 'You are officially like the people on our show. Don't worry, it happens every day.'"

Olivia Wilde is ready for her close-up.

QUESTION: "We are convinced by you as doctors."

"The most common question is 'How do you remember it all?' The second most common question is 'Is it as much fun to do as it is to watch?' I get that a lot on the subway in New York. The medical stuff, people will ask, 'Do you know about this thing?' I did it inadvertently to Hugh my first episode. I was talking about this medical condition I had heard about and I was asking him as one would ask a doctor if this person was cured with this remedy and he looked at me for a long beat and he said, 'You know, I'm not really a doctor.' 'Oh my God, I'm so sorry. I know that.'"

QUESTION: "Has your own experience with doctors changed?"

"Since I've been on the show I have so much more respect for them. I give them much more detailed histories because I think that's what we do wrong with our doctors. We expect them to perform miracles without [us] giving them all the information that they need.

"But what other team of doctors spends that much time and energy thinking about one person's welfare? I would be so happy to have us—five doctors spending day and night killing themselves to find the cure and seemingly not charging you. I think it's because we're made by Canadians that we don't ever concern ourselves with that. It doesn't occur to David Shore how broke each patient would leave the hospital."

QUESTION: "Your fate is determined for you. But is anyone capable of change?"

"I think Thirteen was the character who has changed the most. She's gone from being a very private person holding everything very tightly to the vest, being very stubborn and secretive, to being open to a healthy relationship, to taking care of herself. She has changed drastically. She's proof that people can change. House can change. His attempt to be clean is a change in itself. He wants to change and that in itself is a change."

Olivia Wilde on . . . Olivia Wilde

QUESTION: "You are a Cockburn [parents Leslie and Andrew Cockburn are journalists] so you grew up in a household full of heated discussions and typewriters . . ."

"I didn't know any other world. It was exciting. I always had a sense that they were plugged into what was happening and I could ask any question about the world, about politics, about any period in history and I was convinced they knew everything. I always wanted to act . . . I have approached acting like a journalist—investigating the character in the way that you would investigate your subject."

QUESTION: "Did you talk politics at the dinner table?"

"It was very healthy to grow up knowing that debate was always part of the discussion. Lefties are always vying to see who is leftiest. There were always different kinds of people. I had family members who were quite conservative. I learned from an early age that in order to argue with a Republican you have to learn to speak the language of Republicans which means . . . money. If you can convince a Republican they need to hire better schoolteachers and pay them more because in the end a better national grade point average improves the GDP. If you can bring it back to them paying less taxes . . ."

QUESTION: "And Kal Penn left here to go to the White House . . ."

"I asked Kal how working for the administration was different and Kal said well it is different from acting. For instance when it's cold no one brings you a warmy coat. That's how infantile we are in this business. 'It's freezing. Why isn't anyone approaching me with cashmere?' Such a cool thing to watch him explode out of this into public service."

QUESTION: "You have a strong connection to Ireland."

"My dad's Irish so we went back and forth."

QUESTION: "Hence the Wilde?"

"That was part of the reason. It was a tradition to have pen names in my family. My uncle [Alexander] wrote 'Beat the Devil' [column in *The Nation*] under a pseudonym and I always thought there was something romantic about it. When I was five or six I went through a period of wanting to be a horror fiction writer. My step-aunt was Sarah Caudwell, who was a great mystery writer, and I remember asking her what my pen name should be. I was always excited by the idea of it.

"Once I became aware of the lack of privacy in this business I was attracted to the idea of having a barrier between the business and my family. Protecting myself and also protecting them. Being able to forge my own path. I think growing up in D.C. with them being pretty well-known journalists I was constantly being identified as being part of the brood and honored to be so but eager to set out on my own . . . You think about Sigourney Weaver, who got the name from Fitzgerald, and she found that really informed her as an artist.

"I was doing a fantastic production of [The Importance of Being] Earnest at the time, playing Gwendolen. I was really inspired by Oscar Wilde and immersed in the works and respecting how he stood up for his individuality and his principles. He had a sense of humor through all the humiliation, which is I think what is necessary on order to survive this world."

"And B, because it is a solid Anglo-Irish name."

QUESTION: "You studied in Ireland?"

"I was eighteen. I went to the Gaiety School of Acting in Dublin. I love Dublin. The Celtic Tiger allowed it to be an artistic hub. Anywhere you looked there was a hole in the wall where someone was doing a production of a Beckett play. There was this great, exciting vibe. It was a very good time to be there. It had a big impact on how I would approach this business. You'd go see a play and go have a beer with Colm Meaney afterwards, who had been in the play, and there was no BS. I was going to go straight from there to college in New York to study acting and my teacher there told me to come here for a year to see if I really wanted to be in the business."

QUESTION: "If you could be an actor without having to be famous would that be ideal?"

"Of course. Then you could concentrate on your work and never screw yourself with your own fear and insecurities. The best actors are the fearless ones and it's hard to be fearless when you know someone is immediately going to criticize you, but you have to get over that."

QUESTION: "I read about you and Julie Christie . . ."

"She is a great mentor and a great guide because she has a very realistic approach to this business. She is very humble, too humble. She'd say, 'I wasn't so good when I was younger . . .' She has a great way of being outside of it all."

QUESTION: "And you look to Hugh Laurie?"

"I ask Hugh for advice all the time. He's a great fountain of wisdom. He's so self-deprecating. He's very kind and sensitive to whatever questions I have and his advice is pretty spot-on. He's someone who is profoundly uncomfortable with celebrity but I think has handled it extremely well and has transformed into a famous dramatic actor. Actors tend to think once you are in one genre you're stuck there."

QUESTION: "Tell me about *Tron: Legacy*."

"It's a complete departure. It was important to do something I was really afraid of and I had never thought of myself as being able to do a sci-fi action film. I loved it so much and it was really exciting but it really made me appreciate *House*. We have such incredible writers, you take for granted the fact that everything is logical, well thought out and that it tracks, even from something that happened years ago. In TV the writers really are in control. It's their medium, I think, and in film it's the director's. I'm used to talking to the writers all the time asking for advice, discussing characters with them. I do the same on a film set and the writers seem quite shocked, like 'Actors don't usually talk to us.'"

QUESTION: "How did you fit that in?"

"We filmed that during our hiatus, set to set. We wrapped *Tron* at six-thirty on a Monday morning in Vancouver and the same day I was back in L.A. on the *House* set."

QUESTION: "You find it refreshing to do something different?"

"I think balancing out is important. I think now I want to do something completely different. My husband [Tao Ruspoli] and I did a film

[*Fix*]. That's something I shot when I first joined the *House* cast. I could only do that being married to the director—no other director would have dealt with my schedule."

QUESTION: "You want to do more movies?"

"When people have seen you in a lab coat they can see you in any official position with power. So if you have played a doctor you can play a cop, a politician, a firefighter. Anything with an official badge. People take me seriously, which is great. My goal is to be able to traverse the genres of film and try to skip between comedy and drama seamlessly and easily—like Cate Blanchett or Meryl Streep. The great roles are few and far between but they are there.

"I did a Paul Haggis movie with Russell Crowe and squeezed it in in two weeks. Credit to our producers that they give you enough notice . . . The show is always in first position so anything you do has to work around *House*. If you can find something that is willing to work around *House* and if you are willing to never sleep and take red-eyes a lot. . . . When the next hiatus comes I'll do a couple of projects in then."

QUESTION: "Do you take any vacation?"

"When everyone starts telling me I'm too old then I'll take a vacation. It's really important to take a few days off here and there and I always feel so recharged and inspired. That's when you have the chance to read and see some theater and remember why you're doing what you're doing. . .

"I feel very anxious if I haven't read the paper in the morning."

QUESTION: "Here, it's all about words . . ."

"It's really exploring language. Some people are able to say, 'Well, the script's not there but the director's amazing,' if the script's not there. . . . I can't allow myself to overlook bad writing but I have more of an appreciation myself from them."

QUESTION: "Do you do any writing yourself?"

"I do and I'm trying to do it more. I think this is my year to finally follow through with that stuff."

QUESTION: "So what are you writing?"

"I like to write nonfiction stuff, my own thoughts on different situations. Short fiction as well. I have to get to the point when I am willing to show it to the public. I'm building a Web site which is kind of funny. I have this resentment and discomfort with the Internet but the only way to stake your claim is to have your own place. Taking them on on their own ground.

"I appreciate what the blogosphere has done for democratizing journalism but I think it's frustrating there is no fact-checking entity and the idea of truth has now disintegrated on the Internet . . . I think that instead of just resenting that I have to have my own place where I'm saying my own piece. I like the idea of saying I'm going to interview Julie Christie on . . . on monogamy. Not on 'me and my day' and what macrobiotic restaurant we went to."

QUESTION: "You should get on that because you don't have enough else to do."

"You're right. I should really stop being so lazy."

6

IF IT'S HAPPENED ONCE

 The Odd Medicine of *House*

> "If it's happened once we can do it. This is the great
> thing about doctors—they write everything down.
> So there are case reports of absolutely everything
> out there, on the Internet or in journals. If you can't
> find one instance in the last fifty years of someone
> saying this has happened then it's probably not
> okay. If it's happened exactly once then you are in
> the realm of odd."
>
> —DAVID FOSTER, M.D.

Every week, *House* ventures boldly into the medical realm of odd.
Dr. House's Department of Diagnostic Medicine takes only the
cases that have flummoxed everyone else. Mark, husband of House's
ex, Stacy, for example, has seen five doctors before Stacy turns to
House; Jason, who forces House to diagnose him at gunpoint in
"Last Resort" counts sixteen in three years; financier Roy Randall's
son Jack ("Instant Karma") has seen seventeen doctors. In the pilot,
Foreman repeats the well-known med school axiom that if you
hear hoof beats, you think horses, not zebras. But these seventeen
doctors have eliminated all the horses—House only gets zebras.

The medical cases are the weekly conundrum, the puzzles that
House needs to occupy himself and allow him to connect to the
extent that he can with the world, something that Dr. Nolan (Andre

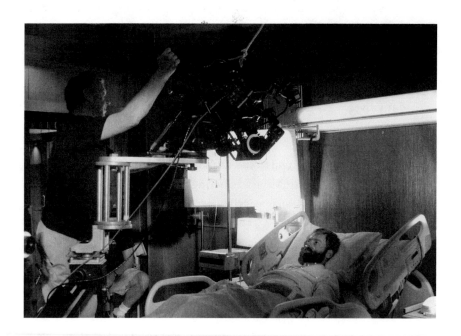

"*House* ventures boldly into the medical realm of odd."

Braugher) helps House to understand in season six. It's a common feature of the case of the week that it somehow reflects events in the main characters' lives. The case then serves a dual purpose: as a one-week procedural mystery and as a plot device to advance the overarching story lines. That's a lot to ask of a disease.

Unearthing the identity of the villain of the week isn't the point. Viewers aren't watching so they can say "I *knew* it was subacute sclerosing panencephalitis" ("Paternity"). They watch because of what the diagnostic process says about the doctors and patients involved, how it causes them to act and react. David Foster is the senior *House* medical consultant and a supervising producer. Dr. Foster explains why he wants to use a disease that makes you lie, for example. "The medical story that unfolds has to be a medical story that only we can tell. One that gives rise to House commenting on the nature of the character of the patient who faces a medical dilemma that we will resolve in a House-like way."

Some ailments are devilishly Housean because of the way they present. They either look like something else or the symptoms they bring about in patients mimic the kind of philosophical and ethical land mines and tank traps we encounter in our daily lives. This isn't even counting the stuff that patients consciously lie about:

- Stacy's husband, Mark, told House he took Stacy to Paris on honeymoon. A PET scan shows he thinks he was telling the truth when he was lying which means he's delusional, possibly a symptom of acute intermittent porphyria. ("The Honeymoon")

- The woman who swears she hasn't made love since she split with her husband sleepwalks and has sex with her ex (a condition called sexomnia). ("Role Model")

- The writer who has aphasia (loss ability to speak) and agraphia (loss of ability to write) because he tried to treat the bipolar disorder he kept from his wife. ("Failure to Communicate")

- The physically perfect teen model is actually a hermaphrodite—"The ultimate woman is a man," says House. ("Skin Deep")

- A police officer dies from bacterial infection caused by pigeon droppings he is using to fertilize his marijuana plants. ("Euphoria, Part I")

- The death row inmate (played by LL Cool J) whose murderous rages were caused by a pheochromocytoma brought on by heavy metal in his prison tattoos. ("Acceptance")

- Leighton Meester's underage teen temptress Ali ("Informed Consent"), hits on House not because of House's (undeniable) attractions but because of the *Coccidioides immitis* in her brain.

- The girl whose short stature isn't caused by dwarfism like her mother's but by Langerhans cell histiocytosis. ("Merry Little Christmas")

- Dave Matthews plays a virtuoso pianist with severe neurological disabilities who can get a life but lose his talent if his brain is sliced in half. ("Half-Wit")

- A woman has abulia, the inability to make a decision, manifested when she can't make a choice in a street game of three-card Monte. ("House Training")

- A caring father who causes his son (age eight) to grab Cameron's ass and bite Chase and his daughter (age six) to begin puberty and stroke. By holding hands with them, the male enhancement cream he's taking is flooding their bodies with sex hormones. And dad's new, young girlfriend is his daughter's teacher! ("Act Your Age")

- Brain damage causes mirror syndrome, in which the patient loses any sense of self and mimics whoever they think is in charge in any situation. ("Mirror, Mirror")

- Anhedonia, the inability to experience pleasure, a symptom of familial Mediterranean fever. ("Joy")

- The special-education teacher whose patent ductus arteriosus in her heart reduces the stress she feels when she has high blood pressure. ("Big Baby")

- Alien hand syndrome. A patient's hand develops a mind of its own: I'm hurting you and I really can't help it. ("Both Sides Now")

- The young girl who may or may not have been molested bleeds into her brain, causing her to lie. Perfect. Everybody lies and she can't help it. ("Known Unknowns")

- The porn star whose own lifestyle is too clean, causing his body's immune system to rebel. ("Teamwork")

- Ted, who collapses at the altar as he is about to be married to Nicole, has a Chiari malformation in his brain that was exacerbated by electroconvulsive therapy he had while undergoing "conversion therapy"—a futile attempt to make him straight. Among the side effects: Ted starts lactating. ("The Choice.")

The strange and obscure condition in question may or may not be the cause of a patient's medical issues or character defects. Jasper, the boy with the amorous dad, has an excuse for his aggressiveness but the kid in "The Jerk," he's just a jerk.

One quintessentially House-like case is presented in "The Social Contract" in the form of Nick Greenwald, a book editor whose frontal lobe disinhibition causes him in the manner of an AM radio host to say exactly what pops into his head. He comments on the size of Taub's nose and how he'd like to "do" Thirteen and Cuddy. In other words, he's just like House, who in the same episode calls Taub "Cyrano de Berkowitz" and makes his usual inappropriate comments about his female colleagues. House has no clinical excuse—he's just an ass—but when Nick's zingers start to hit closer to his own home, House says he knows how the guy feels.

When Nick says his developmentally disabled daughter is simply below average and he sometimes regrets marrying his wife (who isn't so sharp, either), he's driving away his family. It's classically Housean—if this is what happens when we say what we think, no wonder we tell so many lies. Just when it looks like Nick's condition, and his self-alienation from his family, are permanent, House figures out Nick has the incredibly obscure Doege-Potter syndrome. Nick's body is overreacting to one small fibroma. Remove the fibroma, says House, and he'll be a happy hypocrite again. In other words, just like the rest of us.

At times we're made to wonder whether the treatment isn't worse than the disease.

Take the eighty-two-year-old woman who comes to the clinic in "Poison." Her personality has changed: She's loving life, checking out guys, fantasizing about Ashton Kutcher. In fact, House reminds her of Kutcher: "Same bedroom eyes," she says. When House diagnoses syphilis it's not a surprise to her; she got it on her prom night in 1939. The syphilis is curable but she doesn't want the treatment. She likes feeling sexy and making a fool of

The PPTH pathology lab

herself with young doctors. "I really don't want to play canasta for the rest of my life," she says. House seems to like her, appreciating the trade-off she's making. Even if the syphilis is killing her she's doomed to feel good as it proceeds.

"My father-in-law is a doctor. He likes the show . . . The only way we cheat is we kaleidoscope time a little bit. Medical tests come back the next day. People get better a little faster. Or get worse. He always says, 'Robert that disease would never . . .' 'I know, I know.' I get that a lot. He is actually very impressed with the show. Our guys are very good, and very thorough. There's nothing on this show that couldn't happen medically. I believe everything on this show is medically possible. Possibly improbable but certainly possible."

—Robert Sean Leonard

In "Heavy," a voluptuous woman diagnosed with a thirty-pound tumor says she likes the curves the tumor gives her. She doesn't want to change the way she looks and her husband loves her body. But House deduces it's not her husband the woman wants to please; it's the other men in her life she's sleeping with. House persuades the woman to have the operation, reasoning that the woman shouldn't worry about her looks so much. "Men are pigs. . . . They'll pretty much have sex with anyone." Jeff, the nice guy in "No More Mr. Nice Guy," loses more than his pleasant demeanor. "I'm not so sure I like ketchup anymore," he says at the end. And miserable genius James Sidas makes a possibly counterintuitive lifestyle choice in "Ignorance Is Bliss."

The most intriguing and Housean case of all is of course House himself. In the Emmy-winning "Three Stories," we find out what happened to House's leg and the fact that it was House who finally diagnosed what was wrong. The treatment option that Stacy elects for her comatose partner leaves House with the painkiller addiction he has been treating and not treating and treating again the whole series. House has gone to extreme lengths both to maintain his addiction and to try to cure it. It's a question that comes up in medicine and is given a typical Housean twist on the show: "So, Patient X, do you really want to get better?"

One of these conditions is a fake, invented by House to appease a patient convinced he's going to get sick and die when House thinks it's in his head (House is wrong). The rest are real (answer below).

alveolar rhabdomyosarcoma
Anton's blindness
Erdheim-Chester disease
erythropoietic protoporphyria
Fitz-Hugh-Curtis syndrome
hemorrhagic telangiectasia
hereditary coproporphyria
immune reconstitution syndrome
Kelley-Seegmiller syndrome
Korsakoff's syndrome
Lambert-Eaton syndrome
Langerhans cell histiocytosis

lymphangioleiomyomatosis
male pseudohermaphroditism
neurocysticercosis.
Ortoli syndrome
paraneoplastic syndrome
pheochromocytoma
primary antiphospholipid syndrome
Sjogren's syndrome
subacute sclerosing panencephalitis
Von Hippel-Lindau syndrome
Wernicke's encephalopathy
Wilson's disease

ANSWER: House cooked up Ortoli syndrome in "Brave Heart."

Whether it's sexiness, happiness, niceness, honesty, life, or death, House's patients have something significant at stake that's in serious jeopardy. It's part of David Foster's credo for *House* that even though the audience knows it's fiction, the show has to stay grounded in reality. We're only going to believe the stakes and jeopardy that House is grappling with if the rules we recognize from the world at large are applied. It means occasionally someone has to die. It means that the disease can't be utterly fantastical. Says Foster, "If you take those rules and ignore them then you've lost your stakes and jeopardy because the audience will say you're just going to make it up anyway."

David Foster entered the medical profession because he's always loved listening to people telling their stories. Foster interned at Beth Israel Hospital in Boston and practiced in that city for some years. Through Neal Baer, a friend who was a producer at *ER*, he took baby steps in writing for TV. Gradually Dr. Foster shifted the direction of his life 180 degrees from a lot of doctoring and a little writing to the other way round. He consulted on a Hallmark Hall of Fame movie, on pilots that never got made, and on *Gideon's Crossing*. Then Baer hired Foster to work on *Law & Order: SVU*. He graduated from adding medical terms to scenes to writing whole scripts. When he came to *House* in the first season he was a consultant who could freelance scripts. In his second year he was hired as a story editor and worked his way up from there.

"I like people who see the world differently and seeing the world through their eyes," says Foster. "I worked at an inner-city health clinic and ran a detox center—prostitutes and drug dealers. I like to hear people talk about their lives that are different from mine and their view on the world that is different from mine . . . One of my patients came in and complained that a prostitute stole his dentures off the side of his bed. Who would do that? Who would steal dentures off the side of the bed?"

It has happened that something a writer has proposed breaches the boundaries of reality and Dr. Foster has said no to David Shore. "I have rarely ever said what you are talking about is absolutely impossible. I have said it but it's a very rare occasion." What about sixteen accessory spleens (an idea from consultant John Sotos used in "Ignorance is Bliss")? "Very odd," says Foster. "It has happened." Same goes for Maggie, the patient in "It's a Wonderful Lie" who develops breast cancer in cells behind her knee. "As a show we're different from other medical shows," says Dr. Foster. "Most of them deal with what usually happens and we tend to deal with what is plausible but not what usually happens. As a writer and a doctor I find that incredibly fun and creative and the most exciting. How can I take something and do it in a way that isn't down the middle."

Bobbin Bergstrom is a qualified nurse who serves as the on-set medical adviser for the series. Bobbin's job is to help preserve reality, making medical procedures look convincing and telling patients how much their latest complication or ultra-invasive test is going to hurt. Occasionally she's slightly skeptical of what the writers have come up with and it's part of her job to help keep it real. "I'll say, 'Please show me the research you have so I have something to say to Hugh.' They are very intelligent actors. Hugh is very smart and he won't just buy any kind of ridiculous. Omar will always ask me with that great Omar look as if to say, 'Really?' It's better if they know that I've not personally seen it but I've verified it as one in a million. I'm not going to say 'yeah' all the time. Our writers are brilliant and they do their best to make sure everything is accurate."

Because the stories are grounded in reality, art can, unfortunately, find parallels in life. When Bobbin Bergstrom saw alien hand syndrome on the script for the season-five finale she was, as she puts it, "beside myself." She'd never seen it and couldn't find out much about it. But it was a "magnificent" show. A few months later she found out that the wife of someone she knows had sadly contracted the very same condition. "Every one of these writers is so well educated. Book smart and people smart."

The show isn't above teasing us. In "Joy to the World," the audience is led a long way down a path toward believing that House is witness to a hitherto never-before scientifically verified virgin birth. In fact he's making it up to save the woman's impending wedding. A virgin birth would have been too fantastic. "People get mad or shocked before they've seen the whole thing," says David Foster. "'That's unbelievable!'"

In fact, the writers nix some stories because they don't think the audience will find them credible. In "Deception," House memorably treats a clinic patient who has an infection after using strawberry jelly as a contraceptive. (When the woman asks how long she should refrain from sex after treatment House tells her, "On an evolutionary basis, I'd recommend forever.") From whose fevered imagination did this spring? No one's; it's a true story, told by Harley Liker, one of the medical technical advisers on the show.

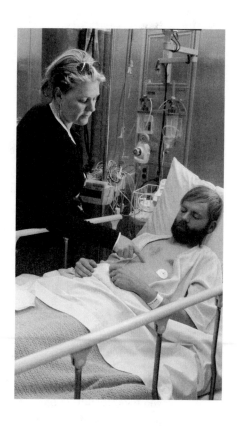

Bobbin Bergstrom preps another patient.

DAVID FOSTER: "He had another story along that same line about frogs."

QUESTION: "What do they do with the frogs?"

FOSTER: "The same thing as the jelly."

QUESTION: "A live or a dead frog?"

FOSTER: "Dead I believe but I'm not really sure."

"It's too unbelievable for TV," says Foster. "You have to suspend your disbelief and believe it really did happen. In real life there is no requirement because it really did happen and no one cares."

> **"The tasting of the vomit . . . I checked out. That's not entertaining to me. That just freaks me out."**
>
> —ROBERT SEAN LEONARD

Then there is the stuff that is just gross. In "Histories," House tastes some not-so-fresh vomit for the saltiness that might indicate a chemical imbalance.

The young Hurricane Katrina victim's reverse peristalsis ("Who's Your Daddy," in which the girl's digestive system sent waste up and out instead of down and out, ranks high in the yuk factor charts. Ask Bobbin Bergstrom. "The bowel that exploded over Omar ['Not Cancer']. That was pretty gross. [But] the little girl from Katrina? It's hard to top pooping out of your mouth." How about the clinic patient who circumcised himself with a box cutter? ("Autopsy") Or the man who used toenail clippers on his nasal hair and got athlete's foot up his nose? ("One Day, One Room")

BOBBIN BERGSTROM'S MEDICAL STORIES

"The toenail clipper: You want a comparable story? A sweet old man probably in his late seventies comes in with a goopy, gooey eye infection in each eye. He was wearing a fairly odd-looking band around his head. I find people fascinating so I'd sit and talk to them. 'Sir, what is that on your head?' 'Well,' he said, 'my wife, she was a much younger woman and she left me. This is the band from her underwear and this is how I think of her.' Okay. Back to the eyes. The doctor comes in and is looking at his eyes and he doesn't know. The third time the old man comes in, I see something. 'Doctor, I think I've figured out what's wrong.' The patient has his pants round his feet and he's scratching his booty and rubbing his eyes with the same hand. His eyes were *E. coli*'d out. People do weird things . . . Most of the things you see in the ER are sex games."

So where do the writers come up with their ideas? Other than Dr. Foster, the writers haven't spent years on hospital wards being exposed to disease and decay. The Internet means it's not so difficult to find something obscure. The trick is to integrate the medical condition and its resolution into a story line. Take the worm treatment in "Teamwork." David Foster says writer Eli Attie was fascinated by the idea that there are so many more incidences of autoimmune diseases and allergies because we have oversanitized our living environment. We don't live on farms any more getting dirty; we huddle in cities and clean our hands with almost moral fervor. The notion is that if we give the body something it recognizes to combat (a parasite, in this case worms), then it will stop attacking intruders that aren't there.

> "There are a few moments when you have to cringe. Like when someone's testicles explode. And I don't even have testicles."
>
> —LISA EDELSTEIN

In a differential diagnosis (or DDx), doctors elaborate possible causes for symptoms a patient is presenting and then eliminate them until one diagnosis, the one that best fits the symptoms, remains. The DDx, often held in House's outer office, is familiar from almost every episode. When a diagnosis emerges House will often treat rather than test. In forty-four minutes of TV, there isn't time to involve the lab much. "We have a number of dramatic devices to move the story forward," says David Foster. Treatment quickly follows theory. "They either get better or it causes something else to happen."

It's not so far removed from our experience with our own doctor but with higher stakes. "The trial is part and parcel of diagnostic medicine. [There are] more risks associated. Frequently we'll cover it with House saying treatment is faster. 'I could do three tests to confirm my diagnosis or I could just treat.' It's a little fast and loose. We're frequently wrong but we're rarely reckless to the point that the person is damaged because of our being wrong."

The process is key. "What you can never go towards is House magically coming up with the answer. What you need is House going piece by piece solving the puzzle." If House divined what was wrong in a very complex case without ticking off alternatives with a DDx , then the show has become *Touched by an Angel.*

Here, a writer has unearthed a condition and created a story around it. Other times writers will think of traits they would like to exploit in a character and figure out a situation to bring that about. Russel Friend and Garrett Lerner, executive producers and writing partners, worked backward from the famous picture of a fetus grabbing a surgeon's finger to create the story in "Fetal Position." Of course, the doctor they had in mind was House. House did seem to have a tender moment when his finger was held but naturally he deflected the emotion in the room with a comment. "Sorry," he says. "Just realized I forgot to TiVo *Alien.*"

Writing "Ignorance Is Bliss," David Hoselton was looking for something that would, in his words, "effectively turn the brain down to low." He could have used alcohol but that was too pedestrian for *House.* Cough syrup proved to be an excellent solution. It's a simple household item everyone has in their medicine cabinet but it's also a major source of drug abuse, which isn't so commonly known. The threat posed by everyday items can make for a more alarming story.

David Foster read about all the problems swallowing a toothpick can cause in a piece in the *New England Journal of Medicine* ("Needle in a Haystack"). It fit the bill perfectly. "I did some research and it happens quite often. It's odd but true. I thought that was a good idea for our show and a good disease for a Romeo and Juliet where the toothpick was central to the story." Foster wrote about House diagnosing a man's diabetes from his hairless hands, too-tight shoes, and doughnut crumbs on his shirt ("DNR"). In the first draft of that scene, House diagnosed the guy by more conventional means than just looking at him. David Foster says that David Shore challenged him to have House do it the more dramatic way. Foster went away thinking it was impossible but he figured out these clues that House might work from.

The writers know that people actually have the conditions that are being used as fictional devices in *House*. Those people associated with a disease might be glad that it's been mentioned at all, especially if it's something particularly obscure, happy that the condition has been put on the radar screen to this extent. It helps to raise awareness. If a disease is more familiar then it helps when it comes to going out and talking about your cause to the world. If House is interested in something and we're interested in House, there's some transference.

Attention to detail, 1: pathology lab test equipment

Even though they take necessary liberties with the speed at which some diseases and treatments progress, and certainly with the alacrity with which test results are returned, writers strive to get it right with the essentials of any condition. After reading a newspaper story about an autistic child and the difficulty he had on a hospital visit, David Hoselton decided to present House with a similar communications issue ("Lines in the Sand"). "I did a lot of research and we hired someone who works with autistic kids and we went to a school," says Hoselton. "We didn't want to pay lip service to it and we wanted it to be accurate. If we blew it, parents would be very upset."

In "Epic Fail," the patient's final diagnosis condition was Fabry's disease, an inherited condition where fatty substances build up over time in the cells. It's very rare, with an incidence of 1 in 117,000 people. It's so rare that if, as is the average, someone with Fabry's starts exhibiting symptoms at age ten, they won't be diagnosed until they are twenty-eight. After the show aired, David Shore heard from a Fabry's disease patient in Canada who said mentioning the condition would help in their battle to have the disease recognized by the government north of the border and to have treatment funded.

House has a special relationship with National Alliance on Mental Illness (NAMI) and has been recognized by NAMI for helping reduce the stigma associated with mental illness. NAMI and *House* worked with the central Housean notion that everybody lies—people with a mental illness are not necessarily more prone to untruth, something that's commonly misunderstood. And even though it's (almost) never lupus, advocates for lupus sufferers have commended *House* for raising public awareness.

Having said that, there's no public-service element in the show. If in the course of watching an interesting story someone takes a lesson away that will improve the way they look after themselves or their family—about vaccinating their kids (in "Paternity," House tells a parent that kids' coffins come in all colors) or not giving a baby raw food ("If only her ancestors had mastered the secrets of fire," House tells the parents in "Babies and Bathwater") or not trying to perform a self-circumcision, that's a cherry on top.

A response to a story from someone who is familiar with a particular condition is often, "Well, that is not my experience. What was portrayed isn't what happened to me." To which David Foster would reply, "That's correct. We're a show about the one in a million, the oddball case, the stuff that if it had happened in the way that it happens commonly, other people would have figured it out before it got to House. We will portray a common illness presenting in a very rare way. We'll do rare ones but also common ones which give you that 'could happen to me' feeling."

Are the medical consultants and writers concerned they'll run out of medical conditions to write stories around? In short, no. While we as sentient people have an infinite capacity to lie and screw up, so do our bodies. *House* mines the unusual but the more familiar ailments coming at us in disguise are more disquieting ("I didn't know my earache could be a heart attack") and there's so many of them. "What's bad for humanity is great for us," says Dr. Foster jauntily. "Way into the future we will be able to piece together medical mysteries and House is just a fascinating character."

David Foster was not always so confident. "The second episode we shot here after the pilot was 'Occam's Razor,'" he says. "When we finished that episode I said, 'I've told every story I know. I've used every piece of information I have. I got nothing left. I'm tapped out. I'm done.'" Six seasons later, it's clear he was wrong about that. Still, at the time, "It was alarming. I honestly felt that way. Somehow we made it through."

INSIDE DAVE MATTHEWS'S HEAD

How to Fake a Medical Procedure

> "We have Dave Matthews's head on a stake
> somewhere from an episode where we did some
> brain surgeries on him. They molded his whole
> face and actually it's a pretty good replica. We had
> three; he got one. There's a picture of him with it
> next to him and it's pretty eerie."
>
> —MIKE CASEY

In addition to their work as prop masters, Tyler Patton and Mike Casey rig up many of the medical procedures that viewers see most weeks on *House*. What appears on-screen is often a combination of Tyler and Mike's work with visual and special effects. There has been cause more than once for a doctor to drill into a patient's skull, for example. The drill itself looks like a standard home improvement model but around here, they're not using a drill to put up shelves. The writers and the director will let Tyler and Mike know just what effect they want to achieve. Says Mike, "If they want to drill into the head and then they want to have blood gushing everywhere—which is one of our favorites—we can do that."

At the prop meeting the team will discuss how to make the effect in question happen. It might be easier to have Elan Soltes, visual effects supervisor and his department (VFX), add the drill bit in postproduction. VFX will often be asked to create the effect of bone, blood, or brain matter being ejected as the drill bites into the skull. Tyler and Mike have a rubber drill bit they can use if they have to get close to an actor's head. For cutaway shots they can use a brain-matter-filled skull covered with fake skin that has been made by one of the specialty shops. The fake brain tissue can be drilled into for a biopsy.

QUESTION: "Do you have fake brains in storage?"

TYLER PATTON: "We have people that we call and they make the brains. We do have a lot of stuff. If they say, 'Do it right now,' Mike will go to the store and get some lasagna and I'll go to the OR and start putting some drapes up. We can make it happen."

In the past, Elan Soltes and the VFX department created more of the voyage-into-the-body shots—what he calls the "Magic School Bus shots"—than they have recently. While a lot of what Elan and his team does is computer generated, he also works with models. His first trip into a body in season six came in "Brave Heart" with the reckless cop who is convinced his heart is going to give out like those of all the men in his family before him. Elan's job was to explain using a model how an aneurysm in the man's brain might grow and block the nerve that sends signals to the heart. The shot traveled down the nerve into the chest cavity, where the heart beat slower and slower and then stopped.

Elan Soltes explains how the shot was set up:

"I commissioned a model of a part of the brain stem where we can see the aneurysm grow, which was actually a condom painted red that we could blow up and see push against a nerve, which was a piece of latex. It's all done with the magic of latex."

The model of the brain stem is about two feet square so a camera can fit inside to take the shot.

There is another model of a skull with a layer of skin and blood vessels that the camera pushes through, then a model of the brain, then the model of the brain stem itself. Elan also uses a model of a chest cavity that is larger than life size with a heart that beats by way of an air pump and lungs that can rise and fall. A lifelike sheen is provided by methacyl, a food thickener giving the viscera their veracity. Elan uses reference books like *The Architecture of the Human Body* but he takes a little bit of dramatic license now and then. "That guy's aneurysm would take months or years to grow," he says.

The challenge in making these models is to figure out how to see what's going on—the human body is a dark place inside. Elan remembers as a kid shining a flashlight through his hand and the glow the skin would allow. He lights his bodies through layers of latex as well as directly to provide that same look. Elan is aware that once he's gone into the body, it's difficult for the viewer to remain oriented so as soon as the injection has started, say, he'll pop back out to let us know where we are. The models Elan makes have a high degree of realism. Suspiciously high. "We had a critics' tour and I was asked to do a demo," says Elan. "I brought over some of the models and there was this woman who insisted we were stealing cadavers. I said no. . . ."

....

The Princeton-Plainsboro operating theater, as re-created on the FOX lot, is uncomfortably realistic. The show's art department coordinator works with the major manufacturers to acquire large pieces of equipment, such as MRI machines. Set decorator Natali Pope will find smaller piece, such as a gamma camera, a kind of nuclear scanner. It was being used on a regular gurney bed, which was not correct, so Natali contacted the company that makes the authentic "couch" the patient lies on. "I got a used one," says Natali, "but it is the right equipment." "There's some new medical device in the script and you think, What the hell is that?" says Mike Casey. He can either get one from a manufacturer or have one replicated. Companies that provide equipment want it to be used correctly so on occasion, in the same way that food products are taken out of their original jars and repackaged, a machine will be altered so it can't be recognized.

QUESTION: "What was the hardest prop to find?"

MIKE CASEY: "It was a bite block for electroshock treatment. We had some made but they had this horrible taste because of the rubber that was used. The real ones taste even worse."

Much more alarming than the large medical equipment are the prop guy's collection of endoscopes. First they have a real endoscope with a camera mounted on the tip that would be inserted in a real patient's mouth. The camera can be remotely manipulated by the technician. There is a channel down the middle of the scope through which a biopsy sample can be taken or water or air can be introduced. It's an expensive piece of kit that someone from the manufacturer came on set to demonstrate. Tyler also put together an endoscope from parts he found on eBay. Apparently car mechanics like to use scopes to diagnose engine problems. Tyler and Mike aren't going to use one of their real scopes on someone. They'd use one of their fakes.

As the subject lies on the operating table, one end of the fake scope is placed in his mouth. While the doctor holds the tube in place, under the table and out of sight, Mike moves the sleeve of the fake scope up or down. With a real scope, the whole thing is going down the patient's throat while here, the end of the tube stays still and the outer sleeve moves to look as if it is going into and out of the body. If the scene calls for the scope to be pulled out of the patient's mouth in a hurry, Tyler and Mike have a cut-off rubber scope that can be pulled away from the mouth very quickly. Later, Elan Soltes can make it appear as though the tube is being pulled up and out of the patient's stomach.

"Scalpels: Some are safe; some are super safe and made of rubber. We have real ones, too, because occasionally we have to cut something. To look at it, you won't know it's not real. Any time anyone hands anyone anything, even if you just put it down, even if it says 'super safe' on it, every time they're going to check it before they hand it to an actor. Better you cut your hand than someone gets slashed open."

—TYLER PATTON

Tyler and Mike can also perform a convincing-looking biopsy. In a scene for the show, two doctors might do the procedure. One will be looking at a monitor to see where the other doctor needs to insert the business end of the equipment. Video playback technicians will add the right image onto the monitor in postproduction. Doctor number two takes the biopsy equipment and presses it to the skin; the needle retracts back into the device, making it look as if it's penetrating the skin. The biopsy tool is a stainless steel instrument of torture. "The new director wanted to use this evil-looking one," says Tyler, holding the shining medieval-style implement. The subject can't help feeling a tinge of fear as the fake needle is pressed against the skin.

The same technique works for the various spring-loaded retractable syringes. Some are rigged so that as the plunger is pulled out, liquid will flow down and fill the chamber. "Those retractable syringes are about eight hundred dollars each because they are so small and precise," says Tyler. "We have 20cc, 10cc, 5cc, 3cc syringes, about four of each. . . . Season one we had one 5cc retractable syringe. Our stock grows and grows."

In most of the scenes in the OR, there will be blood. Special effects makeup head Dalia Dokter uses all sorts of blood. Dalia consults with medical adviser Bobbin Bergstrom and Dr. David Foster to see what type of blood she needs, a darker blood or a lighter blood depending on the situation. One type Dalia uses frequently is called "My Blood." This she likes because it doesn't leave a stain. If three or four takes of a scene are needed, she can use this product, clean it off, and put it back on. Another type is "Mouth Blood," which is safe to put in the mouth. "I could use that for cuts but it is specifically for the mouth," says Dalia. "You can swallow a little but don't put it over your French fries."

Amidst their collections of IV bags and urine catheters, Tyler and Mike have their own supply of blood. Like Dalia they have different bloods depending on the color and consistency that are needed and where the patient is bleeding from. They have dark pumping blood, dark mouth blood, watered-down blood that flows quickly. There's drying blood and basic "prop blood," which is labeled "Not harmful if ingested." And "Huggy wipes are essential," says Mike. "They work the best to clean up the fake blood."

One of Bobbin Bergstrom's jobs is to advise actors how to play a medical scene. It's a vital part of making a medical situation look realistic to have the actor react appropriately. Any scene that takes place in a procedure room or at a patient's bedside, or even in House's office if he chooses to inject himself with something, Bobbin will be on hand to provide guidance and answer any questions. She might give a note to an actor or offer the director a suggestion. Her role is more than telling an actor how much something is going to hurt. What kind of energy is someone going to have after dialysis? If they're having a seizure or chest pain, how are these symptoms going to manifest physically? "They don't always clutch their chest if they have chest pain," says Bobbin. "There are lots of ways a person can be exhibiting a heart attack."

"I should ask my accountant if I can write off medical expenses because I'm doing work for my job when I'm at the doctor's office. When they take my blood pressure, or draw some blood, I watch as closely as I can. I don't like to have to be taught how to do it again. Doing a procedure is the hardest thing to play because you have to concentrate on getting it right and you have to repeat it the same way on exactly the same line. A doctor doesn't have to think about drawing blood and I don't want to have to think about it. I want to just be playing the scene. Everyone does it differently, though, and I do it Bobbin's way."

—PETER JACOBSON

Anyone who has watched their share of medical dramas will have seen hundreds of patients flatline. "Automatically a TV audience will see a flatline and think, Here come the paddles," says Bobbin. In fact, if you look at the latest medical thinking, the protocol is to give drugs and to start chest compressions. In order to maintain medical credibility it's important to adapt to changing circumstances when it's dramatically possible. Bobbin will also advise on pain responses. A test that the audience believes would be intensely painful, such as a bone marrow biopsy, is often undertaken with a lot of drugs in a hospital. A spinal tap, a common *House* procedure, does hurt, as anyone who has had one can attest. "I will tell the patient what I think it should look like and the director will say, 'Give me more,' or 'Give me less,'" says Bobbin. "A lot of times they will increase it because they want it to be bigger."

Audiences are also likely to react when a beeping monitor lets out a long single note. "Beeeeeeeeeep." Nowadays, effects like this and the shots of the monitors are added in postproduction by video playback. Bobbin used to supply effects herself, wearing a blood pressure sleeve that was plugged into the monitor to provide a heart rate. A technician on set will still mimic a flatline on the monitor screen for the actors so they have something to react to at the right moment.

Bobbin says it's difficult for an actor to make the act of dying look real. It's easy to spot a bad dying scene in a movie when somebody flops back in the bed theatrically. To avoid a death scene, a character might bleed out in surgery and the next time be shown being wheeled off to the mortuary or in postmortem care. The actual death itself has been elided.

James Earl Jones's dictator, Dibala, expired in an extremely dramatic death scene. He arrested and was defibrillated and in the director's cut, this passage was stylized with music added for extra effect. "He bled out and stopped moving after he was defibrillated so it was clear he died," says Bobbin. "But instead of 'cough, cough, die' it was a beautiful, sad, realistic, drawn-out death scene that usually you'd lose interest in after a couple of seconds."

QUESTION: "Do people come to your office and close the door and say, 'Look at this'?"

BOBBIN BERGSTROM: "Yes. And frequently it's more information than I care to get from someone I work with. But I don't mind because most of the time they are just looking for reassurance."

Bobbin's been on hand a couple of times when there has been a real medical issue on set. A guy fell off a catwalk on another show Bobbin worked on and she stabilized him until paramedics could arrive. An actor had a mild seizure on the set of *House* and Bobbin tended to him until he could be taken to the hospital. He was back

Attention to detail, 2: pathology lab medical fridge

at work the next day. Bobbin was looking after the actor in a space where some fake blood had been put on the floor and a nurse asked if the man had hit his head. "A couple of people when this guy had his seizure were just staring at him," says Bobbin. "They were looking at their sides [scripts]—I even did for a split second."

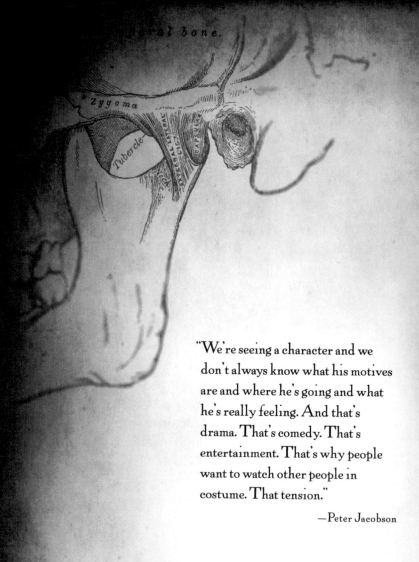

"We're seeing a character and we don't always know what his motives are and where he's going and what he's really feeling. And that's drama. That's comedy. That's entertainment. That's why people want to watch other people in costume. That tension."

—Peter Jacobson

TAUB

Peter Jacobson

Chris Taub nearly didn't make it through the first five minutes of House's season four selection process: He is in row 'D,' that is arbitrarily fired by House when Cuddy tells him he has too many candidates, and just as quickly unfired when House sees he has eliminated an attractive woman. Taub's first contribution is to suggest House perform elective breast enhancement surgery on the prospective NASA astronaut to conceal her lung operation. Taub tells her that people with dreams don't care when someone laughs at them ("The Right Stuff"). Taub's going to need that kind of thick skin. He shows he has it in "Ugly" with the kid with a huge growth on his head. The boy's treatment is being filmed for a documentary and while many on the team mug for the camera, Taub makes a play and questions House's diagnosis. House fires him; Cuddy hires him back and Taub moves himself to the front of the selection pack.

"The first episode where they delved into Taub was 'Ugly,' with the guy with the big broccoli thing on his head. We knew I had been a plastic surgeon and here we got into the whole thing. Sometime before they shot that they invited one of L.A.'s preeminent plastic surgeons to come talk to the writers and I sat in on the meeting. It was really fun: this big, successful plastic surgeon and the writers were peppering him with questions doing their research."

—PETER JACOBSON

This is Taub: confident, a little sneaky, anxious to get on the team.

"What is interesting about Taub is that while he made a killing as a successful plastic surgeon in New York, where he was doing mostly boob jobs and nips and tucks that the fancy people want done, he is clearly an exceptional doctor. I like to think that he wasn't always a plastic surgeon and he might have had other practices and he is a really, really smart doctor."

—PETER JACOBSON

Intrigued, House checks up on Taub at his old practice. Taub's married but got caught fooling around (with his partner's daughter) and had to leave. "Some people pop pain pills," says Taub. "I cheat. We all have our vices." Taub now has the dubious honor of being deemed interesting to House. House has dirt on him and can torture him: He won't bother with someone boring. So House calls Taub "mini-stud" and says he's not a real doctor. Much later (in "Lockdown"), when Foreman reads Taub's file, we discover Taub peaked very early—he published in the *New England Journal of Medicine* at twenty-six. He may be trying now to live up to that prodigious promise.

QUESTION: "House is tough on Taub. His failings are human failings . . ."

DAVID SHORE: "He's a philanderer."

QUESTION: "Once or more than once?"

SHORE: "I think many, many times. That's what's interesting to me, that I think he does genuinely does love his wife and he really doesn't want to do it. But he gets sucked into it and makes bad choices and then regrets it."

Taub is a little older than the average on the team and Cuddy recognizes he'll stand up to House and House tells Cuddy he hired Taub because she wanted him to ("Games"). Taub is on the team, he's happy, but there's obvious tension at home with his wife, Rachel (Jennifer Crystal). She's not telling him things, too: In "Adverse Events," Lucas finds she has eighty-three thousand dollars in a secret account. She's buying Taub a Porsche, which he always wanted. When Rachel gives it to Taub, he says, "We need to talk."

Taub is obviously making a lot less at PPTH than he was in private practice and it's another source of tension at home. In "Let Them Eat Cake," Taub muscles in on Kutner's online second opinion clinic for 30 percent of the action, only to get caught by House. And in "Here Kitty," Taub almost gets scammed by a smooth con man. Taub is a guy who looks out for the main chance. Judging by his angry response, Taub is clearly shaken up by Kutner's death. In "Painless," Taub and Kutner discuss suicide. Taub says a colleague tried to kill himself and he should have done more to stop it. Kutner guesses that person was Taub and Taub says no.

In "The Down Low," Taub joins with Thirteen and Chase in the ill-judged prank of Foreman that begins with Foreman believing he makes less money than his colleagues and ends with the three taking a pay cut to give Foreman a raise. "The phrase 'who's your daddy' comes to mind," says Foreman. Taub has another awkward conversation with his wife to look forward to.

In the cycle of firings and rehirings, Taub is in the Thirteen camp of wanting to work for House rather than the Chase/Foreman camp of having to. With House gone and Foreman in charge, Taub quits to go back to plastic surgery. "I came here to work with House," he says ("Epic Fail").

> "When I first heard I was quitting I was, 'Okay what's that about?' I knew it was not going to be permanent. It was never presented to me as anything other than 'we're just shaking things up' and it's a great dramatic device. It deepens the conflict for me in my life. To quit, come back, and come back again makes it that much harder for my wife and for me and ups the stakes in everything."
>
> —PETER JACOBSON

When House goes about reeling his team back in, Taub, like Thirteen, is easy prey ("Teamwork"). House feeds the apparently uninterested Taub and Thirteen details about the porn actor and they come up with the diagnosis. Nose jobs and crow's feet are boring; this is where the action is and Taub wants back. What about his wife? "I reorganized my life to spend more time with her but apparently I don't love her as much as I thought." Returning to PPTH is not a popular decision at home. Taub spends Thanksgiving at work. "Life's too short to worry about money," Taub says. "She's happy to cut back on a few things. Like sex" ("Ignorance Is Bliss"). Taub is going back to ducking and diving. In "Locked In," Taub takes credit for a diagnostic idea of Kutner's and gains House's approval for the move.

Taub is someone who has to make up with his wife a lot. In "The Greater Good," Taub tells Rachel he wants to have kids. He didn't before and now he does. But she doesn't. Perhaps she has compromised enough while Taub hasn't. When Chase punches House, Taub takes a photo, shows his wife, and says he did it and she responds amorously. Taub says he told House some ground rules. As if. It's another lie that House might appreciate.

> "He's a little raunchy ethically and personally but he's a good person committed to being a good doctor and being with his wife . . . He's the philanderer who stays with his wife, the family man who has a seedy side. That's an interesting dynamic. There are a number of public figures who have the same thing."
>
> —DAVID FOSTER

Taub and Rachel reach crisis point in "Black Hole." "Chris, I love you but I swear if you start talking like I'm on the witness stand again I'm gonna break your neck," she says. While Rachel laments they don't do anything together, Taub's colleagues agree she thinks he's cheating again. He swears not, but can this philanderer change his spots? And how can he prove it? Taub tries: He invites Rachel to work for a make-out session in the parking lot (coitus interruptus courtesy of House), then asks Rachel to marry him again, a move House approves: "Good for you," he says. But then House watches Taub talk to a nurse (Maya) he obviously knows. Taub touches her on the arm. House's dictum on the impossibility of change is being proved right once again.

When Taub finds out that their patient, Julia, has an open marriage ("Open and Shut"), Taub's interest is pricked. Julia's justifications all sound like arguments for Taub to give in to his philandering self. "We decided things work better when people tell each other the truth," says Julia, obviously not a watcher of *House*. House ensures that Taub has to spend all night with Julia working tests. She says she doesn't want to settle; that she needs to get the 10 percent she doesn't get from her husband, Tom, whom she loves, somewhere else. The devil on Taub's shoulder is taking notes. Again, Taub is spotted flirting with Maya again but claims nothing's going on.

Taub decides to bring up Julia and Tom's lifestyle with Rachel and it's predictably a disaster. She immediately thinks he's cheating. But later, saying it's the lying she can't stand, she offers Taub the same deal (what House calls the "Golden Ticket") with some conditions. "You want more than me," she says. "You want that thrill." But before Taub can do his worst, Rachel stops him. She can't go through with it. Taub relents. "I've been an idiot," says Taub. "I don't need anything else. I just need you." Taub is genuinely conflicted. When he says something like this to Rachel, he believes it. But when he sees Maya later in the parking lot, it's inevitable that they will kiss and drive off to find somewhere private.

In "The Choice," House sabotages Taub's efforts to set up clandestine dates with Maya even though he's supposedly handed in his Golden Ticket. Taub calls off his public affair and thanks House for saving his marriage, but that was not House's intention. However, Taub isn't going to be able to shake off his particular predilection and on the evidence, it isn't clear he really has any desire to do so.

Peter Jacobson on . . . Taub

QUESTION: "Is Taub's flaw in a Housean universe such a major one?"

"I don't think so. It's just a solid fastball flaw right down the middle. I don't know a whole load of people that do but everywhere you look there are hints and indicators that that is what happens. To be part of that mainstream flow is a nice thing for me to play . . . For me it's most interesting when characters in general and certainly my character get caught. That's where the dramatic tension is."

QUESTION: "Your marriage is only ever shown in tense situations."

"Whenever we go to my apartment and my wife, I'm always a little bit tense. The show is House and us and I don't think House would survive without the interesting vicissitudes of our characters but I think they wisely keep it contained. If they're going to go outside the hospital and get in deep I feel it has to connect back to House; otherwise I feel like what is really the point? At the Chase/Cameron wedding there were a couple of shots of my wife and I sitting in the audience loving the wedding. The only time there has been a shot of us without a story line. That's as far as you need to go with the marital bliss."

QUESTION: "We see that you can't stay away from the puzzles."

"No matter what. He is a really curious, smart doctor. No matter how much abuse is being heaped on him, ultimately Taub wants to figure it out and he wants to win. Not necessarily be House but be the one who solves it."

QUESTION: "Is he a people person?"

"You don't get a whole sense of real bedside manner. In 'Ugly' there were a couple of moments to show that if he is not the warmest guy in the world, he is going to show a sweetness and a sensitivity and a confidence for this kid because he is a middle-aged man who has been round the block in his profession and he is good at what he does. And part of being good is knowing how to relate. And if they are going to have me conflicted about all these life issues of fidelity or suicide, he's a human being living in the world and dealing in emotions. I don't think anyone can be a robot."

QUESTION: "Is Taub going to blow up?"

"I don't know but the fact that is even a question is gratifying."

QUESTION: "Taub takes credit for punching House . . ." ("Ignorance Is Bliss")

"It is steeped in a certain level of dishonesty. Clever, and as long as there is a means to a sufficient end he will take it.

"When I first read it I thought, Oh, come on! It wasn't until the read-through when it got half up on its feet and life was being breathed into it and the actors were engaging in the moment, then it really killed."

QUESTION: "Someone said Taub is slightly sleazy."

DAVID SHORE: "Kutner's death may have had an impact in that regard and he may turn a little toward the light side."

QUESTION: "His buddy is gone."

SHORE: "And in such a dramatic way that is going to make Taub think every day is precious, or a Cameronesque attitude that every human is precious."

QUESTION: "Kutner and Taub had an interesting relationship. The online scam . . ."

"I loved that. Especially when House got us at the end with the live dead body. It's a little tiring to play the same shock and terror four or five times but it was fun."

QUESTION: "As an actor how much fun is that?"

"I love that. The crazier, the zanier, the better. There have been a few things—when House made me come to him and prove I knew how to play racquetball in the morgue ['The Social Contract']. It is always great as an actor to step outside what you are normally doing in any show."

QUESTION: "Taub's wardrobe . . ."

"So exciting. Brown today. Always coats, shirts, and ties for me."

QUESTION: "What does he wear at home?"

"Same thing. He sleeps in his shirt and tie. He rolls up his sleeves for bed. He's a successful guy, sort of conservative. It's important to him to show he's making some money even if he's not. He and Foreman have a little unspoken sartorial battle going on. He can carry it off so much better than I. All the stuff I have is nice but just a little bit staid."

Peter Jacobson on . . . Peter Jacobson

QUESTION: "Do you have any medical people in your family?"

"Not a one. Lisa Edelstein's dad was Kal Penn's pediatrician in the seventies . . . Lisa and I worked together fifteen years ago. We had one scene is *As Good as It Gets*. We were the two Jews at the table that Jack Nicholson abused in the restaurant. It was a memorable scene. But there is not a single doctor in my family."

QUESTION: "Now there is."

"Occasionally you get the really weird person who says, 'Can you help me?'"

QUESTION: "It's the white coat."

"I try very hard to avoid wearing the white coat off the set."

QUESTION: "How do you find the medical stuff?"

"To me I do all the research I can to have an idea of what it is. That's the hardest part, tracking the medical journey because we shoot out of order. If you're really doing your work as an actor you should always know what came before and with this show more than anything I've ever done, when you are talking about this medicine you really have to have the history at every moment."

QUESTION: "Are you able to appreciate it as a TV show as well as from a professional standpoint?"

"Not really. I know it's a good show. It's usually the third showing I can step back enough and set aside the actor ego. The first run through is always, 'Oh, that sucked.' 'Oh, my hair really is falling out.' 'Oh, what a nose.' I get through the vain BS then I get to what is going on in the scenes and then the third show I can watch. Some actors don't ever watch it. I think it's helpful."

QUESTION: "The schedule is hard?"

"We make it work. As long as it doesn't in any way impact the working of the machine, the ADs know I have a family in New York and they very generously try to get me as long a weekend as they can. Oftentimes it doesn't work and I know every time I go in, there is nothing I can really do about it."

QUESTION: "There is a rhythm to the show . . ."

"There were two days last season when I was doing three episodes on the same day because there were couple of makeup days. There was an overlap day so I was doing the episode we were finishing, the episode we were starting, and then there was another scene I was picking up for another episode."

QUESTION: "So it was three lots of wardrobe . . ."

"And three medical things I was trying to keep in my head. Ultimately it is a fabulous, not-so-hard job. I would not say that if I was Hugh. He is on another level. He is carrying this show and day in and day out he has to show up. I think I have a pretty cushy job. I am working my ass off on a lot of days but in the bigger picture, this is a lovely way to spend time."

Peter Jacobson on . . . the Selection Process

QUESTION: "You didn't know who was going to be selected?"

"I got the part and then I heard there are actually going to be thirty new actors trying out for this position and I thought, This is ridiculous. Then I heard that five of us would be contracted to become a regular—Olivia, Kal, Edi [Gathegi, aka Big Love], Annie [Dudek], and me. Then they can do whatever they want. There were several actors who stayed on to the end and they could have gone with them, or none of us. When it got down to the final five there was constant speculation amongst us as to who might make it."

QUESTION: "You didn't pull any Taub-like tricks on the other actors?"

"It might have worked but weirdly we got along really well. It was a fun time. When you are in a situation that is so inherently nerve-racking if you have five neurotic actors there is a certain shedding of pretense and we all were open about it. 'You're going to get in, they need a black guy,' 'No they don't, they need a Jewish guy,' 'They need an Indian,' 'You're a babe.' Honest talk. It made it easier because we were just being silly."

QUESTION: "The actors were feeling the same pressure as the characters."

"That was the weird thing. My wife said, 'That's you' at first but when she heard what the process was, she said, 'You don't want to take that job; you worry every day of your life that you're going to get fired, so why would you embark upon four months of worrying every day about being fired?' But it was so out there, up-front crazy it actually became kind of fun."

QUESTION: "How great was that when the final word came out?"

"Fantastic. Really great. The tricky part is I live in New York. My wife and son are in New York and I go back and forth. So I'm doing a lot of travel. I was already away for three months and my son was just five and these are hard years to be away. A part of me knew there would be a moment of relief if we could just be together. But that of course is two percent. The ninety-eight percent is I want the job, I need the job, and I'm thrilled I got it."

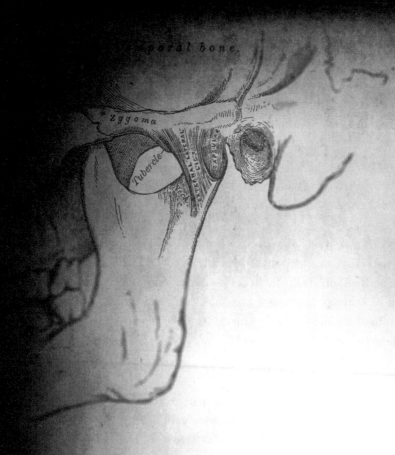

KUTNER

QUESTION: "You must have known Kal Penn was leaving but you didn't know they were going to shoot him in the head?"

OMAR EPPS: "I don't think he knew, either! We all assumed they find him and it would be pills or something. But it's so David Shore. The epitome of going out with a bang."

In "Simple Explanation," Kutner has gone missing. His dog is sick, Taub says. He probably went to a comic book festival, Taub suggests. There has just been a case where Taub steals credit for an idea of Kutner's. Foreman and Thirteen go to Kutner's apartment and they find Kutner's body, gunshot wound to the head, a gun by his side. Thirteen and Foreman work on the body but it's useless. He's cold. Kutner is dead.

> "That was Kutner's body but he wasn't in the episode. A lot of us thought he should be there. The first part of the episode was 'where's Kutner?' and we thought that was tipping it and it won't be shocking but it was so shocking. It didn't need to be any more shocking."
>
> —Peter Jacobson

Greg Yaitanes directed the scene. The writer Leonard Dick wrote that the body isn't shown, but Kal Penn was lying there. "Kal was there and that's what made those performances even better—he was in a pool of blood," says Yaitanes. "There is blood all over the actors." The whole episode was overcast, dark and unsettling, matching the mood of Kutner's shocked colleagues. Kal Penn's fellow actors were surprised, too. "It seemed a little outrageous," said Peter Jacobson. "I thought it was a surprising choice," says Robert Sean Leonard, but the outrageousness and the surprise were intended to push House toward a breakdown. "It made sense ultimately," says Peter Jacobson.

QUESTION: "Were you shocked about Kutner?"

GREG YAITANES: "Well, I knew something was up when I called to get my script and they wouldn't send me one."

House would no doubt accept the choice that Kutner made if there were a reason for it. He chastises the team for not seeing it coming but no one knew anything. Cuddy has hired a grief counselor she know no one will use, offers time off no one will take.

CUDDY: "I'm sorry for your loss."

HOUSE: "It's not my loss."

CUDDY: "Then I'm sorry you don't think it is."

Thirteen and Foreman visit Kutner's foster parents and House goes along. Kutner's given name was Choudhury and House berates the grief-stricken parents for changing his identity, for making him tormented about who he was, for pushing him to this. House is so far out of line and Foreman stops him. "There was a great moment when Foreman reminded him," says David Shore, "but you see that look on his face. House backed down. That's something I'm not sure we have seen any other time. He backed down." Greg Yaitanes remembers the reaction to House of Mary Jo Deschanel, the actress who plays Kutner's mom: "The disgust and repulsion and the embarrassment and humiliation . . . I remember being very moved by that performance."

Taub is mad at his friend Kutner. He says Kutner's an idiot and he feels pity but no guilt for not seeing his suicide coming. "That's a natural response. I loved how they wrote that episode," says Peter Jacobson, enjoying how the Taub/Kutner relationship was fleshed out only for Kutner to die.

> "Taub put up a wall and shut it out and went to work and then broke and to play that arc was the most satisfying, gratifying episode to play. There is no more of a gem to play as an actor than a character who is struggling to keep the lid on. Every day all we are doing is trying to make it through, put on our pants and be a normal person when we don't always feel like normal people. To play something like that is a real joy."
>
> —PETER JACOBSON

House is desperate for answers. He calls Kutner's friends, looks at his background check (he streaked at a Penn-Dartmouth football game). House goes to Kutner's apartment and becomes convinced that Kutner was murdered. Soon he can't sleep and he starts on his hallucinatory descent to Mayfield Hospital. Cuddy tells House it's okay for him to be upset because Kutner thought like House, pushed boundaries like House. House isn't having it. "If he'd thought like me he'd have known that living in misery sucks marginally less than dying in it."

House is confronted by the inexplicable, and it hits very close to home. "I felt it was incredibly honest," says Greg Yaitanes. "When something completely unexpected like that happens and you don't see it coming, it felt really lifelike in the fact that nobody had the answer." Peter Jacobson says, "It can actually be that shocking. They can be hiding a world of hurt and if anybody anywhere thought to themselves, Oh, or related to it or thought of anyone who needed help, if on any level that raised consciousness, then it's a great thing."

> QUESTION: "This happens: People take their own lives and no one sees it coming and it can be completely mysterious to everyone else. And House doesn't solve the puzzle."
>
> DAVID SHORE: "That was what was intended there. That's why we didn't do a flashback to something that happened to Kutner, to him doing the act. The last picture we show of him was designed to show him uncertain and for us to look at him and go, 'I just don't know this man.' The man, Dr. House, who can go in a room and sit down with a guy for eight seconds and tell what he had for breakfast three days ago, worked with this guy for two years and on a very fundamental level didn't know him. House had to come to grips with that."

SETS AND STAGES

Designing and Building *House*

> "Most decisions are time- and financially based. As a producer told me, it is show business not show friendship—it's all about the money. Luckily for us, *House* is a very successful show, so I am allowed to indulge maybe more than other shows."
>
> —JEREMY CASSELLS, PRODUCTION DESIGNER

"I don't think Wilson would live in a funky space with exposed beams," Katie Jacobs is saying. Katie and production designer Jeremy Cassells are at the end of a corridor in the *House* offices looking at ideas for the apartment Wilson buys to share with House in season six. The corridor walls are covered with pictures of apartments and apartment buildings: photocopies and pages torn out of magazines. At the center is a draft of a floor plan for the living space. The first idea, cued by the writers, was for a high-ceilinged loft similar to Thirteen's home. Katie wanted something more "masculine." "I thought let's stick with an older building; let's have a newer take on it and just get rid of some of the walls."

Between the first meeting a handful of days previously and this one, Jeremy created a second concept. After an idea that House and Wilson should move to New York City was rejected, Jeremy worked on a New York-style apartment in Princeton. One of the pictures on the wall is of a turn-of-the-century building on Sutton Place in New York. In an older building like this, a big apartment would have a reception foyer, dining room, a study, a library perhaps, a master and other bedrooms, and a maid's room, which could be House's bedroom. Jeremy had also talked to DP Gale Tattersall about adding a balcony, which would give the space more depth.

The question was, How are House and Wilson going to interact in these rooms? "I like all the spaces; [but] I think they are too separate," says Katie. Filling the apartment can wait. Neither House nor Wilson has a lot of furniture, other than House's piano. The men can put their stamp on the place even if they'd probably be happy with a giant TV and a couch. (In "Black Hole," Wilson demonstrates the same character deficiency he showed with Amber when they went to buy a bed: He simply cannot choose furniture.) Katie and Jeremy talk about the backings, the view that can be seen out of the window and whether they'll have to commission a new one. But the main point of the meeting is the apartment interior. House's and Wilson's bedrooms should be very close to each other. "It's great," says Katie. "I just want them off the same hall." And Jeremy promises he'll have a new plan tomorrow.

Plans and sample layouts for the Wilson/House condo on the wall in the *House* production office

"I had some people who worked in the business and they said, 'I can't believe you went to New Jersey to shoot all that,' and I said, 'No, they built it all on the soundstage.'"

—JEREMY CASSELLS

Hugh Laurie reading the day's
sides on the set.

ABOVE: Front row *(from left):* the DP, the director, and the script supervisor working in front of the monitors at video village.

BELOW: Peter Jacobson and director of photography Gale Tattersall.

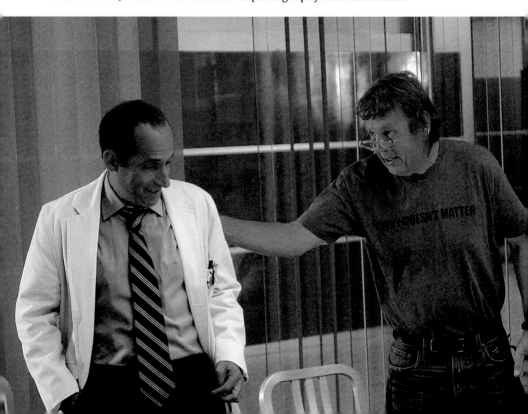

ABOVE: **The season six diagnostic team** *(from left):* **Chase (Jesse Spencer), Taub (Peter Jacobson), Foreman (Omar Epps), and Thirteen (Olivia Wilde).**

BELOW: **Omar Epps, director Greg Yaitanes, and Olivia Wilde.**

ABOVE: House's desk.

BELOW: House's desk up close: the large tennis ball and House's mail.

ABOVE: Gale Tattersall—the "rare breed" of DP.

BELOW: Setting up a shot with Omar Epps.

If the light is __BRIGHT__ red, we're on a bell so please don't come in.

Red light means keep out.

Still-life with House's cricket ball, baseball, and bowls ball.

House likes his music old-school: vinyl and a turntable.

DIRECTORY

basement
MRI
CT SCAN
DIAGNOSTIC IMAGING

main floor
CAFETERIA
CHAPEL
LECTURE HALLS
CLINIC
PHARMACY

second floor
INTENSIVE CARE UNIT
ULTRASOUND
PATHOLOGY LABORATORY
PATIENT ROOMS

third floor
PEDIATRICS
PEDIATRIC ICU
PEDIATRIC OR 1&2

fourth floor
DEPARTMENT OF ONCOLOGY
DEPARTMENT OF DIAGNOSTIC MEDICINE
DEPARTMENT OF LEGAL AFFAIRS

The PPTH directory—note the old oncology department location on the fourth floor.

ABOVE: Hugh Laurie flanked by *House* creator David Shore *(left)* and writer David Hoselton *(right).*

BELOW: Katie Jacobs and Jeremy Cassells with layouts for the Wilson/House condo.

Jennifer Morrison (Allison Cameron).

Lisa Edelstein (Lisa Cuddy).

ABOVE: Thirteen hears a word to the wise.

BELOW: Medical adviser Bobbin Bergstrom helps Jesse Spencer with the medical details.

Chase takes down House . . .

Jesse Spencer and costume designer Cathy Crandall.

House with Kutner, the unsolvable puzzle.

Wilson in his office.

. . . who finds a soft landing.

Dalia Dokter applies makeup for House's eye damaged by Chase.

Greg Yaitanes working out a scene with
Hugh Laurie and Robert Sean Leonard.

ABOVE: House relaxes on the beach, if only in locked-in Lee's imagination.

BELOW: House and Cuddy at an eighties party—Cuddy is Jane Fonda; House has the wrong eighties.

Jeremy Cassells is in the business of visual deception. Jeremy operates on a grand scale, or he makes the viewer believe it is a grand scale. When House spent the weeks at the psychiatric hospital in New Jersey that are covered in "Broken," it looked as if everything was shot on location. Not so. Jeremy's production design job covers a lot of ground and design is part of the ever-moving train. "There are so many good heads of department, they do it so well and they all interact with Katie." Together—design, art, construction, set dressing, cast, and crew—they can pull something off like building a New Jersey hospital on the lot in Century City.

"For the end of the season visually, I had the idea of losing House behind two doors in a place like Oz. If you have the idea of him checking in you have to sell the visual of it."

—KATIE JACOBS

To create Mayfield Hospital, the team had a much longer lead time than for a regular episode. Jeremy had to come up with a look for the whole institution. "It was difficult to design because everybody thinks immediately of One Flew Over the Cuckoo's Nest," Jeremy says of the classic 1975 movie, "and hospitals aren't like that anymore." Still, Katie wanted to retain the idea House was in someplace hard-edged and uncompromising when he goes through detox.

Starting in Princeton and working outward, Jeremy looked online for a suitable building. The first places were like country houses; then he found Greystone Park Psychiatric Hospital in Parsippany, New Jersey. He showed Katie the entrance that he thought was a strong image. "She said, 'I love that place,'" says Jeremy. "Problem, though: It's in New Jersey." It was also abandoned and derelict, so they couldn't have shot the interiors there even if it had made economic sense to do so.

The production department looked for a comparable building in L.A. but there aren't any. They did find a hospital in Ohio that was in better shape but it's difficult to film in Ohio because there's no local crew that can be used. It proved cheaper to go to New Jersey and use a New York crew for the exterior shots. The scene of House entering the hospital took a day to shoot with the New York unit and some key crew from L.A. Jeremy went to New Jersey four times, taking photographs and picking up floor plans to help with his design. Katie, Jeremy, and the writers talked about where the characters could interact even though the set was built before the script was ready. So there was a telephone bank, a pharmacy, bedrooms, and treatment rooms. Jeremy and the construction crew paid extraordinary attention to detail. They made knives to recreate the moldings for the door casings, the baseboards, and the chair rails; the glass in the set had distortion built into it so when the camera was moved across it reacted like old glass.

....

Construction coordinator Steve Howard was charged with the physical building of Mayfield Hospital, as he is with all *House* sets. Working on four stages on the FOX lot and thirty thousand feet of warehouse space at an off-lot site, Steve supervises building work on an ever-changing village. (No other show has more than two stages.) Employing from thirty-five up to sixty workers, Steve remakes ten to twelve "swing" sets in eight days for each episode. (A swing set is a set specific to the episode.) Split over two stages, the hospital plus the permanent sets and the swing sets total about fifty thousand square feet.

"In the hiatus I took two days off. Mayfield took two months. And one of the hard things was we didn't have the full script so Jeremy didn't know what rooms to put in the middle of the hospital. We knew there were going to be some character rooms but we just had to leave a big blank. Here it is we are two weeks away and it was, 'Let's go.'"

—STEVE HOWARD

Suddenly the perpetual motion train was rerouted when the writers decided to get House back to PPTH ahead of the original schedule. At first, Jeremy was going to design the office for Dr. Nolan, House's psychiatrist, on a stage but with the shortened stay, the right-hand side of the dayroom was repurposed into Nolan's office. The switching of the set meant all the dayroom scenes were filmed first. "Gerrit and Marcy asked me if there was a way to utilize the backing and the space I already had so I changed it around and painted it a different color and tried to give it a different look." Pulling off the switch so fast was, in Katie Jacobs's words, "a tribute to construction and to Jeremy."

"They went off and filmed the exercise yard for two days and we changed the set over in two days. But the backing is the same. If you look out the back, Nolan has the same view as the dayroom. We moved the backing so it is a little different. My premise was he was on a different floor."

—JEREMY CASSELLS

Katie Jacobs directed the two-hour "Broken" episode. The sets were designed and the piece was cast before the writing was completed, giving the two-parter a different creative impetus from a standard episode.

"Katie did such a great job with that. So much of the story end was her contribution. But that looked great. I have gotten that feedback from so many people and I'm not sure if it is a condescension to TV or what, but people say it would have been a great movie."

—DAVID SHORE

"Broken" was shown as a movie in a theater for the cast and crew and David Shore's was the common reaction. Jeremy Cassells, though, was aware of the backing and a couple of brushstrokes that would be invisible on a TV but which showed up on the big screen. "My wife says, 'What are you talking about? I never saw that was a backing out there.' Everybody said it looked great so maybe that's just the way I am, hard on myself." Jeremy said he knew a lot of carpenters who worked very hard making the hospital. It was a little sad for him to take it down. All in the name of moving the story forward, the hospital went up, and came down early. "I thought the writers came up with the great idea at the end," Jeremy says. "That House was free to go but his medical license wasn't."

QUESTION: "House's bedroom, the dayroom, the pharmacy. Where are they?"

STEVE HOWARD: "They've all gone."

QUESTION: "So can we deduce House is not going back to the institution?"

HOWARD: "Well, it's not going to be cheap if he does."

QUESTION: "If he goes this season you're going to be really mad."

HOWARD: "Some people are going to be extremely mad."

....

QUESTION: "You are making them a stage?"

KATIE JACOBS: "They are great characters. We're putting them together. Creating opportunities for them."

Design of the Wilson/House apartment moved quickly. Jeremy resubmitted drawings and the set designers created a miniature 3-D scale model of the apartment in a day. That way Katie Jacobs was able, by way of a small periscope device, to see how a shot might look from a particular vantage point in the apartment. Katie likes to see a lot of depth in a shot, which is a challenge for Jeremy. At Mayfield and at the design stage of the apartment there are no drapery treatments on the windows, which means the backing has to be very convincing.

Katie was thinking about House's room. "He can't have a single bed. Maybe he'll have a king in a kid's room so he will be a little cramped." She was looking at bathtubs. How much is the tub going to cost? Is it cheaper to buy one or build one? Are they going to want to fill it (which is a special effect)? (The tub that was chosen, which House uses without Wilson's permission, is called a "Picasso.") Each decision at the design stage has these sorts of

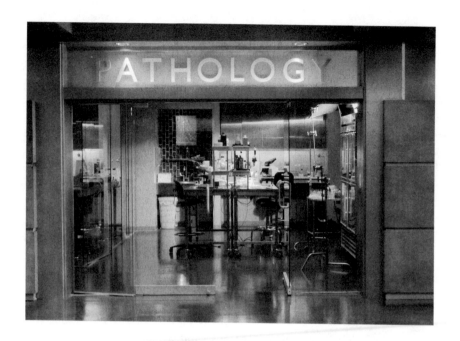

Real but not real: the pathology lab exterior

repercussions. "It affects grip; it affects electric and their budgets. Gerrit and Marcy have what they want to spend and you adjust."

"I take my building cues from Jeremy. He develops all the prints out of the art department. I'll get the prints so I'll get a rough idea to get a budget going. The producers will look at how much money it costs and determine what we can do and sometimes we can't do everything. There is a huge amount of time written in, [perhaps] time-wise we can't do it, either."

—STEVE HOWARD

The story has to be propelled forward at a particular pace. Windows are built on runners so they can be removed for a camera to come in. Camera access also means that rooms are slightly larger than in the outside world. A bedroom has to be big enough for a camera to be the objective view. "You have to make it easy for the crew; otherwise the saw comes out," says Jeremy. "My key grip Shawn

[Whelan] likes to put in a 'grip window,' as he calls it. Which is basically a hole in the wall." There have to be a lot of doors, but not everywhere, "otherwise every wall would be a door." "There is a pressure that we have to make six pages of dialogue a day," says Jeremy.

Jeremy Cassells went to art school in Glasgow in his native Scotland. He was traveling with the intent of getting into the film business and was about to head out to Australia when he met someone making a low-budget movie. Jeremy asked if he could help. Soon he was driving around the country with movie sets in the back of a van until he settled in L.A. and worked his way up to art director, working on movies like *Mortal Kombat* and TV shows like *Profiler*.

"What I enjoyed was it doesn't have to last for very long and nothing has to make architectural sense," he says. "It's always changing. Every day I come in, I might think I have everything under control and suddenly I have to build a whole new apartment for House and Wilson."

On the set, more deception is under way. At PPTH, the emergency room is in the basement of the hospital, but on the set it's located next to House's office. If the camera were to shoot out of House's inner office down the corridor, the ER would be visible to the left. David Shore likes to get the actors out in the corridors walking and talking so the team needs to be able to walk out of House's office without passing the ER. So every time they walk, panels are put up in front of the ER and repainted: another scheduling issue to take account of. A different part of the set, the second floor, is being changed and repainted to create Wilson's never-before-seen oncology department, located on a hitherto unmentioned fifth floor. By the elevators in the lobby are signs that only go up to the fourth floor. They'll have to be amended.

DAVID SHORE: "Every now and again we get a new floor . . . It doesn't completely make sense because there is a skylight on the fourth floor."

QUESTION: "Completists are going to complain that there didn't used to be a fifth floor . . ."

SHORE: "It's like the design of the starship *Enterprise*."

Certain parts of the hospital, such as the ER and the observation area above the operating theater, appear small. The lobby looks huge. "That's what I love about my job, that you can fool the camera," says Jeremy Cassells. "And therefore the audience with the lens choice."

"It's a backwards way of working. When you are doing a pilot or a movie you key off the script. In this department we can't key off the script. We have to create and give opportunities for the script."

—KATIE JACOBS

House has expanded into its current space over time. The first *House* sets were used for the pilot in Vancouver and brought down to Los Angeles. The set was small—if there was a scene set in an OR, a patient room was changed for the purpose. "What we really should be doing is build an operating room because we're going to be doing a lot of stuff in the operating room," says Gerrit van der Meer of his thinking at the time. "I also realized we didn't really have a big lobby entrance. We had a lot of patient rooms and offices. We also didn't have enough stage space. We decided to expand." A lot of sets were made bigger but the lobby on Stage 15 was still small, "so to deal with the space problem we decided to put a second floor on the set." Then-production designer Derek Hill designed the entrance as it is now and added the mezzanine.

"We basically doubled the size of the hospital in the hiatus between season one and season two when I started. [It took] about seven weeks. It was very scary. We pulled it off. A few things weren't quite complete but we were able to finish in the first week. That set the pace for this show and it hasn't stopped."

—STEVE HOWARD

The PPTH lobby photographed from the permanent second-floor balcony

"It was an engineering feat," says Gerrit of the new lobby. The second floor had to be able to hold a hundred people and heavy equipment like scissor lifts for camera movement, so structural engineers were brought in to advise on construction. "That took a long time," says Gerrit. The lobby is less of a set and more of a regular building constructed inside a soundstage. "We have to make it safe enough if there's an earthquake," says Steve Howard. Half the walls are shear walls designed to hold steady in an earthquake to protect the structurally supporting I-beams.

An unexpected complication was found under the floor of the set. Engineers had to dig down to put in steel posts and supporting concrete forms, more than forty of them. Under the floor of Stage 15 were the remains of a full-size ice rink built by the studio for the movies of former Olympic champion ice skater Sonja Henie, who was one of biggest movie stars of the 1930s and '40s. It meant the crews had to dig through layers of wood and asphalt as well as a giant latticework of metal pipe that carried the freezing agent for the ice. "We had crews that worked under the stage that were like mining crews digging out and cutting the lumber and setting up the forms," says Steve Howard.

"After we started the season the writers started writing to the idea of having a second floor. Up to then it was, 'Why does Gerrit want a second floor?' After the first few episodes it was no longer my floor; it was everyone's floor."

—GERRIT VAN DER MEER

Construction works fast: Steve Howard built Lucas's apartment in five days. All the sets are lightweight so the walls can be moved for the camera. If there's a table in the kitchen, the wall behind the table has to be moved by the grips to fit the camera in. Doors have a hollow core. The walls are made of quarter-inch-thick plywood and the framing material is three-quarters of an inch by two and a half inches. If a set is taken down it can be folded very small and stored at a separate storage facility. Many times a set will be adjusted and used for a different character. Kutner's apartment, for example, is "long gone." Says Steve Howard, "We go all the way up to Katie and David Shore to approve that. We used his hallway for another set, added to Thirteen's hallway. His set was unique so there was no way we could save it. We can reuse single-sided walls, windows, and doors. We have some walls we have used on twenty sets."

Steve Howard started working in construction specifically to gain experience for the movies on the suggestion of a friend who helped movie producer Dino De Laurentiis build a studio in Wilmington, North Carolina. Steve was born in Santa Monica, California, and his father was an actor in commercials and small films. He has lived in Morristown, New Jersey, near where the real Mayfield Hospital was located, and his grandmother worked as a volunteer there.

Steve Howard's main mill where sets are made has to be moved from stage to stage. "We make a lot of sound, a lot of dust–a bit of a mess," says Steve Howard. "It's nothing you can do anywhere near the company. You have to dance around. It's a tough part of scheduling for the ADs working around us." He often jumps from Stage 10 to 11, sometimes to 14 or 15, occasionally working out on the street. "We can move it all in an hour," he says. He has a second mill at the lot as well as one off-site.

Steve has machinery for making moldings, for milling wood and metal. All the machinery is on wheels and it all has Steve Howard's name stenciled on it. Steve explains that construction coordinators like himself are all members of Local 44 of the International Alliance of Theatrical Stage Employees and they own their equipment. The grips move walls that have already been shot; up to that point sets are built by carpenters and laborers who belong to different unions and are arbitrated by Steve.

At a paint shop by the mill, the oncology department nurse's station is being finished. Steve took an old nurse's station from outside the ICU and made it larger. It will be broken down into three pieces and taken to the set for shooting. Once it's been filmed perhaps pieces of the station will be saved; most likely its working days are done. Steve never knows how much of what he builds will make it on the screen. "You build an entire set with a kitchen and a bathroom and a big hallway and then you watch the show and you just see the guy's face and a bookshelf behind him."

QUESTION: "Do you get attached to a set?"

STEVE HOWARD: "Not at all. I've done this twenty years. I built the first *Black Pearl* in *Pirates of the Caribbean* and the other large floating ship HMS *Victory*, a three-quarter replica of the original. That I had some feelings for."

QUESTION: "What did they do with that?"

HOWARD: "Cut it up and threw it away. It's all locked in on film and is eternal that way."

The shooting history of Stage 10 on the Fox lot detailed on a plaque
on the building

"We build these sets before the writers have written. It's very different—it's a new space and every Post-it needs to be put up and every item needs to be selected."

—KATIE JACOBS

Once the Wilson/House apartment was designed there were two weeks before the first scene was filmed when Wilson and House visit and Wilson decides to buy the place. In that time, DP Gale Tattersall looked at the plans and figured out the lighting and Steve Howard started to build Wilson's large bedroom and House's small bedroom and the rest of the apartment. The completed condo turned out to be three thousand square feet, with the library the last part to be finished. A new backing was used for the living room. Fully eighty percent of the walls were removable for ease of shooting. Next up for design and construction: the addition of a couple of bedrooms, a hallway, and a bathroom to Cuddy's house. As House and Wilson start to inhabit the apartment they took out from under Cuddy's nose, the strife was inevitable. With the his-and-his bedrooms idea, it was built in.

9

EAST COAST, L.A.

 The Look of *House*

"It's all about tone and how everything is going to blend. I get calls from wardrobe all the time—what color are your tablecloths, what color are your chairs, what color are the sheets?"

—NATALI POPE

House's unironed shirts and sport coats; Foreman's suits; Thirteen's consistent color scheme; the hospital furniture and Wilson's bedspread—all are part of the look of the show. The look is maintained by departments like costume and set dressing with significant input from Katie Jacobs helping to establish a common feel and palette. Costume designer Cathy Crandall will show Katie Jacobs colors for nurses' uniforms in the oncology department and they choose the most restrained colors on offer: This is a place where there are some very sick people so it's an understated and subtle choice.

Cathy Crandall has eight people working for her, each with his or her own strengths for her to call upon. Sometimes eight people doesn't seem like enough. The fact a scene is a brief eighth of a page might be deceiving. A week before filming was due to start on the episode where House, Wilson, and Cuddy go to a medical

The thumbs-up: Katie Jacobs approves costume designer
Cathy Crandall's sample

conference ("Known Unknowns"), Cathy reads in the script that they're going to attend an eighties-themed costume party. As soon as she sees that, Cathy knows she's going to have to outfit a lot of people to look like members of Devo, like Boy George and early Madonna. Later she'll find out just how many people—one hundred, plus House and Cuddy. Cathy did it, of course. "Nothing's impossible," Cathy says. "We never say no."

Cathy Crandall has worked with Katie Jacobs from the beginning creating the clothes for the characters, which is so important for the personality of the show. "We collaborate a lot with hair and makeup to create a look," says Cathy. Around the walls of her office are head shots of actors and pictures that inspire a character's wardrobe. Cathy looks for a recognizable and integrated look for each character. "It says something without saying anything. It's noticeable but it's subtle and it helps define who the character is."

Cathy provides every piece of clothing for the show, from Foreman's suits to flight attendants' uniforms to the medical gowns worn around PPTH. When it came to designing costumes for the eighties party, as well as her usual resources—the Internet, sourcebooks, and the costume houses around town—Cathy had something else to draw on. "We lived it," she says. "I looked in my high school yearbook." Cathy went inside the head of attendees at the medical conference where the party took place. The doctors would likely pick someone famous: the guy from *Ghostbusters* or Mr. T. "The trick was to do it poorly," says Cathy. "Like a doctor would do it, not like we would do it, which would be perfect."

Cathy was working in interior design when a friend helped her get a job on a low-budget movie as a costume PA. The costume designer took Cathy under her wing and she never stopped working. She was assistant designer on a lot of movies and after working with Bryan Singer on the second *X-Men* movie she moved over to *House*.

QUESTION: "What is the biggest thing you need for this job? A good eye?"

CATHY CRANDALL: "Yes, a good eye and good taste. People skills. And a smiling face."

Cathy's clothes are housed in two giant rooms called cages. When Cathy gets the episode script, she'll see how many days each character is involved. "Let's say there are five script days and they need five outfits. I'll sit in here for a whole day and I'll make outfits." Accessible at ground level are the regulars' clothes, the most recently worn nearest the door. House has about thirty feet of rail tightly packed with shirts, T-shirts, and jackets. There's at least two of everything in case one garment gets damaged. Of one of House's shirts, a fetching lavender, there are four, since two were soiled as per the script. Cathy does reuse—as in life, clothes are going to be worn more than once. Every piece of clothing is labeled by episode so Cathy knows when it was last worn so she can judge when it can come back in the rotation.

CATHY CRANDALL: "When Amber died, we broke her wardrobe down and put it in the general population. Who knew she was going to come back? Everyone was frantically trying to find it. 'That was an Amber piece, that was an Amber piece . . .'"

QUESTION: "Did you say, 'Please don't do that to us again?'"

CRANDALL: 'No, I said we're going to be smart next time. We kept Kutner all together. And Amber's stuff is all together."

Up above near the ceiling of the cage is what Cathy calls the "basic stock." When a guest cast member is introduced, she'll look here for clothes. If there's nothing, she'll shop for it and put the clothes back in stock once the episode has aired. In a separate area are the episode holds—clothes that have just been worn and are being held until the episode airs.

"I was dealing with a foot surgeon and he says, 'Can you find out where they get those lab coats? I really like them.' I said I would find out what company Cathy gets them from. Cathy said, 'Do you know how many people ask me that?' Well, they're all silk lined and custom-made. I went back and I said the principals' are custom-made and the rest of them are Medline and he said, 'Yes, that's where we get ours.'"

—NATALI POPE, SET DECORATOR

"Here's Lowcutville," says Cathy, indicating Cuddy's forty feet of rack space. Wilson has maybe ten feet, Taub less. Bags and shoes are kept on the trailer. Here are the regulars' custom-made lab coats, which are off-white, almost gray, so they don't flare too brightly on screen. Thirteen's lab coat has a badge that reads "Doctor Thirteen" rather than "Doctor Hadley." Clothes for the current episode are on the trailer and this is where the three set costumers—two for the principals and one for the background—dress the actors. Once an actor is done for the day, his clothes are picked up, dry-cleaned overnight, and delivered back to the set before the next call time. Every piece of clothing that "works," that has been filmed, gets cleaned like this. Detailed notes are kept of how the clothes were worn so if a reshoot is needed, everything is ready to go. It's a tight ship by necessity—leave things a couple of days and Cathy would never catch back up.

....

"The best way I sum it up is if you move into an apartment and you walk in and there's nothing there and then you walk in six months later and all your world is there, that's all me. The life." So says set decorator Natali Pope of her job. Everything on the set that isn't a prop, she provides. Filling Wilson and House's apartment was a long process. Natalie and Katie first discussed the visuals, whether they are going to get a straight-line couch or one slightly rounded. The first items: the TV, couch, and a poster, were all brought in by House. Usually Natali starts like this from scratch; occasionally there will be an opportunity to change an existing space. During "Last Resort," Cuddy's office was shot up by the hostage taker so the reconstruction of the office was built into the story. It meant the look of the place could change and become less dark.

Natali Pope, the set decorator, dressed Nolan's office in Mayfield Hospital as a professional, nonpersonal space. "House kept bringing it up," she says. "There is nothing personal in here." Natali put one piece of artwork in Nolan's office, situated behind the doctor's head, but it doesn't tell any kind of story. The furniture had an "old-to-new" feeling, described by Natali as mid-century modern reupholstered in a more contemporary fashion. Even though it is a psychiatrist's office there is a glimmer of style, in the shape of the patient's chair. "It has a bit of chrome where you don't see any other chrome in the room," says Natali. "That is my favorite thing to do. I am a huge fan of texture and the chairs are very textured. It gives it a warmer feeling, a life, especially in HD. Light texture like that goes a long way."

All around the hospital and in people's apartments are examples of Natali and her department's handiwork. Wilson's books were moved out of Amber's apartment (where a novel by Cormac McCarthy was on Wilson's nightstand). If a book is sitting spine-out in a bookcase, Natali doesn't need to get permission from the publisher. If House pulls out a Stephen King novel from the bookcase and it has a jacket, there are a whole lot of clearance issues for Natali. Natali has boxes of cleared coffee table books from HarperCollins, a News Corporation company as FOX is, and many of these are in Cuddy's office. A lot of the books in House's office are fake, made by a company called Faux Books that takes real books and guts them for a lightweight book look-alike.

"We were having our concept meeting [for 'Teamwork'] and the director said he would really like to see how this was done and I said, 'Okay, I'll call my porn connection. I do have a connection. There is a company in the valley and they provide me with cleared boxes for DVDs and all that stuff. They make actual porn. They told [the director] what kind of lights they used and what equipment. I have done more than my share of strip clubs and police stations and hospitals and they all have to be different. I don't copy myself. Unless they go to the same strip club. I'm not going to change out the chairs because I'm not touching them."

—NATALI POPE

On House's desk is a pile of fake letters. The top letter is addressed to House with a return address and a franked stamp. So is the next letter, and so on, all the way down to the bottom of the pile. Phones and letters and official hospital documents all carry the PPTH logo. A patient's medical records have a sticky on the corner with a name and the date the patient was admitted. The legal department sends Natali names they can use. The benefactors' board in the lobby includes names of production staff and crew who worked on the pilot episode. To Natali, "the details are what counts. I spend a lot of time on little things you may never see." The plan is never to shock the audience. "You don't want to be noticed," says Natali. Many people use Post-its around the home

The PPTH benefactors' board and *House* pilot wall of fame

to remind themselves of things like a dental appointment at nine o'clock. Natali writes little notes and sticks Post-its in places where hospital staff might, all in the name of making it look real.

House's mailing address is:

Gregory House, M.D.
Princeton-Plainsboro Hosp., #4101
978 Washington Road
Princeton, NJ 08542

One of the patient files:

Rogner, Bruce I, Patient ID 85873, dob 09/10/80

The phone list in the pharmacy starts with Dr. Andersen, Oncology x. 55467

Cuddy's extension is 55788

When she's dressing a set, Natali puts her own taste aside. "I have to think of how I would do a nine-year-old's bedroom with an extremely wealthy father. This kid would have everything," she says, speaking of billionaire Roy Randall's son in "Instant Karma." The teaser scenes were filmed in Greystone Mansion, a city-owned property in Beverly Hills that has been featured in movies like *Eraserhead* and *X-Men*. Natali rented the huge dining room table off a showroom floor; for the kid's bed she bought a setup from Pottery Barn. Once filmed, the bed goes in storage in one of three warehouses, on the lot, in Culver City, or at the off-site facility.

Natali has photographs of her handiwork on the walls in her office. The special-ed classroom from "Baby Boy"; Sharrie's Bar, where House got fatefully drunk in "House's Head"; Nolan's office. Natali fondly remembers the Buddha she found for "Birthmarks" at the Universal Property Department and the tabletop Japanese temple she put together for "Wilson."

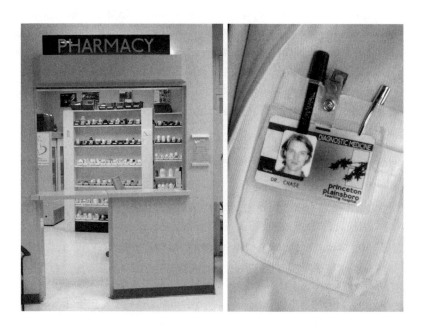

Set dressing large and small: the pharmacy and Dr. Chase's PPTH ID on his off-white lab coat

Of Chase's bachelor party ("House Divided"), Natali says, "There was good stuff cut out of that." She found a bakery in Hollywood that makes bachelor and bachelorette cakes. "I had a custom-made cake with a woman's torso and red lace and a corset." Also in "Birthmarks," Natali made up the funeral paraphernalia for U.S. Marine Colonel John House, House's dad, which included authentic medals and a saddle blanket.

Natali Pope went to documentary school at the University of California at Los Angeles and worked at a model-making company in the art department. She was a set decorator on the movie *Freddy's Nightmares,* and a lot of horror and feature work followed. Natali also has a degree in theater design and worked in black-box theater, where the sets are decorated hardly at all. One of the series Natali worked on was NBC's *Medical Investigations*, a show that began at the same time as *House.* "I watched *House* then—what are we up against?" "I thought coming on here would ruin it for me," says Natali, "but I watched the premiere ["Broken"] with everyone else at the theater and I cried. When Andre Braugher is with his dad, in the theater and on TV, both times I teared up." Natali likes to watch the show because as soon as the actors come on the set, "I am out of there." She likes to see what has been used. "I say, 'I wish they had shot over there because I put some nice stuff over there.'"

"I have an amazing team that pulls it off every day," says Natali. Not every item her team makes is going to be used. For a Fourth of July scene she had people making hats, paper chains, and firecrackers; one guy spent a whole day making a flag. "Katie keyed in on that flag and took that one element to sell the fact that it's July," says Natali. "The way it was edited, it was brilliant." Natali had already done two sets that morning. "Then I had to race on a Tech Scout and you think, How are these locations going to work? I have to have it fully shopped by Friday."

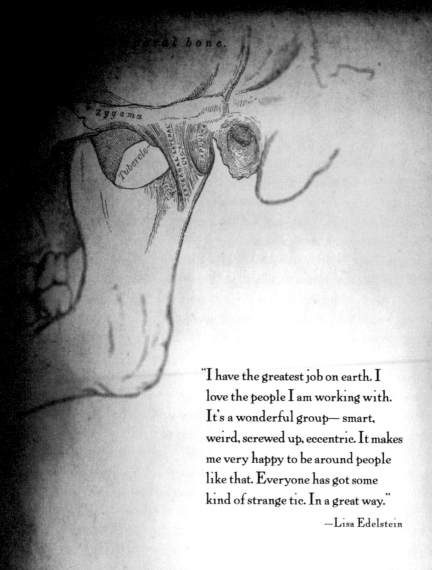

"I have the greatest job on earth. I love the people I am working with. It's a wonderful group— smart, weird, screwed up, eccentric. It makes me very happy to be around people like that. Everyone has got some kind of strange tic. In a great way."

—Lisa Edelstein

CUDDY

Lisa Edelstein

Princeton-Plainsboro is Lisa Cuddy's hospital. She's one of three women chiefs of medicine at a major hospital ("Mob Rules"), in fact the first woman, and, at age thirty-two, the second youngest ("Humpty Dumpty"). It's also established that Cuddy knew what she was getting into with House. "When I hired you, I knew you were insane" ("DNR"). There's history here. As far back as "Control" in season one, hospital chairman and House archenemy Vogler said he knew House and Cuddy had slept together "a long time ago." When House is snooping around Cuddy's bedroom, ostensibly to look for clues as to why Cuddy's handyman fell off her roof, it's revealed Cuddy was an undergraduate at Michigan when House was there. He was already a legend ("Humpty Dumpty").

It's only years later, as House and Cuddy dance at the eighties party at the medical conference in "Known Unknowns," that more comes out. As Cuddy, dressed as Jane Fonda, dances with House, dressed like John Adams (wrong eighties), they reminisce about the last time they danced, at med school, the week they met. They tracked each other down. "One thing led to another," says House. "Then it didn't," says Cuddy. After they slept together, House never called. Now he tells Cuddy he meant to call and come see her but that morning, he got kicked out of medical school by the dean. Cuddy is floored and leaves the party, upset. The timing was off then and it is again now. House is sober and trying at last to make it work with Cuddy but what House doesn't know is that back in her hotel room, looking after her baby, is Lucas.

"Now we know they met in college, although there is an age discrepancy. He was a graduate and I was undergrad. He was a legendary mind on campus and she was quite aware and made a point of being around him because she had a thing for him—physically sexy and brain sexy, a double whammy. They had their one-night stand that we find out was never intended to be just that. I think she is so shocked to find out that his intention was for more than just one night [and it] is very upsetting for her. Every time she tries to move on, there's something . . ."

—LISA EDELSTEIN

How has Cuddy put up with House all these years? Even when House wasn't undermining his boss's authority or legally compromising her or staring down the front of her blouse, he's been an absolute ass. House and Cuddy are flying back from Singapore ("Airborne"), a visit during which House delivers a three-minute speech and racks up hundreds of dollars in charges for hotel porn and room service. On the plane, House downgrades Cuddy's ticket and then switches seats with her when a guy in first throws up.

Nice.

He says things like this (in "Kids"):

HOUSE: "You just don't usually see breasts like that on deans of medicine."

CUDDY: "Oh, women can't be heads of hospitals? Or just ugly ones?"

HOUSE: "No, they can be babes. It's just you don't usually see their fun bags."

Nice.

House names Cuddy's breasts Patty and Selma, after Marge Simpson's cigarette-loving sisters. Why? "They're always smokin'" ("Known Unknowns").

Nice.

Cuddy is very capable of biting back. In the pilot, the first time Cuddy appears it is to unload a litany of grievances on House: his lack of billing; his failure to do consults; the six years of obligations he owes the hospital clinic. House isn't interested.

HOUSE: "It's five o'clock. I'm going home."

CUDDY: [beat] "To what?"

HOUSE: "Nice."

We see the issue: Cuddy is House's boss ("I sign your paychecks") and she has to try to keep him in line. But there are decades of unfinished business between them. As Cuddy and House argue outside an exam room, House can be heard to say, "I can see your nipples." One watching medical student says to another, "No wonder she hates him." But the other knows better. "That's not hate," she says, "it's foreplay" ("Brave Heart"). It's certainly something. Who knows, if House hadn't blown it perhaps what he'd be going home to would be Cuddy. And who knows, maybe one day, it will be.

....

For David Shore, giving House a credible boss was one of the greatest challenges he faced when putting the cast together. "That was a very difficult character," he says.

> "You have two choices with a boss, normally. You have the boss who is stopping him from doing anything and he is pulling end runs on them. If we went that way the boss becomes an idiot.... And you become Colonel Klink. Hogan's Heroes is a very funny show but we didn't want it to be a sitcom. And we didn't want her to say yes to everything [because] then we don't need her. It became this tightrope we had to walk and Lisa does such a great job of somebody who knows House is out of control but knows he's a genius and knows if she can harness him correctly and limit him and mold him and shape him and control him a little, she can have something great here."

Cuddy hired House for his genius but by the time the show starts, his downside is growing. His drug intake has doubled since he was hired. Cuddy tells House he's addicted; he's in denial. "It's not just your leg," she tells him. "You wanna get high" ("Detox"). Still, Cuddy decides House is worth it, worth more, in fact, than $100 million, which is what the hospital loses when she sides with House and not Vogler, the benefactor who is determined to fire the maverick doctor.

By season three the functioning-addict argument in House's favor is harder to maintain, especially in the face of House's most determined adversary, Detective Tritter. Cuddy repeatedly tries to get House to dig himself out of the hole he made but when he comprehensively fails, she has to save him by lying on House's behalf on the witness stand ("Words and Deeds").

> "That was one of the cool things in the Tritter story, that she did lie but refused to celebrate that lie. She hated House for forcing her to do that. She recognized at the end in a very House-like way that the lie was necessary for a greater good. But she also recognized that she has killed her soul a little bit in doing that."
>
> —DAVID SHORE

Cuddy's attempts to start a family frequently intersected with Cuddy and House's off-off affair. At the end of season two, House figures out that Cuddy is looking for a sperm donor ("Forever"). House is happy to help Cuddy with the fertility shots in her butt but not to support her decision to have a baby. In a low moment, when the leg pain is bad, House tells Cuddy she'll be no good as a mother ("Finding Judas") but also, when Cuddy thinks she has found a baby to adopt but loses it, that she'd be great ("Joy"). Seconds after the latter, they (finally) kiss. The foreplay ratchets up—House smashes Cuddy's toilet ("Let Them Eat Cake")—but he fails spectacularly to give Cuddy what she wants or needs. One episode later and Cuddy finds her baby, Rachel ("Joy to the World").

> "She gets stick from people for dressing inappropriately or not flying the flag for women in the workplace, et cetera, et cetera. That's all bollocks. What she does every week is phenomenally complicated and demanding and she manages to be funny and glamorous and downtrodden and tortured. Much like real people."
>
> —HUGH LAURIE

Although she has a rough road at first with the baby (in "Big Baby," Cuddy confesses to Wilson she feels nothing for the child), she makes it work. After Kutner dies, House bottoms out and it's to Cuddy he comes for help. To House, Cuddy's baby is getting in the way, "Go and suckle the little bastard child if it makes you feel good about yourself" ("Under My Skin"). "I need you," he says, and Cuddy babysits House while he detoxes. But House's nadir is yet to come. He tells the world, from the second-story balcony of the hospital lobby, that he slept with Cuddy. "This is beyond asshood," she tells him ("Both Sides Now").

> QUESTION: "She took exception to the fact that you stood on the balcony and declaimed to the world that you had slept with her."
>
> HUGH LAURIE: "Yes. Pretty long-suffering sort."

House hallucinated the sex with Cuddy and he finally admits he is not okay.

> QUESTION: "House was socked with Lucas and Cuddy."
>
> DAVID SHORE: "We don't make it easy for him."

> QUESTION: "It's a low blow."
>
> SHORE: "He had it coming."

It seemed that House had his chance with Cuddy and failed. While House is in the hospital Cuddy is living her life. She hires Lucas, House's private-investigator friend, to find out if someone in accounting was stealing money. "I'm a mother now," she says. "I need a guy I can count on every single day" ("Known Unknowns"). And Lucas was what House isn't, or wasn't.

> "I was hoping they would bring back Tritter, he's so tall and masculine. I never said that to anyone—that was an inside thought. He's more challenging to House than Lucas's character, who is more like a friend to House. Tritter is a direct challenge of his manhood. He's the kind of guy who makes other men feel smaller and weak and inadequate."
>
> —LISA EDELSTEIN

When House, Wilson, Lucas, and Cuddy have breakfast at the convention hotel, Lucas breaks the awkward silence by revealing things Cuddy has told him about House and her. House looks betrayed. Still, Cuddy has supported House like no boss would ever have to. She's like the partner she never became and the lover he fantasized about and the woman he sparred with, insulted, and relied upon as much as his cane. Cuddy has been all this.

In "5 to 9," viewers get to see a day at PPTH from Cuddy's perspective. She's up at 5 A.M., working out and looking after Rachel, checking her Black-Berry, trying to have sex with Lucas before she has to leave for work. Despite moments of vulnerability and concern about Rachel's well-being, she kicks ass all day long at PPTH, firing a staff member who stole drugs and then setting her up to incriminate herself when she finds out it was a whole lot of drugs; stopping a fight between Chase and the head of surgery; defusing a lawsuit from a guy whose thumb Chase reattached against his wishes; and, most impressively, strong-arming the hospital's insurance company into taking different terms by winning a game of chicken. House is, for once, not Cuddy's biggest problem but rather a colleague and something of a confidant.

"Lisa is an absolute joy. There was a show—I can't name it—that won an award. They all got up onstage and waved to the crowd and I was looking at these women [and thought], Oh, I see what you have done here. You've got the beautiful glamorous one, the kooky funny one, the downtrodden miserable one, and I was thinking that Lisa Edelstein does all of that. It takes all those of you to do what she is doing every week and people are giving you the award. It's so unfair."

—HUGH LAURIE

Lisa Edelstein on . . . Cuddy

QUESTION: "She wears these skirts—pencil skirts. It doesn't seem like she could walk in them. If she had to run for a bus, could she?"

CATHY CRANDALL: "Hell yeah."

QUESTION: "She wears heels, too . . ."

CRANDALL: "She could do a marathon in heels, Cuddy."

QUESTION: "How do you walk in some of those skirts?"

LISA EDELSTEIN: "It's difficult to get a good forward stride in a lot of them—that's why you have to swing your hips; you have to get side-to-side momentum going."

QUESTION: "So they have that going for them. They look uncomfortable."

EDELSTEIN: "A lot of women's clothing is uncomfortable historically."

QUESTION: "Cuddy has more wardrobe space than anybody else."

EDELSTEIN: "That's good. She runs a hospital; she needs outfits."

QUESTION: "Her color palette is interesting . . ."

EDELSTEIN: "She likes lots of pinks and reds and black and necklines, choker necklaces and bracelets."

QUESTION: "It makes a statement."

EDELSTEIN: "Yes, I think so. I was able to participate in the way her wardrobe mutated and it's a lot of fun. We have a great costume designer. What's also fun as a girl is that essentially you get to shop twice. There is you and then there is your character. When I'm in a store and I am looking for myself and I see something that is great for Cuddy I can call Cathy. 'You know what? I saw something that would be really wonderful,' and she is awesome about it. Of course most of it is Cathy but I can be in a beautiful place [and think], I can't wear that but my character can."

QUESTION: "So you can switch on Cuddy?"

EDELSTEIN: "I've known Lisa Cuddy for a long time. Shockingly, she has a very similar figure to mine so I can tell what she will look like in clothes just by the eye."

QUESTION: "We don't know so much backstory."

EDELSTEIN: "David Shore and I talked about it the first season. Cuddy wasn't being fleshed out very much and I was worried she would become peripheral . . . Only I cared who Cuddy was and where she came from. I did a little bit of research to understand what my job was [and] how unusual it was for a woman to have that position. I brought these details [and] my ideas for the history of her and House to David and that was a scary thing to do. He was really fantastic and enhanced it in his own way. He didn't kick me out of the room or off the show and used my ideas, which was great. Now we have a much more detailed version. It was great to be able to participate like that."

QUESTION: "Are you the only doctor who hasn't killed anyone?"

EDELSTEIN: "I almost killed my gardener when he fell off the roof."

QUESTION: "But that wasn't your fault."

EDELSTEIN: "She hasn't practiced much the last ten years. There were people I couldn't save like the woman whose baby I ended up adopting."

Lisa Edelstein on . . . House

QUESTION: "Why did it take House so long to say what he felt?"

"He's done all this work on himself in the mental institution and he has come back with a different way of communicating. He has life skills that he didn't have before. How long he will have them I don't know. They are very surprising to her. She had finally come to peace while he was away. She has gone through some changes herself. She realized she had to find stability in her life because now she is a mother. This guy comes back who is one hundred percent more stable, in terms of his people skills at least, than the man she saw leave and go into the institution."

QUESTION: "As a medical professional Cuddy was conflicted when House was an addict . . ."

"He was abusing the drugs. . . . It is hard for Cuddy to comprehend the inability to control drug intake because she is not an addict. If you aren't, you just take the drug when you need it and you don't want to take it any other time. For someone who is, you take it and you take it. . . . In the real world he would have lost his license a long time ago. Any doctor on pain medication has a difficult time practicing at all even if it is prescribed. But this is Princeton-Plainsboro, you know. It is very special."

QUESTION: "Cuddy wipes the floor with Tritter by lying and perjuring herself."

"She would have been in jail fifteen times. What a world! All my good deeds go unpunished."

QUESTION: "You were prepared to go to jail . . ."

"She really believes in this guy. She understands he is a genius, which is why she tolerates his insanity. I think his insanity turns her on a little bit. Great minds are attractive . . . until they directly hit you in the face.

"In some ways she is a mother cub who will fight to the death and she is extremely protective of him. That's why she gets so mad when he is hurtful of her, because it is a deep betrayal. She does everything to make sure he is safe, even to protect him from himself. He is attached to her; he appreciates her for what she does for him. I don't think he is capable of doing much more than lashing out. It is the [classic] story of abandonment. The most abandoned will abandon everyone else to maintain their abandonment. That is not unlike Dr. House."

QUESTION: "Cuddy has done crazy stuff. When you were trying to outdo each other to make the other crazy—smashing toilets . . ."

"She tries to get down to his level but she really is not there. It's a lot harder for her to behave that badly than it is for him. She's also the boss so she really can't permit herself to behave that way. But it's really all foreplay for these two."

QUESTION: "Six years of foreplay. When you get together it's going to be . . ."

". . . pretty rock and roll."

QUESTION: "Twenty-five years from now are House and Cuddy going to be friends?"

"They'll always know each other. They will do this dance for the rest of their lives. They will go through phases when they can't stop having sex with each other, then they will go through phases where they can't stand each other, then they'll go back around again. . . . I don't think certain people can be without their very special form of bickering."

Lisa Edelstein on . . . Settling Down

"Now she has settled to being a mother and trying to make sure she has the timing down and the right employees and the right friends and that's where Lucas seemed like a better choice because he was more responsible. Those are very intellectual reasons to pick a guy and personally I have tried that and it really doesn't work for me . . . A lot of people pick their partners on an intellectual level and are willing to tolerate a lot of things. I myself cannot do it. To me it feels like prostitution. I can't imagine Lucas is the greatest choice. Cuddy is choosing Lucas because it's so much easier and more convenient."

—LISA EDELSTEIN

QUESTION: "Do you think House has terminally blown his chance?"

HUGH LAURIE: "I don't know. TV being what it is, writers are never wont to close any door."

QUESTION: "Lucas is the only guy other than Wilson [that] House has ever related to."

"Right. He can't hate Lucas. He likes him."

QUESTION: "She finds the genius puzzle solver attractive. Lucas the PI is also a puzzle solver."

"She likes creative thinkers. There is a difference. What House has that Lucas doesn't is a delicious dark side. He is the safe version of what you would really like to be with. I don't know how long you can last with safe."

> "House has had every chance in the world at Cuddy. She has given him every chance she possibly could have and he has screwed it up every single time so it's somewhat unfair to expect her to wait. On the other hand maybe she could have picked someone better."
>
> —DAVID SHORE

QUESTION: "She sent House to the wrong address last Thanksgiving . . ."

"That was mean. . . . I think she is being very mean to him that episode and I asked about that because it's bad enough she's with Lucas. He's really working on himself and I don't get it. . . . Cuddy and House have spent six years him pulling her braids and her kicking him in the shins and this is what they do. It's more foreplay for the two of them. I don't think he'd like her if she didn't fight back a little bit. It keeps him intrigued."

QUESTION: "At the end of season five he thought you actually had gotten together."

"He wanted to move in together, which I thought was so sweet. I loved that that was what he thought and that was what he imagined he wanted. He hallucinated having sex in his mind and he thought they should move in together—that's really where he wanted it to go. I thought that was beautiful. But he was so far away from actually creating that in his life."

QUESTION: "Is she going to settle down?"

"I don't know. I would answer that question from my own point of view and I'm not sure why anyone wants to get married. I think everyone should have the right to, by the way, but I just don't know why they want to. I understand having a partner in life and wanting to be with somebody but the rest of it baffles me. So I don't know how to answer it for Cuddy."

Lisa Edelstein on . . . *House*

QUESTION: "You seem to have a great time."

"I love my job—are you kidding?"

QUESTION: "Do you take the work home with you?"

"You do it when you do it [and when] you're not doing it anymore, you forget immediately what you have just done. . . . The only thing is when you have a standing story arc like I did with the baby that was so personal; you don't take it home but you are exhausted. A different kind of exhausted than you are on a regular day. When you are having big emotional scenes it wears you down."

QUESTION: "Do you watch the show?"

"I watch it one time on TiVo. I can't watch live. I don't want to wait through commercials . . . I watch it because I learn stuff and it's part of my job. I learn everything from, 'I can't ever wear those pants again, what was I thinking?' to 'Why do I look like I have a wig on when I have all my own hair?' It's hard to watch with objectivity but you can discover what's good and what's bad about the skills you have picked up and work on what's needed. You catch yourself lying better than anybody."

QUESTION: "Is there any way you can watch it as a TV show?"

"Only the scenes I'm not in."

QUESTION: "Is the comic stuff fun to do?"

"I really like the scene [in 'Epic Fail'] where Wilson comes in and says his toilet is broken and Cuddy says she'll go get her tools. I love to be able to be funny. It's subtle and quiet. You let the joke go and it flies away."

"Hugh and Lisa and Robert have a rapport together that comes across on the screen. So while the plot is basically Cuddy saying, 'No, this is ridiculous, this is ridiculous, okay, you can do it,' they are able to do it with a lot of the humor. We try to make the shows funny and it's oftentimes hard to be funny in the situations when they are talking about dying or disease. The scenes with Cuddy are usually an opportunity to get some humor in the show and the actors are very good at that."

—TOMMY MORAN

QUESTION: "Everybody here is very collegial; there's no undercutting . . ."

". . . I am happy to say. I can't say that about every work experience that I have had. Most work experiences, ninety-five percent have been positive but this is the longest I have been anywhere. Mostly actors are not insane. Most of the people I have worked with are very welcoming and warm and want the work environment to be a pleasant one. I don't get it when someone isn't that way. I'm not clear why you would want to make your place of work a miserable place to come to especially when you are in position to create the environment. When you are one of the main characters on the show it is in your power to make that place pleasant or unpleasant and I don't understand why you would make it the latter."

QUESTION: "Ego?"

"Weird; needy; in it for the wrong reasons; acting out . . ."

QUESTION: "Tell that to House."

"He's doing it because he is miserable; he just has no tolerance, When you are in pain you just can't tolerate things. The Vicodin kind of helped—it softened the edge."

QUESTION: "When you read the script for the first time are you taken with the quality?"

"I love the way they tell stories and that they continue to take risks with format and pushing the limits."

QUESTION: "That dark worldview . . ."

"I don't find it dark; I find it realistic. I am like David Shore in that any magical thinking is for me very dangerous. . . . I love tradition and I love culture but I have a problem with that way of dealing with life."

QUESTION: "Cuddy and House are both on the side of science . . ."

"[They are] both realists. Maybe it's a female thing . . . She suffers from her hopes more than he does. I think he doesn't have any hopes. Maybe coming out of the institution he is allowing himself to have a little bit of hope and she has been beaten down a little bit too long and is trying to move on. It's an interesting dynamic."

CUDDY'S LOOK

"The biggest comment I get working on this show is why are Cuddy's shirts so low cut? And no doctor or hospital administrator would ever wear such a low-cut blouse. I don't see it. She knows her assets—she's a strong, independent woman and she's gonna use 'em. I think it's perfectly natural."

—CATHY CRANDALL, COSTUME DESIGNER

"I love the way she dresses. It's feminine but well structured. She gets to be a little sexy if she feels like it. Cuddy lives almost her entire life in the hospital. Now she has a baby so she makes time for something else but before the baby, that's all she did. That means all aspects of her personality have to exist when she is here. She needs to feel feminine, sexy, and powerful, like she is in control and be able to relax. She has to be able to do all those things in the hospital."

—LISA EDELSTEIN

Lisa Edelstein on . . . Lisa Edelstein

"I have had one of those careers that has been slow and steady with an increase every year . . . I have been working since 1988 when I did my own play in New York, a musical about AIDS that I wrote and composed. That set me on a certain path. . . . I came out to L.A. and slowly started to book cool jobs like *Seinfeld* and *Wings* and *Mad About You*. . .

"I got this show a week after I didn't get *Desperate Housewives*. I'm so glad Felicity Huffman got that part because she is great in it and I'm so glad I have this part because it is perfect for me. I am so grateful for this show because I have been around for so long I really understand what this experience is, I really get it . . . I don't think anyone handed me anything or did me any favors. I really just stuck to my guns and worked my way here."

QUESTION: "You were in the very first episode of the *West Wing* and a pivotal character."

"The hooker. That was a dream in a lot of ways because it was such a wonderful classy project and I'd worked with Aaron Sorkin and Tommy Schlamme on *Sports Night* . . . Aaron told me about the pilot of *West Wing* and there was a part for me he really wanted me to play. I still tried to audition for C.J. but they really wanted me for the hooker. So I'm more hooker than press secretary, whatever.

"That first scene, we are shooting in a hotel room. I'm in a men's shirt and a pair of underwear and I had such a major crush on Rob Lowe growing up—he was the movie star I was in love with in high school. It was a wonderful moment in my life. If I could just go back and tell my fifteen-year-old self that not only would I be a working actor, which is what I had wanted to be since I was a little girl, but I would also be making out with Rob Lowe on this fantastic project wearing nothing but panties and a men's shirt. . . . This show gives me a great feeling, too."

QUESTION: "You know you are on a hit show?"

"So I hear. It is a wonderful experience to hear things like that about the job that you're doing. At the same time, it's too big to comprehend.

I come in and do my job. I get recognized more; I get interrupted in my conversations more; I discover pictures of myself I didn't know were taken more. I have to have better security. I have had to move.

"There are things about it that are disturbing and frightening and things about it that are really lovely. Of course it is nice to be recognized for doing work; that people think your work is good. At the same time, a fanatic can be frightening because there are a lot of people who are very obsessed and some are perfectly harmless while others it is questionable.

"With the Internet there is so much access. Even on the red carpet for the Emmys, you get asked the dumbest questions. This year we were asked for the first time what we were wearing under our gowns. Don't you want any kind of illusion? Must we talk about my tampon? That's how it feels to me. The detail that people are interested in knowing, I don't get it.

"HDTV is an example. You don't need that much detail and need to see. It enhances lines on the face and makes people look older. Now people on the street love to tell me I look so much younger and thinner than they thought and isn't that great. In a way that's nice but actually maybe a thousand people a week see me in person but about eighty-eight million see me on TV looking older and fatter."

QUESTION: "People feel they have the right to say that kind of thing because they feel they know you."

"That's a little strange. You are a product and you are selling and marketing and manufacturing a product."

QUESTION: "Not when you are walking down the street . . ."

"That's what it seems to have become. A lot of it has to do with reality TV. My job is what I do here. I love it, love it, but the rest of it is a little bit challenging. That is how I earn my money, by what I have to deal with outside. I definitely earn a good living so that's what I have to do."

QUESTION: "Do you watch TV?"

"I like TV a lot. There are so many good shows on now: *Mad Men, Big Love, Nurse Jackie, 30 Rock, True Blood.* . . . People who aren't working have told me it's a really difficult landscape in terms of getting jobs because the networks are doing so much reality TV. But it's helped by the fact that there are so many more networks and cable does less episodes so they are able to do more quality. We do twenty-two a year and that's no easy feat."

QUESTION: "After six years it's still fresh?"

"I just love my job. I really do. I love driving to the studio; I like being on fake streets; I like being on sets; I like the people. I'm in the right business for myself. I'm extremely well qualified as a human being to be in this environment. The writing is wonderful. If you're on a show where the writing isn't good or the writers have been so abused . . . That's not what we're having here. So besides the people, there are so many ways we are fortunate on this job."

QUESTION: "All the medical stuff, does that freak you out ever?"

"No, I love it. I love every bit of information I get and I retain it very well. My medical comprehension level is pretty high. . . . My father's a doctor. I would have been a good doctor in another life. I was a terrible student. I had no interest in school. I would never have gotten through med school. I couldn't even get through college. I am a dropout. I have no study skills."

QUESTION: "But you can play one on TV."

"That's right. And I can answer lots of people's questions. And sound good."

QUESTION: "Does anyone ever come up to you on the street . . ."

"No, but I get asked that question a lot."

QUESTION: "Do you ever see someone on the street and say, 'Oh, look at that person . . .'"

"I do. I frequently diagnose people, actually. I can't help myself. People think I am diagnosing them because I play a doctor on TV when actually I have done that my whole life. I should have a disclaimer: 'This is not because I am a fake doctor—I am a medical know-it-all.'"

FAKING IT FOR REAL

 **Props and Special Effects**

> "Those aren't the actual giant tennis balls. The
> actual ones are a little smaller. We had six of them
> at the beginning of season one but we couldn't get
> the actual ones remade. We talked to China but
> they were never the same. They don't bounce well
> anymore."
>
> **—TYLER PATTON, PROP MASTER**

Many episodes of *House* are two shows in one: the teaser that sets
up the episode and the episode that resolves whatever happened
in the teaser. The teaser may look like nothing a *House* audience
has seen before: different location, different actors, different feel.
There have been some impressive sequences: collapsing buildings ("Alone"), Antarctic accidents ("Frozen"), intergalactic travel
("Black Hole"), and numerous car, bike, and ATV crashes. The
miniature movies in episode teasers can require feature-film-
scale work when it comes to the special effects. The most involved,
and dramatic, scene, however, came at the end of an episode: the
bus crash in "House's Head."

"House's Head" was originally intended to be aired after the
2008 Super Bowl and had a big bang appropriate to the presti-
gious slot. The teaser featured House disoriented and injured
after the crash trying to find his bearings in, of all places, a strip

club. Most teasers don't include regular cast members. Showing House (getting a lap dance) was an opportunity to introduce the show's main character to a large postgame audience, much of which might be unfamiliar with the show. But the writer's strike derailed that idea. "House's Head," paired with "Wilson's Heart," became the season-four finales. Wilson loses his girlfriend, Amber, and House nearly kills himself, first trying to remember who was on the bus with him when it crashed and then what symptoms that person exhibited that caused them to be so ill afterward.

The strike delay allowed for more prep time on what was a very complicated shoot for the crash, one that involved a combination of green-screen effects, live action stunts, and postproduction visual effects. Two buses were used: one laid on its side on the back lot at Fox and the other disassembled to use on a stage on a second fabricated bus. That bus shell was built on a rotating spit so it could tumble on its axis like a rotisserie chicken. Despite the fact the bus only fell on its side during the accident, the effects bus was turned over completely. Stunt people fell out of their seats and rolled around the bus as choreographed by stunt coordinator Jim Vickers. For other shots, the actors lay in the bottom of the bus as fake glass was tossed at them: another effect that was used during the rollover sequence.

Director Greg Yaitanes shot scenes with green screens surrounding the bus so footage of a rolling backdrop could be added later. Lighting effects were also used to make it look as though the bus were tipping over and rolling: the lights were moving rather than the bus. Visual effects supervisor Elan Soltes added the actual impact. Anne Dudek (Amber) was made up with a metal bar sticking through her leg as well as impact injuries on her face. In one shot, House's cane, one decorated with the flame motif, cartwheels through the air. After the crash, House hallucinates conversations with the bus's passengers. Those scenes were marked by parallel sets of pulsating lights retreating down through the back of the bus, an effect prompted by DP Gale Tattersall's memories of airport runway lights near where he grew up.

Gerrit van der Meer and Marcy Kaplan are the producers who decide if the expense of a big stunt like this can be borne. "It's a brief moment but an expensive one," says Gerrit of the "House's Head" crash. Marcy and Gerrit would have liked nothing better than to keep a great prop like this one, but a rolled-over bus-on-a-spit is strictly a one-time use item.

Another stunt began "Human Error." A shivering woman is safe aboard a Coast Guard chopper while a diver tries to pick up her companion from a raging sea in driving wind and rain. The couple has escaped from Cuba and want to see Dr. House. Gerrit and Marcy each had experience of working with a big water tank such as the one needed to film the rescue: Marcy on the movie *Down Periscope* in 1996 and Gerrit in England. They found a tank in Pacoima that fitted Marcy's two criteria: "The two A's: affordable and available." A second part of the stunt was filmed in the Santa Monica Airport in a hangar. It wasn't feasible for a full-size helicopter to fly over the tank, nor was it possible to get a real U.S. Coast Guard helicopter, so the work was finished with a miniature. "You put the whole thing together and it looks totally convincing," says Gerrit.

> "We got every kind of pen you need in the world. And a blond wig just in case."
>
> —MIKE CASEY

For "Top Secret," director Deran Sarafian rolled an army Humvee on a spit like the "House's Head" bus for the scene where House dreams he loses a leg in Operation Desert Storm. The scene took about twenty minutes to shoot. Marcy Kaplan was concerned that there needed to be more than one take after so much prep work and setup. "They got in there with a video camera and rolled the thing and [Deran] said, 'Okay, we got it,'" says Gerrit. "I was freaked out—can't you just do it again?" says Marcy. "We put this whole thing together. That's usually not me saying 'do it again.'"

....

Many subterfuges are employed to convince the viewers they are watching people's lives on the line at a hospital in Princeton, New

Jesse Spencer gets a touch-up between takes.

Jersey, when the action is actually taking place in a series of giant sheds on a movie lot in Southern California. As with the bus crash, some of what is faked is done digitally (visual effects); other elements are rigged on the set (special effects). In many cases, when you see a character holding something, they're really holding something. If it's a giant tennis ball, it has to be the right kind of giant tennis ball. Anything that is picked up by the actor is a prop and the responsibility of prop masters Tyler Patton and Mike Casey. Anything in the background is in the domain of set dressing. This is a medical show so patients' injuries and diseases have to look realistic. In many scenes, such as a complex medical procedure, all the visual elements—props, visual effects, special effects, makeup, costumes, set decoration—come together to transport the audience to Princeton-Plainsboro Teaching Hospital.

Prop masters Tyler Patton and Mike Casey have done up their office to look like a Polynesian-themed tiki lounge. Tyler stands at the bar, which doubles as his desk. The walls are decorated with bamboo and palm tree artwork. The small room is crammed with potted plants. Ukuleles and a couple of gun-shaped tequila bottles are on display. Tyler and Mike spend so much of their time at work, they wanted to make their workplace looks like they're on vacation. Some of the pieces they bought; others were scavenged from shows like *Vegas* that went off the air. This is television, so nothing is necessarily as it appears. Those skulls over there—fake. The hand grenade, that's real.

In a brightly lit trailer is the office and studio of Dalia Dokter, who is responsible for all the special effects makeup on the show. Pinned to the walls are photographs of Dalia's work—sloughing skin, giant facial growths, scars, skeletons, rashes, and bloody wounds. Dalia orders the prosthetics and applies the makeup that transform an actor into a patient in peril. In the corner is a prosthetic scalp, complete with straggly hair, featuring a raw open wound the size of a silver-dollar pancake, as used in "Resignation." Dalia cheerfully describes what it is. "She was in the MRI and her head blew off. I had to have this prosthetic made and this would intermingle with her hair and there was a lot of blood in there oozing and dripping down."

On trailers, on the set, and in storage, in their own garages, Tyler and Mike have accumulated a lot of stuff. Everything that's appeared on the show has been saved, as well as the rejected versions of props and objects that may or may not come in handy one day. Mike says, "When we buy groceries, we buy eleven of everything," but that edict seems to apply to all their purchases. What they can't buy or find in their inventory, Tyler and Mike can rent from one of the city's prop companies, such as the Hand Prop Room, or have fabricated by specialty manufacturers.

"What makes the difference between a good prop master and a great one is to take that extra step and think, What would I be thinking in this scene? So when the actor comes to the set and he says, 'Oh, what would I be doing? Would I have a lighter?' And I would say, 'You probably would have a lighter; how about one of these lighters?' 'Oh awesome, a Zippo. Maybe just a Bic. Do you have a green one?' And I say, 'Absolutely.'"

—TYLER PATTON

Based on the script breakdown, the material needed for an episode is gathered at the prop trailer, where assistant prop master Carl Jones sorts it and crates it up for Eddie Grisco to take to the set to give to the actors for each scene. Once the props are used they go back into storage. Tyler and Mike's on-set storage is like the oddest emporium in the world. Material from the most recent season is stored by episode closest to hand. Brand-neutral grape soda cans are kept along with test results and faxes used in the same episode. Here is a scrapbook Thirteen made of a vacation she took to Thailand. In the scene, Thirteen writes on a particular page, so that page had to be reproduced numerous times to allow for separate takes.

"There are other pages in case she wants to flip through. You can't put a prop on the set and say these are your limitations. You can't turn the page—it's not good prop work and you have to think past what they might want."

—TYLER PATTON

Olivia Wilde's own photographs of Thailand were used, one doctored to remove an airline logo from a plane. For another, the photographer was contacted and clearance obtained to use the picture. The scene with the scrapbook appears in the episode for a matter of seconds.

Hanging on a rail are House's canes, maybe fifty of them, with various versions of each design. Tyler hand-painted the cane with a flame motif for Hugh Laurie—those prototypes are here. "There are House's guitars," says Mike. "His boom box. His racket. His cricket bat. His Scotch. Black Fox Single Malt Scotch. The actual bottles are expensive."

The inventory gets more bizarre. "Candy and wrapping paper," says Tyler. "Bongs . . . There's a piece of chest skin." There are fake condiments, and fake cereal, with boxes that look uncannily like, but not the same as, everyone's favorite brands. Nearby is a "disposable head immobilizer." A box holds samples for Cuddy's lipstick that House mistook for his pills in "Under My Skin." The writer wanted a gold lipstick, the director a clear one, so Tyler and

Mike found about forty samples they could choose from. Then, when the right lipstick was found, they bought six of them just in case. As Mike says, they never want to be in a position where someone says, "Okay, we can't shoot that scene because we don't have a two-dollar lipstick."

The outside of the prop trailer is decorated with Tyler Patton's personal dragon symbol. Tyler likes to mark his things, but if he writes "Patton" on a mug, it can't be used as a prop. The dragon symbol comes in handy that way. There's even more stuff in here, neatly arranged in drawers. "Hole punches, staplers, rulers. What kind of ruler do you need?" asks Tyler. "I have a lot of old-school wood rulers because they are hard to find." "We have your smokes in here," says Mike. "That's all the drug paraphernalia. Herbal cigarettes. Crack pipes, if you smoke crack. Fake coke. Fake pot. Fake joints and all the different stuff." Back to Tyler. "Briefcases. There are fifty in here. I had over two hundred for [Wilson] to choose from."

QUESTION: "Are your houses this well organized?"

MIKE: "No, we only have time to do it here."

TYLER: "My garage looks almost identical to this. I have as many things in my garage."

Food is a particular challenge for the props team. In a scene with food, actors will avoid eating as much as possible. Each scene may be shot from different angles, and close up and wide. If an actor eats in one shot, she has to eat in all of them. If she takes one bite out of a whole hamburger in the shot, then she has to do the same every time. This means the prop department has to provide as many items of food as there are shots, plus spares. If the actor isn't going to chew and swallow every piece of food, there's a spit bucket off to the side to take care of business.

In "Epic Fail," the briefly unemployed House tackles gourmet cooking with scientific vigor. House makes a complicated dish with eggs and ragout that Thirteen tries and deems perhaps the best thing she ever ate. "That episode was a nightmare for me,"

says Tyler Patton, who employed a food stylist to help. "He's injecting the egg yolk and taking out the egg. The little egg yolks were
made out of silicone." The injectable eggs were made by Autono-
mous Effects, who makes bodies for the show. "We had to switch
it out with a little piece of tofu with spices which [Olivia] ate. She
ate probably twelve to fifteen of those," says Tyler. "I haven't poisoned an actor yet."

QUESTION: "Some actors will eat everything you put in front of them?"

TYLER PATTON: "Not when they're all working. When they're all starting out they're
still hungry. The day players will eat."

MIKE CASEY: "Robert [Sean Leonard] wanted to eat something for some reason and
it wasn't scripted. The prop assistant said, 'Are you sure?' and he said, 'Yeah,' and
we gave him some trail mix and he had to eat it again and again and again. He
came after the scene was over and said, 'If I ever say I want to eat again, remind
me of this trail mix. I ate more trail mix than I need to eat the rest of my life.'"

TYLER PATTON: "Hugh asked for some cookies. We had a lot of requests for how
they should look and what kind of box they should come in and the only ones we
could come up with were these sugar-free cookies for diabetics. He said, 'Oh,
they're not bad.' By the end of the scene he said, 'I am going to explode.' You're
only supposed to eat three of them and he ate sixty. He went to his trailer, 'Oh my
stomach.' They have to be careful."

Guns and money present other problems. Showing money on-
screen is a particular issue. Technically, replicating money by
filming it is counterfeiting, as far as the letter of the law is concerned, so some restrictions are applied. The money has to be
smaller or larger than real size. Tyler Patton is an armorer and
has been through the same kind of background checks to work
with guns that fire blanks as he would for real guns. The frame of
the gun is real: It's been altered to fire blanks but can just as easily be altered back to fire real bullets. There hasn't been a lot of call
for guns on *House*. When Wilson went turkey hunting, his former
cancer patient Tucker shot at a chemotherapy bag attached to a
tree. The gun fired blanks; special effects had rigged the bag with
a small charge to make it look like the shotgun fired for real.

Tyler Patton is third-generation Hollywood. His grandfather was director of a show in the fifties called *Super Circus*. His mother (*A Swingin' Summer*) and father (*Scampy the Boy Clown*) were both actors and his father has been a producer and AD. At sixteen, as soon as he could drive, Tyler drove trucks for commercials. Mike Casey also got into the business through commercials. Mike was the assistant running the set for three years while Tyler was prop master on his own. Tyler Patton has also acted and still does, as a neurosurgeon on *House*, operating the rig the prop guys designed and built themselves.

"When you're young you look at the people on the film crew, you see the prop guy, he's got everything—he's got the guns, he's got the booze, he's got everyone asking him questions. He's in charge. He's the man. Of course, in retrospect it would have been better to be a camera operator, maybe, or a makeup artist."

—TYLER PATTON

"Almost every day is different," says Tyler about his work. "There's always something new to figure out. We know so much about so many things that we don't care about at all." He mentions drag racing (seen in the teaser in "Whatever It Takes") and how he knows what the drivers wear and what kind of headphones they use, more than a lot of even the more avid fans are going to know. "We have to go talk to the guys," he says, "go to the pit lane and ask, 'What's that thing? Who's that? What's he doing?' Once that little opener is done, there's something else that comes up."

In their office, in addition to the shooting schedules, Tyler and Mike have both typed up their "Five Golden Rules," designed so they don't "lose it" during their long workweek. Their lists have some of the same items, such as "transcend emotional responses" and "don't dwell on others' shortcomings." Tyler has "Stay off the Walkie-talkie unless absolutely necessary," and "accept small problems"; Mike, "be positive." "He assigned my rules to me," says Mike. "I assigned his rules to him. Half the job is everybody getting along . . . We get along because we're still friends afterward. People say how do you do it? It's more time than we're with our wives." "The good thing is it's a very taxing show," says Tyler.

"There's always more than enough to do. We can only have our little fits for so long, then we have to get to work . . . On this show they give us a lot of latitude but we had to earn that trust."

QUESTION: "Where did you get House's cricket ball?"

MIKE CASEY: "I think I got it from India. I wanted to get a legitimate one. If it's not any good, Hugh is going to bust me for it. He has a Magic 8 Ball, tennis balls, a lawn bowling ball. Set dressing put them out and I said I need to go get multiples because unfortunately people take stuff off the set, as ridiculous as it sounds. These lawn bowling balls are really cool but I had to go online and get four of them. I think we've already lost one this season. Maybe it's him taking them."

Along with makeup artists Ed French and Jamie Kelman, department head Dalia Dokter won an Emmy for Outstanding Prosthetic Makeup in 2007 for George, the six-hundred-pound guy rescued out of his home by firefighters in "Que Sera, Sera." "That was a labor of love," says Dalia, looking at photos of the transformation of the actor. Dalia worked with the director and writers to go over the concept and supervised construction of the suit that was made by a specialist makeup lab. They needed an extra trailer to work on the actor and fitting the prosthetic took three people three and a half hours. The job gave Dalia her earliest ever call time: 3:42 A.M. "It was interesting walking through the lot at that time in the morning," Dalia says. "It was kind of desolate." One issue with fake skin is to have it move like real skin and much of the success of prosthetic work is down to the actor. "The actor made it," says Dalia of Pruitt Taylor Vince, the six-hundred-pound man. "It looked like it was part of him. . . . He was a lot of fun and he enjoyed it."

Often Dalia Dokter's prosthetic work contributes to a medical scene. When House and Foreman started performing the autopsy on the cop in "Brave Heart," there's a shot of the saw cutting into the corpse/patient's chest. Dalia had a silicone piece made that included the wound. She colored it and added blood and in post-production, the effect of a man being sawn open was put in. In "Epic Fail," Vince the video game entrepreneur swelled up partly using a prosthetic that was placed on his chest. The actor's chest had already been filmed and was hairy, so the prosthetic had to have hairs punched into it one at a time.

In "Adverse Events," it was the artist's head that blew up dramatically. Dalia sent the actor to the lab and a cast was made of his head and neck for a test version for the director and writer to look at. Then the prosthetic was made and put on the actor for the shot. Dalia keeps all her prosthetics and will occasionally take a piece and make something else out of it. But all the different rashes she's had to make over the years, she hasn't duplicated any of them.

In the normal course of events, Dalia has a week to research and create her special effects. The writer shares their research with Dalia. For the young woman whose skin was sloughing off ("Under My Skin"), "[writer] Pam [Davis] sent me a link and I sat here watching on the computer and I cried through the whole thing. It was the real story of a woman who was taking antibiotics and within six hours she started blistering and her skin started . . . they thought she was going to die. Her hair was gone. The only thing you could see on her face was her eyeballs, it was so scary. But at the same time, she survived. She was beautiful." The skin was very challenging to re-create, with different layers of very thin skins involved. The young man with the large growth on his head in "Ugly" was also researched online, producing a prosthetic with a wig to go over the top.

If you need a tattoo, Dalia Dokter can hook you up. She uses Tinsley brand tattoos. "The trick of a good tattoo is that they're not too black," says Dalia. "If they're too black on-screen then they look fake. If you have them more faded, they look realistic."

Photographs from work Dalia did in season six are clustered in one corner of the trailer. Here's "Freedom Master," who jumped off a parking structure in "Broken," and Alvie, House's hospital roommate pictured after House hit him. ("I loved Alvie," says Dalia.) Here's Vince from "Epic Fail" and the skeletons that were tested for bad DNA in "Brave Heart." It's essential for Dalia to photograph her work because so many scenes are shot out of sequence. A patient might be filmed on the verge of a bloody death and then immediately shot being admitted, when they might have been a lot healthier-looking. Dalia's photos help with continuity.

"I'm tiptoeing through the stages and looking through a patient's window and you can see a tree there and the branches are swaying—it has to be realistic. I walk by and I see one of our crew members, an FX person, sitting in a lounge chair holding a piece of filament and he's moving this piece of string to move the branches. He is there to complete the whole scene. How cool is that? People don't know what it entails."

—DALIA DOKTER

Dalia started training as a makeup artist when she was forty. She taught at the makeup school where she learned her trade before going out and taking the traditional route to a job in Hollywood—knocking on a lot of doors. She worked on short films, movies of the week, then series work, including *Angel* for five seasons. Although her background is in beauty, on *House*, Dalia specializes in effects. Kathleen Crawford and Marianna Elias head up beauty, and hair is a separate department, "But we're all together," says Dalia. "We're a team." Dalia will help with beauty makeup if needed. She'll help props if they have a very heavy episode. If the actor is sitting in her makeup chair and needs bandages (technically a prop), she'll apply them.

Punching House

In "Ignorance Is Bliss," Chase got to punch out House, leaving an impressive amount of damage that Dalia Dokter created. It was a judgment call as to how hard Chase hit House. Resident nurse Bobbin Bergstrom is often involved in questions like this: What is the eye going to look like right away and what is it going to look like in two days' time? "Do they want it to be big, like Rocky with a huge cut," she asks, "which would be unrealistic for one punch." On other occasions there might be a liberty taken: a big punch one day leaves no mark the next.

House's eye, injured by Chase's punch, starts to look better.

QUESTION: "Would Thirteen ever punch House?"

OLIVIA WILDE: "I think Thirteen would find a different way. Her punishing House would excite him too much. There's something about her losing her cool and being physical with him that would make him win. Her way of punching him would be to deflate him in some way or be indifferent."

In this case, Dalia did a makeup test on Hugh Laurie's stand-in Patrick Price, giving Patrick the broken nose, cut eye, and shiner she'd later use on House. The cut was made using a prosthetic made from a tiny piece of latex. Dalia holds it up. "This was the piece that I used on Patrick. I'll fit it somehow on House. I use glue and seal it, blend out the edges. Hopefully it will stay on all day."

QUESTION: "He hit him right in the eye socket and cut his eye—that's a good punch."

DALIA DOKTER: "Yes. And he broke his nose. In two days he'll be fine."

Making up Patrick Price to look like the punched-out House took two hours. Pictures of the result were circulated to director Greg Yaitanes, the writers, Katie Jacobs, and Hugh Laurie to see if any tweaks were required. Patrick has stood in for Hugh Laurie the whole series and other than being shot, this is the best blow House has taken. "Jesse Spencer can throw a mean punch," says Patrick. "Come on, he's from Australia. He's a brawny guy."

MAKING IT ON-SCREEN

11

Visual Effects and Editing

> "It's like building a car. You use this type of engine block—oh, that doesn't work, you put the other one in. What about the flaring on one side of the car? It's a process of building, breaking down and building and breaking down until you get what you really want."

—CHRIS BROOKSHIRE, EDITOR

The final pieces of the *House* puzzle are put together in editing suites and sound studios and on the computer screens in Elan Soltes's visual effects (VFX) department. "We do a lot of CG [computer graphics] now," says Elan. "The whole trend has been less and less of the internal body stuff and more in the teasers to make them more outlandish and extreme." Nothing was more outlandish than the video game sequence at the beginning of "Epic Fail" in season six. In the episode's futuristic game, characters morphed into Thirteen and Foreman as the patient hallucinated. The teaser was like nothing else the show's ever shown. Some viewers may have checked the channel. "I was afraid of that," said producer Marcy Kaplan. "Are people going to turn off?" Not after they watched a second or two.

Elan Soltes is a member of the cinematographer's guild, a reminder of the pre-
CG era of green screens and blue screens and shooting miniatures. As a kid, Elan wanted to be a photographer. He shot video in college and then experimented with the Sony Portapak, a black-and-white camera that used reel to reel tape. He shot some documentaries for public television and got into TV designing titles. When his employer needed a visual effects supervisor for the remake of *Mission: Impossible* they were working on, the job was offered to Elan. "I said I don't know anyone who does that and they said it's the same thing as title design, you'll figure it out."

The video game sequence was conceived over the show's hiatus between seasons. "That was pretty ambitious," says Elan Soltes, who got the heads-up as the previous season was wrapping. "I said we better get going now. It was a long, elaborate process starting with saying to the writers, 'What are you thinking about?' In real life it would take three or four years." With two boys of his own at home, Elan knows about video games. The idea was to take the technology forward, as if Vince, the video game maker in the story, is creating the next big thing. The characters wore virtual reality goggles and stood on pedestals firing guns that were motion tracked. Tyler Patton and the props department fabricated the guns and goggles. Tyler made a prototype gun and had six more made at the shop. The goggles were made out of headphones and hockey masks; the microphone was a piece of a table lamp stand on Tyler's desk that he clipped off. Everything else was a little more high-tech.

"The game we wanted to be somewhere between a video game and an animated movie, which I think we got."

—GREG YAITANES

Elan Soltes drew on his experience as visual effects supervisor for James Cameron's futuristic series *Dark Angel.* The writers' idea was for a postapocalyptic medical lab modeled on PPTH but populated with mutants. Elan and the artists he worked with came up with sketches for the cast of game characters: Sniper Chimp, Lizard Man, and Vince, the patient of the week. Directed by Greg Yaitanes, the sequences were storyboarded out; fifteen technicians at VFX house Encore Hollywood created the game environment.

The completed first-person game was called "SavageScape." As the characters moved through the feeding area in the hospital/lab they were attacked by prehistoric pterodactyls and "brats"—mutant bat/crow hybrids—and fought them off with their laser guns. "It was insane," says Elan. "But we did it. We're getting ready to do the Saturday morning animated version."

Elan recalls other teaser work. A boy hallucinating about aliens ("Cane and Abel"); filling an auditorium for piano virtuoso Dave Matthews using just eighty extras ("Half-Wit"); blowing House's leg off ("Top Secret")—"that was another little gag," says Elan—the building collapse in "Alone"; the trainee NASA astronaut's test flying sequence with a heads-up display, ground flying by at five hundred feet and the trippy tribute-to-*2001* sequence when she started hearing with her eyes ("The Right Stuff").

> **"We're competing with movies and while viewers are not watching us on a movie screen they are watching us on 50-inch TVs in living rooms across America. It's got to look good."**
>
> —DAVID SHORE

> **"We try to be yucky.** There was one writer who liked to stick needles in the eye so we did a bunch of those. Everybody seemed to like those."
>
> —ELAN SOLTES

Often VFX are used for smaller "fixes" that help speed along the ever-moving production process. During the video game sequence, director Greg Yaitanes called for a wider shot but puling the camera back meant that a light that DP Gale Tattersall had installed in the ceiling was in shot. Elan said shoot it, I'll take care of it later. "I can have a guy sit at a computer for a few minutes and get rid of that light or I can make the crew sit around for half an hour while someone figures out how to rig the light so it's not in the shot." VFX can smooth the edges of a prosthetic, give someone a fast-moving rash or paint a patient's eyes yellow to give them jaundice, a quicker way of doing it than fitting contact lenses. If special effects have rigged a tube to have blood gush out of someone's ear; Elan gets rid of the tube.

Elan is also involved in the wide-ranging and intricate plot to make *House*'s audience believe they are looking at Princeton, New Jersey. Steve Howard hires a greensman, part of whose job is to tie up palm trees to make them look like something you'd find on the East Coast. Wilson and Tucker's turkey hunt ("Wilson") was filmed in Los Angeles. "We are shooting in Griffith Park so we'll have to make it look like fall in New Jersey," says Elan. "We have these tools that let us modify color a little bit."

"I don't know why they don't say House and his team didn't move to UCLA? It's a lot of trouble to make it look like Princeton, New Jersey. I don't know how many people pay attention to that."

—ELAN SOLTES

During what Elan calls the "kitchen sink meeting," a production meeting with other department heads, the decision will be made as to what's a special effect (an effect made on set) or a visual effect (put in afterward); what makeup is responsible for; and so on. It was all hands on deck for the Antarctic episode "Frozen," where House diagnoses, and flirts with, Mira Sorvino's character, Cate, who gets sick at a research station in the South Pole (that was actually built on the set). "Frozen" was *House*'s Super Bowl episode. "I said, 'Okay, I need to basically have the visual effects be kick-ass,'" says Katie Jacobs. "Elan and [editor] Dorian [Harris] and myself worked more labor intensively and put a lot more into that teaser knowing that it was going to be following the Super Bowl . . . We threw everything at it."

The Antarctic set was designed and built on the lot in seven days. The beginning of the teaser is a shot flying over the Antarctic ice toward a guy who is sliced up by the rotor of a windmill. (It's a red herring; he's not the patient of the week.) Most of the shot was made with computer graphics, except for a section of the windmill, some of the snow, and the Snow Cat that the transportation department found in Oregon and shipped in.

The idea for the teaser was to have the horizon go on forever into the white using a backing, polar lighting, and driving snow but CG snow never looks as convincing as real fake snow. As ever with any kind of effect, the key was to find the balance between what is tried on set and what's added in postproduction. In Hollywood there is a specialist for everything, so of course there is a company called Snow Business for this kind of job. Between Snow Business and Elan's computers, the elements were mixed for maximum effect.

"We like the gory. Elan does a great job of taking us inside the body. *CSI* changed all that. People want to see the fingernail flying off into the wall on *CSI* that they recover with their tweezers. Audiences come to expect that level of visual excitement."

—DAVID FOSTER

....

Around the corner from Elan Soltes's office sit the three *House* editors: Amy Fleming, Chris Brookshire, and Dorian Harris. Sitting at banks of television screens, the editors take the film that has been shot and turn it into what FOX broadcasts on a Monday night. Once or twice a day data and files comprising what was shot the day before (the "dailies") are imported into their AVID editing machines. The editor starts to cut immediately—it's helpful to find out if there are any technical problems with anything that's just been shot. After shooting has finished, the editor has four or five days to deliver a cut to the director.

"The acting is beyond compare. The casting is so good but actors have to play up to everyone's level. When you step onto a set with Hugh Laurie you have to be damned good. You have four different takes of Hugh Laurie and he is absolutely fantastic in every one. You have a lot of great options."

—CHRIS BROOKSHIRE

On the set, one scene is filmed multiple times from different points of view, distances, and angles. The editor makes the creative decision that one of these shots works best following another following another. "There is a language to the way things are shot," says Dorian Harris, "and there is a language of editing. It follows certain prescribed rules." "We're trying to get the audience to understand the story," says Chris Brookshire. "We're trying to tell the story in a really creative, efficient, and exciting way from the raw material."

"Let's say there is dialogue of Wilson berating House for making a bad decision. It would mean a lot more if instead of showing Wilson berating House, if we see some reaction shots of House absorbing what Wilson is saying and reacting to it. It makes a better show. It's the actors' choices, the director's choices, the editors', the producer's [choices]. A lot of different processes."

—CHRIS BROOKSHIRE

The first cut that is delivered usually runs eight or nine minutes over the airtime. The editor has made the first set of decisions using their knowledge of who the director and writers are and their experience with the visual language of the show that has evolved over the years. "We kind of know what the show will eventually look like so we try to bring the show to a certain point along the way," says Chris.

The extra nine minutes gets lost as the cut moves along. The director has four days with it; then it goes to the producers. It's likely that no "director's cut" in cinema or TV history has ever been shorter than what the producer wanted but it might behoove a director to make the cuts himself rather than leave it up to the producer. "Often it is in their interests to bring a leaner cut to the producers so there is not as much at play," says Dorian Harris. "Ultimately it is David Shore and Katie Jacobs who decide what is in or out." The producers will know more about the longer-term arc a story is taking and in choosing a shot they can foreshadow something an editor may not be aware of. "I want that reaction to be angrier because later on down the road we are going to develop a story line," says Chris. "I need to see that anger surface."

Many of the skilled professionals working on *House* made their way to L.A. without a job after getting experience in TV, indie films, or commercials elsewhere in the country. Amy Fleming went to film school and enjoyed editing, "constructing pieces and reconciling the written intent with what happens in production." She moved out to L.A. from Chicago, where most of the work is in commercials.

Dorian Harris saw editing as a way to learn a craft from the bottom up and wasn't interested in production work. She assisted in New York, eventually editing on her own with Robert Altman. Dorian's husband is also in the business, as an AD and unit production manager in features. Chris Brookshire slept on someone's couch and started work as a PA. He worked in editorial on features but realized he would learn more, and faster in, TV, and started with *Law & Order.*

It's essential while cutting material that the story continues to make sense throughout and is consistent from beginning to end. The story cannot fall apart. It's a rule of thumb with the first cut not to remove any dialogue. The *House* writers are so careful to interconnect the various threads that are running through each episode that one line coming out in act one probably means something has to change in act three. In some cases ADR lines can be added. ADR is "automated dialogue replacement," lines added to make up for something a microphone didn't pick up or a line that was added or rewritten. An ADR is off-camera; occasionally a scene will have to be reshot to maintain the integrity of the story.

The editors also cut the production sound, which is the sound that's recorded on set. They add temporary sound effects and music, which is later replaced by rerecorded sound. There is a network cut that goes to the network and broadcast standards and practices, and ad sales at the network also weigh in on the cut. The music has to be cleared and paid for with NBC splitting the cost between the production and distribution and overseas partners. Once the picture and sound are "locked," meaning the editors' work is done, the episode is turned over to outside departments who "on-line" the picture, which means bringing it up the highest HD quality and cleaning up the sound. Before long, it's delivered to the network and on the air.

"One of the appeals of TV for me is that you can't stay on something forever. You can't belabor the process and at a certain point it's going out the door. We're expediting shows but we are not overindulging. I have worked on small films for over a year that could have benefited from a shorter postproduction process. There is a certain self-indulgence to a movie."

—DORIAN HARRIS

"You can often overwork something when you should have gone with your gut instincts that you thought were right," says Chris. "You start to question and make it more muddied." Says Dorian Harris, "On very few shows do I feel we don't have enough time."

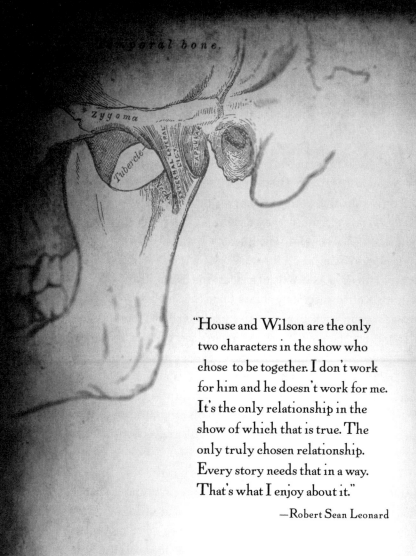

"House and Wilson are the only two characters in the show who chose to be together. I don't work for him and he doesn't work for me. It's the only relationship in the show of which that is true. The only truly chosen relationship. Every story needs that in a way. That's what I enjoy about it."

—Robert Sean Leonard

WILSON

Robert Sean Leonard

What do we know about Dr. Wilson? He's head of the oncology department at PPTH. From his sweats it seems he has some connection with McGill University in Montreal. There are three former Mrs. Dr. Wilsons (one a repeater?) and a recently deceased partner in whose apartment Wilson lived for a time. He is Jewish. He drives a sensible car and dresses like a bank manager. He is very caring and a little needy. And House is his best friend.

When it appears as if Wilson has left the hospital, and House, after Amber's death, Kutner succinctly points out to House what Wilson meant to him: "He paid for your lunch, likes monster trucks, and was your conscience" ("Not Cancer"). From the pilot it's clear that Wilson believes House cares about him. But even with the common courtesies, House has a funny way of showing it. In "Wilson" in season six, when the two men are living together in Amber's old apartment, House wakes Wilson up at six-thirty playing George Michael's "Faith" excellently but loudly on his guitar. He takes all of Wilson's dinners out of the freezer to make room for his frozen Margarita shots. This is the least of it. What's in this for Wilson?

If Taub is a serial philanderer, Wilson is a serial marryer. House is addicted to pills, Wilson is addicted to commitment. With his women, though, Wilson may take on more than one commitment at a time. Wilson starts season one married but there are obviously issues at home because Wilson spends Christmas/Hanukkah eating Chinese food with House. He tells House he loves his wife. House laughs. "I know you love your wife," he says. "You loved all your wives. Probably still do. In fact, you probably love all the women you loved who weren't your wife" ("Fidelity"). In season two, House catches Wilson "sniffing" around Debbie in Accounting ("Autopsy"). And Wilson shares a confidence with Cameron. He's not a constant guy.

> "My wife wasn't dying. She wasn't even sick. Everything was fine, I met someone who . . . made me feel funny . . . Good. And I didn't want to let that feeling go. . . . You can't control your emotions." ("Spin")

(The question is, which wife?—there have been three.) Wilson has hidden talents. His acting ability he tries desperately to keep hidden. In "Private Lives," House stumbles upon Wilson's youthful turn in the zero-budget porn flick *Feral Pleasures* ("He discovered he was part stag . . . but all man . . ."). Wilson insists a body double did the actual feral porn. When House is about to go on his date with Cameron ("Love Hurts"), Wilson gives House very specific advice. Talk about DHA—dreams, hopes, and aspirations. It's obviously worked for him. And in "House Training," House tracks down the second ex-Mrs. Wilson to find out about Wilson's dating technique. Wilson wanted friendship; she jumped him. He sucks you in, she says. He's always there until one day, he's not. Perhaps if you hadn't had sex before you connected, muses House. Sex with James is fantastic, she says. No one works harder to give a woman what she wants.

By the end of the second season, Wilson has left his third wife because she was having an affair ("Sex Kills") and House and Wilson are roomies for the first time. They settle into a routine: House eats Wilson's food and sabotages his attempts to find a new place. He puts Wilson's hand in a bowl of water while he sleeps so Wilson pees on the couch. Wilson's response is disproportionately small: He files through one of House's canes ("Safe"). (Wilson can adopt Housean tactics. In "Alone," he kidnaps House's new guitar to encourage him to hire a new team.) Wilson keeps searching—in "Fools for Love," House mentions Wilson's affair with a patient, now his interest in a nurse in pediatrics.

> " 'Wilson' is from Wilson's point of view. In a funny way it always has been. Wilson is Watson to House's Holmes and I have always had that feeling that the whole thing is Wilson's observation of House. Even though Wilson is often absent it is Wilson's perspective on House. It is Wilson's affection for House. He is the one person who genuinely likes House and doesn't want anything from him and doesn't need to give him anything. There is a sort of parity there."
>
> —HUGH LAURIE

"My marriages were so crappy I was spending all my time with you," says Wilson. "Your real fear is me having a good relationship." That's as likely as the Loch Ness monster. House has nothing to worry about.

Until Amber.

> "My friend Pam Davis wrote a great scene where I'm trying to give a woman a breast exam and House has spiked me with meth or speed or something, I'm flying on some drug . . . ("Resignation"). That was really fun. That was a little bit Buck Henry. I got to do some Cary Grant stuff having trouble putting the gloves on."
>
> —ROBERT SEAN LEONARD

House constantly tests Wilson. In "Daddy's Boy," he keeps borrowing money from Wilson to see how much in dollars and cents Wilson values their friendship. (Wilson goes to five thousand dollars for House to get a car, money House uses to buy his motorbike.) With Detective Tritter, House goes too far.

First Wilson tells Tritter he prescribed all of House's drugs ("Que Sera, Sera"). When House steals Wilson's scrip pad to write his own prescriptions, Wilson accuses House of pushing so hard their friendship will break, proving to House he's right about human relationships ("Son of a Coma Guy"). Even as Tritter shuts Wilson's practice down, House is unmoved—he's not going to do a deal with Tritter that forces him to admit he has a drug problem. "You were either going to help me through this or you weren't," says Wilson ("Whac-a-Mole"). Exasperated, Wilson makes his deal with Tritter—House admits he forged scrips in exchange for rehab and not jail time ("Finding Judas"). "I'm gonna need thirty pieces of silver," Wilson says to Tritter.

> "Did House break into my drawer and steal my scrip pad? Of course he did. If he didn't he wouldn't be House. I know that about him."
>
> —ROBERT SEAN LEONARD

To this point, Wilson has been one of the leading proponents of the functioning-addict viewpoint of House, the notion that he's a positive force in the universe despite his addiction. Wilson saves House from Vogler by standing up for House at the board meeting where House being fired is top on the agenda. "Okay, he's screwed up. He's miserable. And he should probably reread the ethics code, but it works for him. He's saved hundreds of lives" ("Babies and Bathwater"). Only Wilson picks House over Vogler's $100 million donation. Even Cuddy votes out House at first and it looks like Wilson is going down. House has been unwilling to save himself, or Wilson. Vogler offered House a chance if he would make a speech promoting a drug he developed, a chance House accepted and then exploded.

> **WILSON:** "I've got no kids. My marriage sucks. I only had two things that worked for me. This job and this stupid screwed-up friendship, and neither mattered enough to you to give one lousy speech."
>
> **HOUSE:** "They matter. [beat] If I could do it all again . . ."
>
> **WILSON:** "You'd do the same thing."

House's anti-relationship recidivism is unabated. In "Half-Wit," House fakes terminal brain cancer to get drugs and when he's busted, allows his colleagues to think he only has months to live. Understandably they are upset by his deception. "You don't have cancer," says Wilson. "You do have people who give a damn. So what do you do? [laughs] You fake the cancer, then push the people who care away."

From the evidence of his friend's lavender shirt, House figures Wilson is seeing someone ("Frozen"). In "Don't Ever Change," he discovers it's Amber, the ultra-aggressive candidate he didn't hire because she couldn't bear to be wrong. "She's a Cutthroat Bitch; you cry over *Dark Victory*," House says. "Why does scary need pathetic?" House asks, then answers his own question.

> *This isn't just about the sex—you like her personality. You like that she's conniving. You like that she has no regard for consequences. You like that she can humiliate someone if it serves . . . Oh, my God. You're sleeping with me.*

> **QUESTION:** "When he finds out about Wilson and Amber, House says, 'My God, you're sleeping with me . . .'"
>
> **ROBERT SEAN LEONARD:** "To me it was, 'Yeah, so?' I mean the qualities that attract you in a friend are the qualities that attract you in a mate sometimes. I saw the logic of that."

But it seems as though Wilson has changed Amber. She won't drop him in exchange for a job, as House offers to do. Wilson's love and respect beats a fellowship. In "No More Mr. Nice Guy," House and Amber agree to joint custody of Wilson. Amber has little time to change Wilson. When Kutner and Thirteen search Amber's apartment in "Wilson's Heart," they find a raunchy home movie Wilson and Amber made. A first for Wilson, not Amber. Yet in a mattress store he is paralyzed with indecision when Amber makes him choose what to buy ("Living the Dream"). Wilson tells Amber he's always wanted a water bed, buys it, and regrets it at once.

> "He goes out and buys a water mattress and the second he gets home he says, 'I don't want a water mattress.' He tried at least but he didn't get it right. I think he's so screwed up he doesn't know what he wants. Like when Amber said, 'Do you want the water mattress? If you want it you buy it.' I think he's so messed up he doesn't know what he wants anymore."
>
> —ROBERT SEAN LEONARD

Despite their differences Wilson is definitely committed, again, and Amber is, too. Then, in "House's Head," dawns the realization Amber was on the crashed bus with House. In "Wilson's Heart," Amber dies when Wilson turns off the machine that was keeping her alive. She had gone to pick up a drunken House from a bar when House called looking for Wilson. House risks his life taking Alzheimer's meds and with deep brain stimulation to try to remember what symptom he saw in Amber before the crash. He realizes she took amantadine pills for the flu but her heart and kidneys are shot. There's nothing to be done.

At the start of season five, Wilson is leaving PPTH.

> HOUSE: "I'm sorry. I know I didn't try and kill her. I know I didn't want her hurt. I know it was a freak accident. But I feel like crap and she's dead because of me."
>
> WILSON: "I don't blame you. I wanted to. I tried to. I must have reviewed Amber's case file a hundred times to try to find a way . . . but it wasn't your fault."

HOUSE: "Then we're okay. I mean you're not but maybe I can help."

WILSON: "We're not okay. Amber was never the reason I was leaving. I didn't want to leave you because . . . because I was trying like I always do, to protect you. Which is the problem. You spread misery because you can't feel anything else. You manipulate people because you can't handle any kind of real relationship and I've enabled it. For years, the games, the binges, the middle-of-the-night phone calls. I should have been on the bus not . . . You should have been alone on the bus. If I've learned anything from Amber it's that I have to take care of myself. [puts box under arm] We're not friends, House. I'm not sure we ever were." [leaves office]

Like characters before and after him, Wilson can't make a clean break from House. He tries. In a fateful move, House hires the PI Lucas Douglas (Michael Weston) to spy on Wilson to see if he's pining. Wilson has another job; he says he's moving on ("Not Cancer"). He's gone for four months. But House's father dies and Wilson is dragged back in by House's mom, who calls Wilson to try to get her son to go to his estranged father's funeral ("Birthmarks"). When Wilson is pulled over and arrested on the way there, it turns out there is an outstanding warrant for his arrest in Louisiana. Of course, House was involved. At a New Orleans medical convention fresh out of medical school, Wilson threw a bottle at a mirror in a bar, setting off a fight. House bailed him out because he was bored and Wilson wasn't boring.

At the funeral home, House tries to get Wilson to admit he's dumped him because he's afraid of losing him. He baits Wilson until he throws a bottle of bourbon through a stained-glass window. Wilson is still not boring. House knew Wilson snapped in New Orleans because he was getting divorced (from Sam). He does have trouble losing people. Wilson concedes House is right and admits, "That strange annoying trip we just took was the most fun I've had since Amber died."

"Wilson is so screwed up. He takes so much crap from someone who is supposed to be his best friend. It's almost worse than a woman who is in love with a guy and taking that much crap. Their relationship is far more intimate. And why [does he take this crap]? He just loves this guy."

—LISA EDELSTEIN

So House and Wilson get back together. House is worried Wilson has changed when he was away. He hires Lucas and they tail Wilson, discovering he has a new girlfriend, Debbie, an ex-prostitute ("Lucky 13"). Wilson wants to help her with tuition for law school. But Wilson faked the girlfriend, proving that nothing's changed. They enjoy their tricks. Eventually House and Wilson live together in the apartment Wilson shared with Amber.

Real insight into Wilson's neediness comes from revelations about his brother. From "Histories," it's known that Wilson has a brother he hasn't seen in nine years. In "The Social Contract," House finds out that Wilson's brother Daniel was found sleeping in the lobby of an office building in Manhattan and is in a psychiatric ward. Wilson says he didn't tell House because they don't have the conventional social contract: Wilson keeps stuff from House; House doesn't lie to him. Wilson tells House his brother is schizophrenic. Danny used to call every day when Wilson was in med school until one day, Wilson didn't have time to talk and Danny ran away. House jumps on the idea that Wilson's guilt shaped his whole life. "You developed your people-pleasing talents the way an Olympic athlete develops his muscles," says House. "Talk about an overreaction to a single event." Wilson understands they are different.

> *"My whole life is one big compromise. I tiptoe around everyone like they're made of china. I spend my whole time analyzing. What will the e ect be if I say this? Then there's you. You're a reality junkie. If I offered you a comforting lie you'd smack me over the head with it. Let's not change that." (Wilson)*

In "Locked In," House deduces that Wilson's new girlfriend works at Danny's care facility. "She's a caregiver like all your other failed exes."

"[It explains] his caution, yes. He comes from a dysfunctional family. A lot of plaster fell on his head from that incident. He ran away from home. He's never been the same since. A lot of this is sketchy . . . In my mind I think his parents are shits and they took a lot of the pain from the older brother and transferred it into blame on the younger for not helping them because they're pathetic parents."

—ROBERT SEAN LEONARD

In season six, Wilson is focused on House's recovery. Off the pills, perhaps he can make it work with Cuddy. "You see," Wilson tells Amber's ghost, "he really is getting better" ("Brave Heart"). Then they find out about Lucas.

In "Known Unknowns," Wilson's patient Joseph Schultz dies. Wilson feels guilty he wasn't with him at the end and is prepared to commit professional suicide by delivering the paper at the medical conference admitting to euthanasia. House tries to reason with Wilson but Wilson isn't backing down. "If there's one thing I've learned from you, it's that I should do what I think is right and not worry about the consequences." "Worked out great for me," says House. So House drugs Wilson, steals his pants, and gives his paper masquerading as Dr. Perlmutter.

> **"I wasn't conscious of this when we were developing this and Hugh and other people have mentioned it; one of the things I am very proud of is this is a rare one-hour series that explores male friendship the way we do. I enjoy it and we have fun with it."**
>
> —DAVID SHORE

When House sees Wilson in the lecture room he veers off Wilson's script. "I am incapable of turning away from a responsibility," House/Perlmutter says, playing Wilson. "My friends take advantage of that fact far too often." After Wilson has yelled at House for drugging him and stealing his pants, he thanks House for telling him he's okay, that he did everything he could for Mr. Schultz. "You're a good friend. Cuddy should know that," Wilson says. "She should know I drugged you so you wouldn't confess to murder," replies House.

In "Wilson," we see what a great doctor Wilson is precisely because he cares. (House teases Wilson about his concern. "I know you're in there," House says in "Need to Know." "I can hear you caring.") Wilson remembers his patients' names, for one thing. In "Known Unknowns," Wilson calls the dying patient Joseph with great tenderness while it's not clear House even knows Thirteen's name is Remy ("Big Baby"). Wilson deduces that a patient had a relapse because he didn't tell Wilson about the exploits of his grandchildren (whose names Wilson knows), indicating depression indicating a return of his cancer. It's a Housean feat of diagnosis but House himself would never care enough to know a detail like that about his patient.

Wilson's friend Tucker appears. Tucker was a patient—Wilson saved Tucker's life five years ago and they became close. Tucker calls Wilson "Jim," another reason for House not to like him (everyone knows Jim's name is Wilson). Tucker has a young girlfriend but as his prognosis worsens, he turns to his ex-wife and daughter for comfort. With House-like aggressiveness, Wilson tries an ultra-risky procedure on Tucker. House warns Wilson he has to be able to handle the consequences of failure. The double dose of chemo works on Tucker's cancer but it destroys his liver in the process.

With House, Wilson tries to get a new liver for his friend. Then, as a last resort, Tucker asks Wilson if he can donate some of his liver to save his life. Having acted like House in treating Tucker, Wilson reacts to his failure like Wilson, not House. When House sees that Wilson is even considering a donation, he calls him a doormat. Wilson says he'll do it; the man is his friend. "They're all dying," says House. "They're all your friends." Despite House's objections, Wilson asks House to attend the operation.

> **HOUSE:** "No."
>
> **WILSON:** "Why?"
>
> **HOUSE:** "Because if you die I'm alone."

House watches the operation from the viewing room. Wilson has saved Tucker. In recovery, Tucker says he's going back to his girlfriend. The person you want to be with you when you're dying isn't the one you want with you when you're alive, he says. That's not acceptable to Wilson; you can't pick and choose like that. When Tucker's girlfriend comes in the room and calls him "Jim," he corrects her. "Actually, it's James."

Wilson now proves to House he's not a doormat. House tells Wilson it's okay to be angry. So he calls his second ex-wife, a real estate agent, and gazumps Cuddy on the apartment she was going to buy for herself and Lucas. "She hurt my friend," says Wilson. "She should be punished."

KATIE JACOBS: "I think they are both fantastic doctors and to me what is interesting is that what goes into making a fantastic doctor. Not necessarily does a fantastic person make a fantastic doctor."

QUESTION: "House and Wilson would make one great doctor."

HUGH LAURIE: "They probably know that. They would be a fantastic doctor and probably a pretty fantastic human being."

ROBERT SEAN LEONARD: "If Wilson and House could melt into one person that would be an interesting combination. Wilson is very good at being the maître d'. He's the greeter. If that's all he had to do that would be great."

Wilson has learned a lesson from House. House prevented Wilson from putting a different lesson into effect when he drugged his friend and stopped his suicidal speech on assisted suicide. This is what's in it for Wilson, a corrective force for the guilt and neediness that stifle him, the same attributes that help make him a great doctor. When Amber died, House recognized the sense of unfairness that Wilson struggled with, something that fit right in with House's worldview. "This is about you needing to be prepared for the worst. So you become an oncologist. No surprises there, worst happens all the time. But Amber. She was young and healthy. Her death came out of nowhere" ("Birthmarks").

"It's possibly a bad job for Wilson emotionally but good for his patients. I think if you have a mystery disease there's no one you would rather go to than House, if it's fatal. If it's not fatal, anyone else on earth perhaps, so you don't have to put up with the crap but if you have cancer there's no one you'd rather have than Dr. Wilson."

—DAVID SHORE

Like the parent of a hapless adolescent, House wants to protect Wilson even when Wilson doesn't want to be taken care of. When Sam Carr (Cynthia Watros), the first Mrs. Wilson, reappears ("Knight Fall"), House strives to make sure she won't repeat as the fourth Mrs. Wilson. In an initial skirmish, House brings a transvestite prostitute as his dinner date but the ploy backfires when "Sarah" and Sam get on like old friends. House cooks Sam and Wilson an elaborate dinner and waits for Wilson to visit the bathroom before laying his cards on the table.

> **HOUSE [*SMILING*]:** "You're a cold hearted bitch who ripped his heart out. I watched him struggle for years to overcome the damage you did. There's no way I'm just going to let you wheel him back in so you can do it all over again."
>
> **SAM:** "And all this?"
>
> **HOUSE:** "Phase two of getting to know my enemy."
>
> **SAM:** "You're wrong about me. But I'm glad now I don't have to pretend to like you. Except for when James is standing next to me."
>
> **HOUSE:** "Same here. Only difference is, I'll outlast you."

House hires his other rival, Lucas, to check up on Sam, but there's nothing, only her sealed psychiatrist's records which House decides are out of bounds. As he has always done, House sees Wilson's qualities as defects. Meanwhile, House and Thirteen have been treating a man living in a medieval camp who abides by a modern version of courtly love from William Chaucer's time.

> **HOUSE:** "The code that our knight claims to live by, all that crap about honor and chivalry. Wilson's naturally like that. Which is why he's . . ."
>
> **THIRTEEN:** ". . . a great guy . . ."
>
> **HOUSE:** ". . . a sucker and a target. Someone's gotta look out for him."

House and Wilson. Theirs is the pivotal relationship in *House*. They are the yin and the yang. Most of Wilson's patients die; most of House's survive. House can't get on with anybody; Wilson gets on with everybody. Wilson is usually boring; House never is. House writes clearly; in "Daddy's Boy," Wilson starts a DDx on the whiteboard and his penmanship is terrible. Even jokingly they know what they have going.

> **WILSON:** "You can be a real jerk sometimes, you know that?"
>
> **HOUSE:** "Yeah. And you're the good guy."
>
> **WILSON:** "At least I try."
>
> **HOUSE:** "As long as you're trying to be good you can do whatever you want."

WILSON: "And as long as you're not trying, you can say whatever you want."

HOUSE: "So, between us, we can do anything. We can rule the world."

[WILSON SIGHS] ("FIDELITY")

WILSON'S LOOK

QUESTION: "What about Wilson's wardrobe?"

CATHY CRANDALL: "He's so conservative, Brooks Brothers all the way."

QUESTION: "He's going to wear beige and brown . . ."

CRANDALL: "Occasionally he'll pop out a red tie. He's conservative and old-school. He dresses the way he thinks a doctor should."

QUESTION: "If he's going on a date maybe he'll switch out a tie."

CRANDALL: "Maybe. When he was dating Amber he would wear a pink shirt or a yellow shirt or maybe a nice mint green shirt if she picked it out. But she wasn't around long enough."

Robert Sean Leonard on . . . Wilson and House

"They're guys, so I think they don't often reflect on things that women in relationships do. At the end of the day I think it's very important to the audience that House and Wilson stay friends. I think it's a very successful relationship on the show. Part of the reason it's successful is that it's always right on the verge of ending, at least from Wilson's point of view. Maybe not from House's."

QUESTION: "What attracts House to Wilson?"

"I like the guy. I think he's really appealing. A lot of interviewers ask why Wilson spends time with House, this horrible guy . . . Even I know that the attributes of the lead character of our show match eerily the attributes of a lot of other characters of shows—they're loners, they're misanthropic, they can't hold down women and they play some jazz instrument and when they're home alone at night they drink whisky. They're brilliant. They're really acerbic. They have a dry sense of humor; they're cantankerous. And sorry, what in that list is unattractive? It's human nature. Show me a TV show about a man who is nice and friendly and who writes letters to his mother every week—that's not an appealing guy to me. Everything about House is designed to be appealing, a character. We are talking about fiction here. He's a very, very attractive, appealing character."

Robert Sean Leonard enjoys some downtime.

QUESTION: "And he allows Wilson to be bad."

"People get different things from every relationship and one thing that happens with this combination is that Wilson is dragged into situations where he normally wouldn't find himself, which is good for him at times and at times is not."

QUESTION: "After Amber dies, Wilson goes through subterfuges to date and House has to find out. He wants Wilson to himself . . .'"

"The character of House is clearly disturbed. He has a problem. It goes beyond being nosy or being jealous or being petty. He really has a problem. When you hire a PI to follow your friend around that's a little beyond what most people do. He clearly has a problem."

QUESTION: "What happened with Wilson's brother explains a lot."

"I think we're both pretty abandoned. We're both pretty alone. I think Chase has friends; House and Wilson are alone. There's a lot of video games. There's a lot of football watching. There's a lot of porn. There are a lot of bad eating habits. They have very similar solitary lives, I've always thought that. My big joke is that Wilson gets incapacitated and is in hospital and makes House go to his apartment to get all the porn so his landlord doesn't find it. He comes in with boxes of porn and Wilson says, 'Where's the German stuff? Where's all the German stuff?' And House missed a whole other stash that was under the floorboards. I think they are two very lonely guys."

QUESTION: "Is House a positive force in the universe?"

"He does a lot of good for people. . . . The way I view the world gets a little meshed in with the way Wilson views the world. I believe the world is way too gray . . . Judgment should be very, very sparse."

QUESTION: "The last thing Wilson is is judgmental."

"He's more judgmental than me, that's for sure. If you're an adult and you have no children dependent on you, I don't give a damn what you do. If you hurt yourself, I don't care. There's a part of Wilson that feels that way."

QUESTION: "There have been a lot of people House has been up against—Ron Livingston's TB doctor and Vogler, whose drug trial might save thousands of lives, but they were hypocrites."

"You could also take the incredibly cynical view of what's so great about saving a thousand people. The earth needs more people? I don't know what Wilson believes."

Robert Sean Leonard on . . . Hugh Laurie

QUESTION: "When did you and Hugh Laurie click?"

"Hugh and I clicked the moment I met him I think. I remember very clearly seeing him for the very first time walking up to an elevator.

He had a cane already, weirdly. He wasn't using it but he had it with him I don't know why. I was with Lisa Edelstein. We were in Vancouver shooting the pilot and we had just arrived. Lisa and Hugh and I met that first night in Vancouver and had sushi.

"Hugh and I quickly discovered very early in the dinner that we're both Eeyores in the Hundred Acre Wood. I remember Hugh saying, 'You can't be that guy; I'm that guy. We can't have two guys like that on one set.' We're not very positive people when it comes to worldview. Hugh's very passionate about the show. If you need something done on the show he'll do it. I'll be halfway down the highway with my scarf flapping in the wind. He's the guy to count on, the go-to guy. We definitely have a similar humor and my theater past weirdly overlaps with his comic past. Ken Branaugh, Emma Thompson, Imelda Staunton, Stephen Fry—people that I grew up watching and admiring but later working with. I don't think there were many thirty-four-year-old guys in Hollywood he would have met at that time who would have known who Peter Cook was and could talk about Imelda Staunton and Stephen Fry and Derek Jacobi. That was lucky.

"Hugh is a weird example. He is a very unique performer. He's not a stage actor. I guess he would have defined himself as a sketch show artist or a comedian for years and tried to get into acting in film and landed in this role on his ass. Even he would admit it was a fluke."

QUESTION: "In the U.K., he has this incredible history . . ."

"He has a huge history of one thing and now he's gone in this other direction. I don't think Hugh could have made this turn in London. They have a very deep-rooted idea of who Hugh Laurie is. They're so hard because this is so not what he did before. And you're not allowed to do that."

Robert Sean Leonard on . . . Wilson

QUESTION: "We haven't seen a lot of Wilson's patients."

"You mostly see him ushering them out the back door. Which is something he had in common with Cameron which is something I think oddly we never explored."

QUESTION: "With Wilson it's about helping people."

"I think the reason he went into medicine, he's a smart guy and medicine attracts him and helping people is a reason . . ."

QUESTION: "Would House like to be more like Wilson?"

"I don't think House thinks about it. I don't think he thinks, Oh I should be nicer to people. I think he thinks I'm crazy and I don't think he's wrong."

QUESTION: "Everybody lies. Wilson has been known to lie . . ."

"Wilson lies I would think more than House."

QUESTION: "Let's explore the fact that Wilson is more unhealthy than House—he's not able to liberate his thoughts, his actions, his words . . ."

"He's got to be the good boy. Whatever happened to him in that house with the brother and those parents . . . I think there's a little bit of the life of quiet desperation with him. There are a couple of miles he's never going to travel and then one day he'll be dead. And he won't have traveled them. House has traveled them. He gets in trouble and he gets hurt and a lot of other people get hurt but he travels it."

> **"In my mind Wilson's a much unhealthier person than House is. In my mind as the actor. That's my opinion. I think he's very constipated."**
>
> —Robert Sean Leonard

QUESTION: "He's always searching, though, his multiple marriages . . ."

"That's BS. He's not searching. I'm hard on Wilson but I should be. His marriages are cop-outs. They're more of the same."

QUESTION: "Does he think he's searching?"

"A search for him would be not being the good boy. That's a search for him. For Wilson to marry someone who needs his help, that's not a search. That's a cozy armchair and a pack of cigarettes. That's comfortable."

QUESTION: "A fun story line to do would be bad Wilson."

"Amber tried to do that a little bit."

QUESTION: "She was trying to liberate him by getting him to ask for what he wants . . ."

"That's what I mean. Even if he did marry the right person, like Amber, who forced him to search, he still wouldn't succeed. He'd still die without traveling those two miles. I think it's tragic and sad but sorry, I think that's who he is. A lot of people are like that. I may be one of them. House is not. . . . Yes, he hurts people but he does it cleanly and quickly and truthfully. Wilson's way more screwed up, I think, and way more hurtful. In my mind he's hurt way more people more deeply than House has ever."

QUESTION: "Robert Sean Leonard thinks Wilson is far more messed up than House."

DAVID SHORE: [Laughs] "I'm not sure he's far more. I think that's great that Robert thinks that . . . Look, if the guy was as well adjusted as he appears to be to the world, I don't think he'd be House's friend. Wilson is probably burying things. I think he wants to be more like House and House is friends with Wilson because he is envious of Wilson in some ways."

QUESTION: "Because the road to hell is paved with good intentions . . ."

"He tries to do everything right, he tries to keep everyone happy . . . He tries to be the good boy. You hurt way more people doing that than being Peter Fonda and hitting the road."

QUESTION: "So we're never going to have bad Wilson . . ."

"It wouldn't be entertaining because bad Wilson is the water bed. Even with bad Wilson it backfires. I don't think that's something House desires. He doesn't want to bring that out in Wilson the way that Amber did. House is fine with the way he is. It pains House to watch him struggling. Watching armadillos. They roll up in a little ball. When you see one of those on its back you think 'ahh' and I think that's how House feels about Wilson."

Robert Sean Leonard on . . . Robert Sean Leonard

"When I think of *House*, I think of this trailer I'm in, the makeup on my face, Ira [Hurvitz, script supervisor] giving me a note about the script. Of stuff I want to wrap by six-thirty because my wife's making dinner. That's my day. The show isn't what most people experience. To me, that's the show. In Iowa, they turn the TV on at 8:00 P.M. and there it is. One episode bleeds into another.

"I'm the laziest man certainly on this set and possibly in Los Angeles. I don't like working. When I first auditioned for this I also had an audition for the show *Numbers*. I had to decide whether I was going to go screen-test for *Numbers* or for this, and *Numbers*, there were just too many scenes he was in. Too many lines. I thought, Ah, it's just so tiring. I'm okay with being the Schneider of *House* [Dwayne Schneider, the super of *One Day at a Time*]. You come in every eight scenes and say, 'Hey you know the pipes are . . .' I like the role. I like the guy who has two or three scenes an episode.

"I love my wife, I love my life, I love my daughter, I love my dogs, I love my garden. I'm very lazy when it comes to work. I'd much rather be home. One of the jokes with me on the set is I tend to be the 'that was good enough' kind of guy. If a shot's done, I'm ready to move. Someone says, 'I saw a cable in the background,' my first thought is to say, 'Really? Come on.' I always want to move on. I never want to do it again."

QUESTION: "Does that come from a stage background? It's not going to be perfect every night?"

"I hadn't broken it down. Stage work is very different from film work. Film is the most boring job of all time. It's the greatest paradox. People who aren't in film think it's the most exciting job of all time. If you don't like to read you're in trouble because man, oh man, it's about twelve hours of not working for one hour of working every day."

QUESTION: "The same thing over and over . . ."

"I have never really felt it. There are screen actors I really like. I'm not one of them. Brando and Chris Walken are exciting to watch. I'm very cautious. I'm very aware that there's an enormous lens in front of me. I'm never able to shake that. People like Chris Walken must because they seem so alive. They giggle and they laugh and they blink and they scratch their face and they seem so alive. They probably have more fun doing it than I do. I feel kind of stiff."

QUESTION: "One might ask why you do it . . ."

"If theater paid more, I'd do theater. Actors do all three. You need films, you need TV, and you need theater. Not to say this job isn't a joy. It's a great show to be on. The people are great, Hugh's incredible, and the writing could not be better. I've never enjoyed acting on-screen in anything. When I talk to Ethan Hawke or people I've grown up with, there are people who get off on it, I think the way I get off on stage acting. When they talk about Tarantino or this take or *Jaws*, that's how I am with Tom Stoppard. My stories all concern Circle in the Square and public Theater and Joseph Papp. I grew up watching Sam Waterston and Blythe Danner . . ."

QUESTION: "So you have to work in television?"

"There are things I enjoy; they just don't pay. I enjoy reading Philip Roth books and I enjoy playing basketball and I enjoy reading the works of George Bernard Shaw but none of those things pays very well so . . .

"My goal in life. I tell you when I read books about John A. Roebling, the guy who designed the Brooklyn Bridge, I think, Oh my God, who are these guys? I'm so lazy. My goal in life is to make as much money as I can doing as little as possible."

QUESTION: "Do you watch the show?"

"I know actors who hide their heads but I can watch my work. It doesn't bother me in any way but I don't enjoy it. I don't go out of my way to watch it but I don't dive under a couch, either. I'd rather watch *Law & Order*—[my wife and I] both like Vince D'Onofrio. She likes

Nanny 911. It's not that I don't like *House*. I do. I know what happens. I don't have to watch it."

QUESTION: "How Do You Like L.A.?"

"We're still 'staying here' while we shoot *House*. We live in New York and we just happen to be here eleven months of the year. My wife, Gabriella, grew up in Thousand Oaks about an hour north of here and we're staying with her folks."

QUESTION: "How much time off do you get?"

"Each year we get about a month, around May and then maybe two weeks at Christmas. I go back to New York. I feel twice the human being I am when I'm in New York. Maybe that's what home means. It's sad I only get that six weeks a year."

Robert Sean Leonard on . . . Retirement

QUESTION: "Wilson will retire?"

"He will retire. Wilson's a sad case. I don't know. Even so he'll meet House after work. I don't know if they'll be rooming together. There's something a little skid row about that to me. He'll definitely meet at the park bench and have some coffee and bitch about life."

QUESTION: "Do you see House and Wilson in their dotage? Are they still friends?"

"It wouldn't surprise me. What I've noticed in my life is that what changes is family. I don't believe either of them will ever have a family. I believe they really could be Simon and Garfunkel's old friends on the park bench with the high shoes and, whatever the song says. Noises from the city settle on their shoulders. I think they could be those men."

12

EVERYBODY LIES

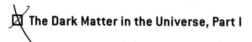 **The Dark Matter in the Universe, Part I**

QUESTION: "Delivering the episode to the network for broadcast, does it ever get down to the wire?"

GERRIT VAN DER MEER: "Every show."

House says it first, in the pilot. Wilson says it ("Meaning"); Detective Tritter says it, and with good reason ("Son of a Coma Guy"); Amber says it ("Wilson's Heart"). Everybody lies. Even fetuses. Anyone telling the truth is greeted with incredulity. "So everybody lies except a convicted murderer?" ("Acceptance"), "Everybody lies, except politicians?" ("Role Model"). That everybody lies is one of the absolute certainties of the show, a constant in House's dark universe. Every patient has an opportunity to lie when they give their history. There are also plenty of motives. "People lie for thousands of reasons," says House. "But there's always a reason" ("Spin"). Since all anyone needs to do to lie is open their mouth, means, motive, and opportunity are right to hand. It happens. Everybody lies.

House: "It's a basic truth of the human condition that everybody lies. The only variable is about what. The great thing about telling someone they're dying is that it tends to focus their priorities. You find *out what matters to them. What they're willing to die for. What they're willing to lie for." ("Three Stories")*

And not just with words. At one point in the pilot the patient, Rebecca Adler, asks Wilson if House is his friend. Wilson says he thinks so—we assume that House has never actually said as much. "It's not what people say," says Rebecca. "It's what they do." Well, in that case, Wilson knows. "Yeah. He cares about me." If we can't trust someone's words, Wilson is saying, paraphrasing House, we can surely trust their actions. Ask that of Detective Tritter in season three as he works to send House to jail. "People like you," Tritter says to House fifty-six episodes after the pilot, "even your actions lie."

QUESTION: "There's a scene when House apologizes to Tritter and he says, 'not good enough because even your actions lie.'"

ROBERT SEAN LEONARD: "I think people do lie and I think the bad guys win a lot of the time. I'm a big fan of Tritter saying that. I would say that to just about anyone in my life. Saying sorry doesn't do it for me."

In "Three Stories," when House says dying makes a person focus, it's revealed that the farmer he's treating lied about being bitten by a snake; it was his dog that bit him. If he'd told the truth, the farmer would have been treated sooner but the dog would have been put to sleep. There are dozens of reasons to lie, Foreman says in "It's a Wonderful Lie." "Only one reason to tell the truth."

HOUSE: "There's a reason that everybody lies. It works. It's what allows society to function. It's what separates man from beast."

WILSON: "Oh, I thought that was our thumbs."

Ask David Shore if he agrees that everybody lies because it's socially necessary, and he'll say yes. But he views the phenomenon in what he describes as its broadest sense, especially as it applies to House.

"There is an inherent contradiction in House and yet a truth within that contradiction which doesn't make any sense and is in itself a contradiction. He believes in the truth above all. He doesn't believe in emotions particularly; he believes in the truth and he believes in anything to get to the truth, including lying."

But the truth is a notoriously slippery eel.

"I don't mean that someone thinks something is black but says it's white but I believe that everybody looks at everything through their own prism. They see their contribution to work as in ated or de ated. They see their relationship to their spouse, to their children, to their friends in a certain way that the other person on the other side does not see it. They see everything through rose-colored glasses.

"So what House means by 'everybody lies' is nobody knows the truth and even more so, nobody knows they don't know the truth. That pursuit of the objective reality is what he is after and he tries to strip himself of anything that would slow him down in his pursuit of an objective reality."

This was something David Shore learned very early on in practicing law.

"I would have a client come through the door and tell you their story and you would go, 'Let's go get that son of a bitch; I can't believe he did that to you.' You would completely believe him and you'd go to court and hear the other side tell their story and you'd know that if that other person had come into your o ce first and told you their story, that you would have said, 'Let's go get that son of a bitch.' And you also know neither one is lying in the strictest sense. They both completely believe their story yet their stories are self-contradicting. And on one level they are seeing events in a certain way that has led to this conclusion. They are not even making things up; they are seeing things through a certain prism."

For House, the truth lies in the answer to the puzzle that is the medical case he has to solve, the reality that provides some order in the universe, at least for him. As far as he can, House removes the human element from the puzzle—he'll only see the patient if he absolutely has to. A perfect case would present as a math problem because "numbers don't lie" ("No Reason"). Fortunately for his patients, House is usually right, which means there's a payoff for the collateral damage caused by his behavior. In "Cane and Abel," Cuddy wishes House had a little humility. "Why does he need that?" says Cameron. "Because other people have that? Why does he need to be like other people?"

Some Lies and the Lying Liars Who Tell Them

- House runs a clandestine paternity test for a pregnant clinic patient to see if the baby is her husband's or her boyfriend's. "The most successful marriages are based on lies," says House. "You're off to a great start." ("Maternity")

- A husband must decide if it's possible his sick wife has lied to him and had an affair before he consents to treating her sleeping sickness. She's treated and recovers, proving she lied. ("Fidelity")

- The baseball player who told the truth about not knowingly doing steroids lied to his wife about not smoking pot. ("Sports Medicine")

- A man lied to his family, saying he worked as a test pilot in the eighties, when he was really on an ashram in India, where he contracted leprosy. ("Cursed")

- The racing cyclist can lie all he wants about blood doping because the blood transfusions he needs to treat his thymoma mask his cheating. ("Spin")

- A woman who is on fertility treatments also takes birth control pills so she can't get pregnant. She has an operation to remove a tumor so she doesn't have to lie to her husband. She asks Foreman to tell her husband the operation means she needs to stop the fertility treatment. "Confidentiality rules stop me from telling your husband the truth," Foreman says. "But my obligation to lie ends there." ("Need to Know")

- In "Clueless," House's married clinic patients blame each other for contracting herpes—could one have caught it from a toilet seat? If not, one of them is lying.

- A painter lies to his girlfriend about how many of his paintings he has sold. He is on three different experimental drug trials to make ends meet. ("Adverse Events")

- A girl who claimed she was an emancipated teen who left her parents because her dad raped her, in fact left because her brother died when she was looking after him. ("Emancipation")

- Mos Def's locked-in character lied to his wife about traveling to St. Louis. Instead he took a temporary job as a janitor in a battery factory, where he got sick. ("Locked In")

- Charlotte lies to her husband about going to Brazil without him—sand flies gave her visceral leishmaniasis and she's diagnosed too late. ("Simple Explanation")

- When Valerie, the psychopath, is cured of her Wilson's disease in "No Remorse," she can no longer lie to her husband that she loves him. Good-bye, trust fund; hello, feelings. "It hurts," says Valerie. "It will," says Thirteen.

- Mickey, an undercover cop, wants to wait for the big bust to go down before he gives the team a full history. Drug-dealing Eddie risks his life to save his partner Mickey but realizes as he's arrested that Mickey, who dies of Hughes-Stovin syndrome, has betrayed him. ("The Down Low")

- High schooler Abby nearly dies from an obscure allergy to semen, but not her boyfriend's—her boyfriend's father's. The father has to admit what he did or Abby will die. House concedes that lying might be easier in the circumstances. "Given what the truth is," he says, "that's a tough call." ("Black Hole")

- Medieval role player Sir William lives by a knight's code that means he cannot try to win the hand of the girl he loves from the King, but he can take anabolic steroids to cheat at sword fighting. An ancient poison, hemlock, interacts with the modern one, the steroids, and nearly ends this knight's tale. ("Knight Fall")

- Tom and Julia have an open marriage. Tom lies to his wife Julia that he has other partners when he knows she does because he wants Julia to be happy. Tom is also concealing from his wife that he lost all their savings. When they seem to reconcile, House says, "That is adorable. Other than you wanting to have sex with other dudes and him bankrupting your family, I think you kids are pretty much home free." ("Open and Shut")

- A mother and daughter never lie to each other, except for the fact that the girl is actually the adopted daughter of a drug addict. ("It's a Wonderful Lie")

Initially House is bemused by the relationship between Maggie and her eleven-year-old daughter Jane in "It's a Wonderful Lie." It seems they are completely honest with each other. Maggie's own mother died of breast cancer and didn't tell Maggie she was sick. Maggie promised never to keep anything from her own child. Jane knows her mom smokes pot and even how she likes to have sex. That much honesty must be concealing something, House thinks. He's right. Maggie refuses to let House test her daughter for a possible bone marrow match because she knows there won't be one. Jane is adopted. Maggie's promise to Jane's birth mother not to tell her daughter she was a drug addict trumps the injunction that she should never lie to the girl herself.

But Jane still won't lie. When mom tells Jane she'll be okay, Jane recognizes the untruth. "You're dying," Jane tells her mom.

"Nobody can help you. It's not going to be okay." Thirteen thinks she was cold; House thinks he's seen Halley's comet in an off year:

HOUSE: "I saw something amazing—pure truth. She told her mother that she was dying. Stripped her of all hope."

WILSON: "That sounds horrible."

HOUSE: "It was like watching some bizarre astronomical event that you know you're never gonna see again."

WILSON: "You tell people the cold hard truth all the time. You get off on it."

HOUSE: "Because I don't care. She cared. She did it anyway. She did it because she cared."

Soon House has a eureka moment, that Maggie has breast cancer despite her prophylactic double mastectomy. Having seen one miracle, someone who tells the truth, he performs another and saves Maggie's life.

"Timing is one of those mystical things to me as an actor. That's the X-factor. The timing for this show with this lead character with everything we'd been experiencing in the world the last few years before House aired I think is incredible. To me, people would rather know the blatant, blunt, truth than to be fed this propaganda to make us feel safe. We're pretty advanced beings at this point. Let me deal with the reality of this. And they get to do that every week on the show."

—OMAR EPPS

Lying Has Consequences

It's not necessarily true that the truth will set you free. Far from it. So he can stop living a lie and come out as a gay man, the mobster in "Mob Rules" has to enter the Witness Protection Program. In "Fools for Love," a married biracial couple find out they have the same father, who has passed on to them a rare genetic disease. The father tried with violence to keep the couple apart when they were young. The truth has come too late and their relationship seems to be destroyed.

Some lies have positive consequences. In "The Right Stuff," House uses a fake breast augmentation to cover up a lung operation he performs on Greta, an air force pilot who dreams of going into space. If NASA knew about the real operation, she'd be disqualified from training. House then lies to the doctors taking part in the contest to join his team, telling them he ratted out Greta to NASA knowing that one of them would try to gain his favor by doing the ratting themselves. House lies to his old friend about the results of a paternity test on his daughter in "Who's Your Daddy." In "Control," House lies to the transplant committee that there are no psychological reasons his patient should be denied a heart. She should be excluded but she's told House she wants to live and House lies to save her life. Other lies are simply expedient, such as Wilson's lie to Detective Tritter about House stealing his scrip pad. Tell the truth and House could have gotten ten years in prison.

"My dad's just like you. Not the caring-till-your-eyes-pop-out part. Just the insane moral compass that won't let you lie to anybody about anything. It's a great quality for Boy Scouts and police witnesses. Crappy quality for a dad."

—HOUSE TO CAMERON ("DADDY'S BOY")

"Everybody does lie. [House is] absolutely right about that. It's very interesting. [Patients] lie to the nurse. They come into the ER and they are drunk. I'll say, 'How much did you have to drink today?' 'I only had one beer, I only had one beer.' 'Are you sure you didn't have two? Something to go with it?' 'No, that's all I had.' 'Do you have any history?' 'Clean as a whistle.' Then the doctor comes in and it's a man and I'll listen. 'Oh, I had twelve beers and took four antidepressants and I've been doing it every day for the last ten years.' I don't know if it's a trust factor or they've been asked so many times by that point. It makes me giggle because it's true."

—BOBBIN BERGSTROM

In no story are the consequences of lying worse than in "Daddy's Boy." The relationship of Carnell, who has just graduated from Princeton University, and his father is riddled with lies. The father told the son his mother was killed by a drunk driver so he wouldn't drink and drive himself. That lie worked because Carnell never drove drunk. Carnell told his father he was studying when in fact he flew down to Jamaica with his rich college friends. Carnell's dad liked him to remember where he came from and Carnell worked long hours in his dad's business. Which was not, as the dad told Carnell's doctors, in construction, but rather in a salvage yard. If House had known about the yard he would have asked questions that would have led to the radioactive plumb bob the father gave Carnell, something else to remind the son of his roots. The lie was fatal: Carnell's immune system is destroyed and he is dying. Carnell asks his dad if he's going to be okay and the dad says he is, he swears. We know that's another lie.

Throughout the episode House has been trying to avoid seeing his parents, who are planning on dropping by. There's no escape, they find him and House greets his mom with a hug. "It's great to see you," says House. "Oh, Greg," his mom says, "don't lie."

QUESTIONS WITHOUT ANSWERS

☒ The Dark Matter in the Universe, Part II

> "You set it out there and what people take from it is
> up to them. I never come to a scene and say they
> might be happy or they might be sad in this scene.
> What they decide about life and what they take
> from the thing as a whole is completely up to them.
> I want to set them up and ask certain questions
> and have them thinking about it afterwards. But
> as they are going along on that ride, I know exactly
> where they are on the roller coaster at any given
> point and after they get off the roller coaster, what
> they make of it that's up to them."
>
> **—DAVID SHORE**

If you had one day of life, how would you choose to spend it? David
Shore and the writers like nothing better than to inject philosophical questions and ethical conundrums into the high-inten-
sity situations at PPTH. In "Son of a Coma Guy," House uses a
shot of L-dopa to wake up a man who has been in a persistent veg-
etative state for ten years. The man's son is gravely ill and the father has roughly twenty-four hours before he'll lapse back into
unconsciousness. The father and son have plenty to talk about;
surely they'll spend that time together? In House's universe, it's
not that easy.

In "One Day, One Room," a clinic patient House doesn't want to treat tries to force House to talk to her. She has been raped. She has one day at PPTH and the awfulness of what happened is plaguing her. Surely she's not going to have any success getting House to talk about any of the great existential questions?

These ethical and philosophical questions—the decorations on the doorknob—serve to raise the stakes. These are often broad ethical questions larger than the fate of an individual patient. Viewers are asked, what might you do in this situation? But no answers are provided. It's for the individual to make up her own mind.

"That's what drives the show, these great ethical questions."

—DAVID SHORE

Take the coma guy (Gabriel, played by John Larroquette). House needs Gabriel to provide a patient history so he can treat Gabriel's son, Kyle. In waking up Gabriel, House is clearly on marshy ethical ground and Cuddy tries, and fails, to stop him. Understanding he has the one day, rather than see his son, the risen Gabriel wants to get a hoagie from his favorite sandwich shop on the Jersey shore. Gabriel spends his day driving around New Jersey with House and Wilson, trading pieces of personal information one-for-one with House and ending up at an Atlantic City hotel.

"What is the interesting philosophical dilemma that this character is in or what is the debate House can have with this character? Those are the things that will make David get interested. The medicine itself is fine but we have learned as a group to think in those terms before we go [to his office]. A lot of times, just pitching him the idea will turn into a philosophical debate about whatever is interesting in this character's life. Those will end up as the themes in the episode."

—GARRETT LERNER

Gabriel has been in a coma since he was hurt trying to save his wife from a fire that was started accidentally by Kyle, who was twelve at the time. Now Kyle is an alcoholic with a failing heart. House deduces he has a genetic condition that was passed, sweet irony, through his mother's DNA. Gabriel says he wants to donate his heart to his son—Kyle has no chance of getting a donor organ because of his alcoholism. Gabriel insists, even though there's a chance he could be woken again in the future and cured. He couldn't save his wife but he can save his son. To preserve his heart, Gabriel needs to hang himself, a slow and painful death, and with House's help, he does.

Gabriel never gets to go back to Princeton to see his son. He never even gets to eat his hoagie. Not knowing what he should say to Kyle, Gabriel asks House, if you could hear one thing from your father, what would it be? House: [pause] "I'd want him to say ... 'You were right. You did the right thing.'" When Kyle asks House what his father said to say to him, House repeats the line. "You were right ..." In the circumstances, it's meaningless and Kyle asks House what his father was trying to tell him. I don't know, says House; he was your father.

As usual, House took the shortest route from A to B. There was a problem (Kyle needed a heart) and the solution (his father) was right there. In "Sleeping Dogs Lie," Hannah needs a liver transplant and her girlfriend Max is prepared to donate part of her own liver. Cameron finds out Hannah is preparing to leave Max and wants to tell Max before she undergoes such a risky operation. "It's immoral," Cameron says. "Look, let's say you're right," says House. "We tell, she changes her mind, our patient dies. How is that

> "Much as I enjoy discussing the relationships between House and Wilson and House and Cuddy and all those sort of things, and they are part of the warp and weft of the whole, I really marvel at the gems that are sprinkled through. I think of all of that as structure—all the medical mystery is a structure, the beautifully wrought iron framework, but the real genius is the decoration of the doorknob."
>
> —HUGH LAURIE

moral?" House has cut through any inconvenient ethical under-growth. And Cameron needn't fret: Max knows about Hannah's plan. She thinks Hannah won't be able to leave her if she takes half her liver.

QUESTION: "Do you watch it and think, that's dark?"

GREG YAITANES: "I don't think it ever betrays the character. It might not be my worldview but it's the character's and I respect that."

In "Fetal Position," House diagnoses a pregnant woman with maternal mirror syndrome. It's a very simple issue for House—deliver the unviable fetus and save the mother. Cuddy disagrees and wants to operate to save the baby. To Cuddy, House's fetus is a baby (talk about a moral question). House agrees to operate on the fetus/baby, which grasps his finger during the procedure (put that in the hopper).

HOUSE: "You let your maternal instinct get the best of you and nearly kill two people. Case like this, you terminate, mom lives ten times out of ten. You do what you did, both mom and baby both die nine-point-nine times out of ten."

CUDDY: "Sometimes point-one is bigger than nine-point-nine."

House makes snap decisions like this—right or wrong, this is what I'm doing. He bulldozes through ethical hurdles that would make most people pause. In "Three Stories," he gives the most comprehensive set of clues as to his worldview. House can answer an ethical question "yes," or "no." For everyone else, that makes his universe a very challenging place to live in.

HOUSE: "I'm sure this goes against everything you've been taught, but right and wrong do exist. Just because you don't know what the right answer is—maybe there's even no way you could know what the right answer is—doesn't make your answer right or even okay. It's much simpler than that. It's just plain wrong."

Life Is Meaningless and It's All We Have

"Nothing matters. We're all just cockroaches, wildebeest dying on the river-bank. Nothing we do has any lasting meaning."

—House ("Living the Dream")

House would do anything to avoid having a weighty discussion with a patient. He'd do almost anything to avoid talking to patients at all, including paying them fifty dollars to leave the clinic ("One Day, One Room"). He often leaves people he does talk to bemused, insulted, or contemplating violence. After she saves House's bacon by lying on the stand for him, Cuddy makes House do clinic duty. He diagnoses a young woman with chlamydia and realizes she's been raped. Eve only wants to talk to House but he doesn't want to treat her—she's physically okay, no puzzle here. She doesn't know why she wants to talk to House, to which he says, "You've got to have a reason. Everything has a reason."

"He approaches every issue from a fundamental perspective. He never says, What does the law tell me to do? He says, What do the basic ethical principles tell me to do? And he recognizes that a lot of the questions that doctors face are very, very difficult and complicated questions."

—David Shore

Cruelly, House says she's trying to exert control . . . like a rape. "If we were to care about every person suffering on the planet, life would shut down," House says to Cuddy, repeating a theme of his: Why should I care about this person right here as opposed to any other? But Eve is persistent. After refusing to speak to a psychiatrist, Eve takes an overdose of sedatives and wakes to find House by her bed. He's only there because he's been told to by Cuddy. Eve says she wants to talk and House has no idea what to say. Eve becomes more of a puzzle to him. He asks Eve what happened and she says he doesn't really want to hear. "Sure I do," says House.

"You're lying," says Eve. House tells her it wasn't her fault and other platitudes. She knows all that. She wants to talk. House wants to know why she trusts him—to say she doesn't know isn't rational.

HOUSE: "Everything is rational."

EVE: "I was raped. Explain how that makes sense to you."

Eve asks House if anything terrible has ever happened to him. Wilson tells House she is looking to connect and that's what scaring him. He says tell her the truth. House tells Eve he was abused by his grandmother. She believed in discipline and made him sleep in the yard or bathe in ice when he screwed up. Eve questions the story, saying House wouldn't keep calling her *oma* ("grandma" in Dutch) if she did that. "What the hell can I do that you're not going to dismiss as just being because I was raped," she says. "Nothing," House replies. House says his story is true for somebody; what does she care if it's him? Is she going to base her life on who she got stuck in a room with? "That's what life is," says Eve. "It's a series of rooms and who we get stuck in those rooms with adds up to what our lives are."

"We are selfish, base animals crawling across the earth. Because we've got brains if we try real hard we can occasionally aspire to something that is less than pure evil."

—HOUSE ("ONE DAY, ONE ROOM")

When Cuddy tells House that Eve is pregnant, House tries to persuade her to terminate. Eve believes abortion is murder. "True," House says. "It's a life and you should end it." Eve says every life matters to God. Okay, what about Hitler? What about the father of your child? She doesn't want this type of chat. Why can't he talk about anything emotional? "There are no answers. If there are no answers, why talk about it?" But House relents and asks Eve if she wants to go for a walk. They sit in the park, where

House says he imagines that one of the runners going past will break a leg. As it inevitably must, talk turns to God.

HOUSE: "Either God doesn't exist or he's unimaginably cruel."

EVE: "I don't believe that."

HOUSE: "What do you believe? Why do you think this happened?"

"I need to know that it all means something," Eve says. "I need that comfort."

HOUSE: "Yeah. You feeling good right now . . . ?"

EVE: "I was raped. What's your excuse?"

Eve asks if the guy who did this to her is feeling bad. House isn't interested in that. "I'm interested in what you're feeling."

EVE: "You are?"

HOUSE: "I'm trapped in the room with you, right? Why did you choose me?"

EVE: "There's something about you. It's like you hurt, too."

House says the story was true. But it wasn't his grandmother. It was his dad. "I'd like to tell you what happened to me," says Eve. "I'd like to hear it," says House. Eve made the connection to House and she got him to talk to her. Later, House is playing foosball with Wilson. Cuddy tells him that Eve terminated her pregnancy and has been discharged. She's talking about what happened. It's meant to be a successful conclusion but House says, "All we've done is make a girl cry." Then why did he talk to her?

HOUSE: "Because I don't know."

WILSON: "You gonna follow up with her?"

HOUSE: "One day, one room."

In "Lockdown," with the hospital sealed because of a missing baby, a series of "one day, one room" scenarios are set up. Thirteen and Wilson play "Truth or Dare" (Wilson is hopelessly outmatched); Cameron and Chase rehash their marriage; Taub and Foreman drop narcotics and for a moment look like they're going to reenact Oliver Reed and Alan Bates's wrestling scene in the movie *Women in Love.* House finds himself in the room of Nash (David Strathairn), a patient on morphine with just a few hours to live. At first House is his matter-of-fact self: Nash says House didn't take on his case to which House says he only takes on one case in twenty: "A lot of the people I turn down end up dying."

Nash is dying, and he's dying alone. He tells House he had an affair and lost his family when his daughter was six. He says he wants to speak to Gracie one more time, but when he calls his now-grown-up daughter, House deduces he knows she's out so he can hear her voice on her voicemail message. This is what haunts Nash. House is more immediately open with Nash than he was with Eve if no less bleak:

HOUSE: "I like being alone. At least I convinced myself I'm better off that way. And then I met someone in a psychiatric hospital of all places. She changed me. And then she left. We're better off alone. We suffer alone and we die alone. It doesn't matter if you're a model husband or father of the year—tomorrow will be the same for you."

NASH: "Today would have been different."

House decides to force Nash's hand by calling Gracie back and saying to Nash he should tell her what he needs to tell her. Nash is only just able to say he loves her. Then House performs another favor for Nash, upping his morphine dose so he can drift off painlessly. When there's no one there to record the event, House can go against everything he believes in and apologize to Nash before he fades away.

HOUSE: "I'm sorry I didn't take your case."

NASH: "Me too. Gracie was the cutest six-year-old you ever saw."

At the end of the episode, the camera brushes over a Latin inscription: *Omnes te Moriturum Amant.* Before, House has scoffed at this notion, that everyone loves you when you're dying. No one loved the dying Nash, but a chance encounter with House at least allowed Nash to reach out to his daughter from the very brink of death.

"David is brilliant at hiding those themes within a very humorous and poignant show. The show breaks my heart and moves me and makes me laugh out loud. And it's beautiful that he's able to wrap those messages within it."

—GREG YAITANES

If it's true for House that life is essentially meaningless, then he's also stuck to the position that it's all we've got coming to us. He has been consistently relentless in his assault on faith and refuses to use any of the common platitudes. "I always wondered exactly what was on the other side," asks the dying Ezra in "Informed Consent." To which House replies, "Nothing." In "Damned if You Do," an episode in which it turns out a nun is being poisoned by her old birth control device, House gets to tackle religion with some of the workers on the front lines of faith. A nun is having visions and seizures.

NUN: "Sister Augustine believes things that aren't real."

HOUSE: "I thought that was a job requirement for you people."

SISTER AUGUSTINE: "Why is it so difficult for you to believe in God?"

HOUSE: "What I have difficulty with is the whole concept of belief. Faith isn't based on logic and experience."

QUESTION: "House is a scientist and people on their deathbed are looking for solace and he isn't going to countenance it."

DAVID SHORE: "It is something I think about a lot. You have to do religion in a show where people are facing death. The notion that they are not thinking about God or about the lack of God is a form of insanity. You can't face the end of your life without thinking, Is there anything after this? and in our show we almost always have someone facing the end of their life.

"I think the reason we have got away with it isn't that America is filled with closeted atheists—it has plenty and we appeal to those people—it's that we don't just set up straw men as the antagonist. When House tells that dying person there is nothing there, Wilson gives him crap and has a good argument in response. We confront House with things that are very difficult to answer and raise these questions and House stays firm in his point of view. It is important to us that the people who disagree with House aren't simply portrayed as stick figures, House just beating up on somebody and the person not fighting back—it can be fun in a clinic story, not on the big-picture issues."

In "House vs. God," House goes up against Boyd, the teenage preacher, whose symptoms can be explained by the fact he has herpes. House restates the position that defines his core: "There's nothing in this universe that can't be explained, eventually." In "97 Seconds," House and Wilson argue about allowing a dying man to believe there is something more to look forward to. "His beliefs are stupid," says House.

WILSON: "It's over. He's got days, maybe hours left. What pain does it cause you if he spends that time with a peaceful smile? What sick pleasure do you get in making damn sure he's filled with fear and dread?"

HOUSE: "He shouldn't be making a decision based on a lie. Misery is better than nothing."

WILSON: "You don't know there's nothing. You haven't been there."

HOUSE: "Oh, God, I am so tired of that argument. I don't have to go to Detroit to know that it smells."

WILSON: "Yes. Detroit, the afterlife, same thing."

And yet when the man claims to have died for ninety-seven seconds and seen the afterlife, House is prepared to stop his own heart to find out if there's anything to it. He does it in the vicinity of Amber, knowing the Cutthroat Bitch will do anything to keep him alive. House is open to belief if scientific proof could ever be found. It's in the nature of faith that science is unlikely to ever prove anything to the contrary. So House will continue doing things like baiting Mormon candidate Cole by saying his religion's founder Joseph Smith was a "horny fraud." Cole punches House ("Guardian Angels"). You can't say House isn't prepared to suffer for his beliefs. In the meantime he'll try very hard to aspire to something that is less than pure evil.

The Ends Justify the Means

QUESTION: "Means and ends. You kidnap people. You have committed felonies . . ."

HUGH LAURIE: "Gets the job done."

CAMERON: "But I know I'll never have that sort of . . . excitement."

FOREMAN: "You miss people trying to kill you?"

CAMERON: "No. I miss people doing whatever it takes to get the job done. I guess that's why I'm having trouble giving it up." ("Whatever it Takes")

"I supposed it is part of the childish and very male side of House that causes him constantly to set himself apparently difficult tasks like . . . can you throw this crumpled-up piece of paper into the rubbish bin from here? I bet you can't roll the cricket ball down the hall and hit the fire extinguisher . . . whatever it is. House is doing that to himself all the time. Having set himself the challenge he is absolutely fixated on doing whatever has to be done—hit the fire extinguisher or whatever. The tasks he set himself just happen to be medical ones. Though he could probably spend the whole day doing that [as well] with crumpled-up paper."

—HUGH LAURIE

Any physician for whom housebreaking skills are a job requirement (for Foreman) is likely to cut some corners. In his quest for the truth (the answer to the medical puzzle), or to be proved right, or simply to get his own way, House will stop at nothing.

Welcome to the house of fun.

- House coughs on a scrubbed-in surgeon to prevent an operation from proceeding. ("Detox")

- House tortures the politician (who must be a liar) by removing his oxygen mask to get him to say what drug he took. ("Role Model")

- House turns the tilt table way up with Sebastian Charles, the sainted TB doctor, attached. It's "Abusive and unprofessional," says Foreman, but it shows up a problem with Sebastian's heart that wouldn't otherwise have been spotted. ("TB or Not TB")

- House tries to bribe a surgeon to perform a liver transplant with twenty thousand dollars and when that fails he blackmails him by threatening to tell his wife about his affair with a nurse. And he tells the wife anyway. ("The Mistake")

- House puts a suicidal and terminally ill patient in a coma against his wishes to try to save his life. ("Informed Consent")

- House stabs a screaming and delirious clinic patient with a paralytic to quiet him down before giving him a sedative. A dangerous way to get some peace. ("One Day, One Room")

- Posing as a limo driver, House kidnaps soap star Evan Greer after seeing changes in his acting on TV. ("Living the Dream")

- House gives a deaf kid a cochlear implant even though he doesn't want one. "It was a caring act," says Wilson. "Which you did in a way that was immoral and illegal. But baby steps." ("House Divided")

- House drugs, gags, and ties up Wilson's Canadian vet neighbor and forcibly relieves him of the phantom pain in his amputated arm. ("The Tyrant")

A subset of this notion is the Hail Mary technique of Treat First, Ask Questions Later, employed in many differential diagnosis sessions. If everything else has been ruled out, the patient must have what is left up on the board. If they then treat and the patient doesn't die, then the diagnosis is correct. "If I'm right, I save his life. If I'm wrong, he's dead no matter what I do" ("Distractions").

Everybody Screws Up

"Occam's razor. The simplest explanation is almost always that somebody screwed up."

—HOUSE ("OCCAM'S RAZOR")

Ask Foreman ("House Training") and Chase ("The Mistake"): The consequences of a medical mistake can be fatal to the patient. It follows from House's willingness to do whatever it takes to save the patient once he thinks he's found the answer. Because if he's wrong, then look out. Rarely, as in "Brave Heart," when House and Foreman perform an autopsy on a patient who is alive, a screw-up has a positive outcome, in this case bringing a cadaver back from the dead like Lazarus. It's high-stakes poker that House indulges in—40 percent of lawsuits at PPTH are down to him, Cuddy says in "The Mistake," and she's also said she sets aside fifty thousand dollars for legal expenses for his insane acts ("DNR"). It's part of the cost of doing business with House.

Gerrit van der Meer tells a story about someone close to him who was diagnosed with lung cancer and the man was saying his good-byes to people. But the original diagnosis was completely wrong and it turned out to be a bad case of pneumonia. Gerrit says that medicine is an art rather than a science, to which House would probably have a loud retort. It's the human element—lying, screw-ups, the role of interpretation—that makes it an art.

"My son is just about to start reading philosophy at university. Proud dad. And I picture the first week of ethics between eleven and one; they will be discussing precisely that. What is the point of us struggling to save the people who come before us if by doing so it causes the deaths of thousands?"

—HUGH LAURIE

"That's where I heard the term *dead ringer* comes from. They would attach a ring to your toe and the ring to a bell and someone would sit in the cemetery and if [a recently buried person] moved and the bell rang they'd come and take you out. Let me out of here! A dead ringer."

—MARCY KAPLAN

HOUSE: "Success only lasts until someone screws them up. Failures are forever." ("Broken")

Killing People Is Wrong

"Peter Blake and David Shore both liked the idea about killing Hitler, killing someone who deserves to be killed but having to wrestle with the guilt about that. And Peter developed that into this story."

In "Occam's Razor," Chase asks Cameron, "Have you ever taken a life?" Cameron doesn't answer. Two years later, Cuddy asks House if he helped a terminal patient in his request for assisted suicide. "If I did, would you really want to know?" House asks, and Cuddy wouldn't. At the end of the episode, it's implied that Cameron has helped the patient die. House finds her crying in the chapel and he puts a hand on her shoulder. "I'm proud of you," House says ("Informed Consent").

Moving forward a couple more years and Chase allows the dictator Dibala to die. And in "Known Unknowns" Wilson helps his end-stage lung cancer patient hasten the end by slipping him the code to his morphine pump. Driven by a need to atone because he left the patient alone to die, Wilson tries to present a conference paper the first line of which is "Euthanasia. Let's tell the truth, we all do it." Killing people is wrong, right?

QUESTION: "Everyone has killed somebody."

DAVID SHORE: "Wilson assists somebody . . . There is a significant moral difference between what Chase does [with Dibala] and what Wilson does. The patient in the Chase case did not want to die. That would fall under the significant moral difference category I think."

QUESTION: "In the Dibala episode Chase is asking Foreman to perjure himself . . ."

SHORE: "That's not the same as what Cuddy did [for House with Tritter] but Foreman has got himself into that. His decision to burn the evidence [means] he is in bed with Chase more than he would like to be. If he were to tell the truth he would have some explaining to do. Not as much as Chase, obviously."

When Dibala first comes to PPTH, it's Cameron who questions whether the dictator should be saved. "We fix Dibala, he gets on a plane and executes half his country," she says. After Chase stops a young man from killing Dibala, Cameron says maybe next time don't yell out a warning. Chase and Cameron debate justifiable killing. Cameron says, "Am I trying to kill our patient? Of course not. But if he died am I supposed to pretend that wouldn't be good for the world?" Ultimately Cameron treats the patient as the law, her oaths, and her training demand. Contending with a higher authority, Chase causes Dibala to die. Earlier, arguing with Cameron from the opposite viewpoint to the one he ultimately takes, Chase outlines some of the consequences of taking a life:

CHASE: "Only psychopaths can kill other people without having some kind of breakdown."

CAMERON: "Not if it's justified. Look at soldiers."

CHASE: "Even when it's justified."

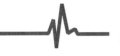

GUILT IS A USELESS EMOTION

House's impulse to reject what can't be measured like a pound of apples means he's light on some of the more abstract emotions (pleasure and pain are more likely to be quantifiable). He's not big on hopes or expectations; remorse and guilt are just counterproductive. It was Wilson's guilt at not staying with his dying cancer patient that almost made him admit to a roomful of doctors that he euthanized a patient. Chase's guilt about Dibala doesn't go far enough for the priest who insists Chase turns himself in, and is eventually too little for Cameron as well.

In "Humpty Dumpty," House tells Cuddy she's not happy unless things are right with the world. Cuddy is feeling bad because her gardener lost a hand after falling off her roof. "Your guilt. It's perverse and it makes you a crappy doctor," says House. "It also makes you okay at what you do." That's it? "Now, would the world be a better place if people never felt guilty?" says House charmlessly. "Makes sex better. You should have seen [Stacy] in the last months of our relationship. A lot of guilt. A lot of screaming."

House struggles with what may or may not be guilt in "No Remorse." He cuts up a couple of Cuddy's framed photographs in her office to make fun of Lucas and Cuddy is very upset. He's destroyed a picture taken by her now-dead father and she has no copy. House is contacted by Wibberly, a guy House screwed over in med school and to whom he apologized as part of his rehab. House finds out that what he did to Wibberly, switching a test paper, pretty much ruined the latter's life, since, as a direct result of House's action, he never qualified and now he's losing his house. At the time, House is treating Valerie, the psychopath who has no conscience and can feel no guilt. House has an unsettling conversation with Valerie, who intuits that House might perhaps like an override switch on his own feelings now and again.

House does feel guilt; he just can't direct it. He refuses to apologize to Cuddy and gives Wibberly five thousand dollars to cover some mortgage payments. Wilson nails House. He says it's easier for House to give a guy he doesn't care about money than to apologize to someone who used to love him. It transpires that Wibberly lied and his failure had nothing to do with House; he just wanted to see if House was still the same bastard he had been in med school. House tries to force his money on the thoroughly defeated man proving that yes, he is the same bastard. When he goes to talk to Cuddy (perhaps to say sorry), Lucas is there and he leaves. To expiate his guilt he trudges to Wibberly's house and shoves the check back through the mailbox.

Change Is Impossible

"I wanna get better. Whatever the hell that means. I'm sick of being miserable."

—HOUSE ("BROKEN")

House hates change. In "Lines in the Sand," House doesn't want to go in his office until an old bloodstained carpet that was being replaced is put back. After he's admitted to Mayfield Hospital, House eventually admits he wants to change. He's broken. But it's been one of House's maxims that people can't change. House encounters an Orthodox Jewish woman who a few months before was a music executive who did heroin. Rather than think someone could find religion and change that drastically, House looks for a diagnosis that explains her behavior as delusional. (He's wrong, it turns out: She had changed.)

"In both the universe of this show and in the universe I live in, I believe people can change but not a lot. You won't change at all unless you want to change and if you want to change, it's baby steps. It's one thing I find a little too pat, probably about the movies more than TV, the epiphany and everything changes. I think we should be trying to change and we should be trying to make ourselves better but the idea that we are going to fundamentally turn into a different person, is I think simply naïve. We are who we are and that doesn't mean we can't strive and we can't make choices. On the other hand we are the choices we make. This is one of the battles between House and Wilson."

—DAVID SHORE

In "Merry Little Christmas," House sees a quick fix for a girl whose short stature is caused by a lack of growth hormone, not her mother's dwarfism. At first, the girl doesn't want to change; she wants to be like her mother. House tries to persuade the mother to start treatment for her daughter:

House: "You and I have found out that being normal sucks. Because we're freaks. The advantage of being a freak is that it makes you stronger. Now, how strong do you really want her to have to be?"

The girl's stature is different from House's misery, or even his leg pain, in that there's a permanent medical remedy. House is more like the writer who undergoes experimental surgery to try to overcome his bipolar disorder ("Failure to Communicate"). There's no quick fix.

The trumpeter John Henry Giles ("DNR") recognizes House as a kindred spirit. "I know that limp," Giles says. "I know the empty ring finger." Giles sees that House is as obsessive about his work as Giles is about his music. "You got this—the thing you think about all the time that keeps you south of normal." It's what makes us great, Giles says. "All we miss out on is everything else," meaning relationships. And then it's over and it's too late.

Can House change, even when he wants to? In "Known Unknowns" House goes to Cuddy's hotel room to offer to babysit Cuddy's daughter. On Wilson's urging he's making a first step. He's off the painkillers, House and Cuddy have just had their moment at the eighties party, apparently, he's changed. Then he sees Lucas with Cuddy's baby. So much, so far, for that.

The idea that people *can* change is at the essential to the second-time-around romance of Wilson and Sam or, as House describes her to his friend, "The soulless harpy you were married to before we met." ("Knight Fall")

WILSON: "People change, House."

HOUSE: "Sure. They get older. Ovaries start drying up and nice guys like you look attractive again."

House makes it his business to break Sam and Wilson up. As he did with Cameron and Chase, House says he is merely performing a service by hastening the inevitable. With intimate knowledge of what drives Wilson crazy, House is able to booby trap the condo with domestic don'ts Wilson blames on Sam: Don't put the milk in the door of the fridge; don't put banana peel in the wrong trash can; don't put large dishes in the bottom of the dishwasher. Wilson was so uptight he never mentioned any of these foibles when he was married to Sam. House wanted Wilson to stand up for himself and he does, way up. Sam and Wilson have a big row and air decade-old recriminations. Wilson calls Sam a selfish bitch and House's work is done.

Except it isn't. Sam comes back and tells Wilson she has changed. Wilson says he's trying to. They should have had that argument ten years ago, Wilson says. Clearly that would have been impossible. He had to change first.

You Can't Always Get What You Want . . .

QUESTION: "Is it true to say you can't always get what you want? Can you ever get what you want?"

ROBERT SEAN LEONARD: "You can. But then it's killed in a bus accident. I don't know if you keep what you want. In my personal view it's totally random. There are lovely, incredibly giving, caring people who are run down by buses and there are people who are the beasts of all time who get away with murder and who live great lives. I always think about it on the highway. I'm from New York–New Jersey and this freeway living is new to me. You're three miles back on the 101 and you can sense you're getting ready to get on the 405. People start drifting right and traffic slows down. Then there are the people who zip all the way to the front and get right in. When I see that, I think I don't know, that guy may get in a horrible accident or his mother may die of a horrible disease later that day, but my first thought is, I bet that guy is okay. I think those guys do okay actually."

. . . You Just Get What You Get

"People get what they get. It has nothing to do with what they deserve."

—HOUSE ("DYING CHANGES EVERYTHING")

Roy Randall, the billionaire in "Instant Karma," thinks he is being punished by the gods for his unbroken run of business success. First his wife dies, then his son becomes incurably sick, and he believes it's his fault. Randall insists on seeing House because he is the best doctor. But he also insists on deliberately cratering his own fortune, thinking that restoring the karma will save his son. House diagnoses the son and saves him. Randall thinks his financial self-destruction worked; House knows it was the medicine.

"To me I think it's random. You get what you can get."

—ROBERT SEAN LEONARD

"I try to be as good a person as I can but I don't believe St. Peter is there with a little record book waiting . . . checking off. I don't believe there's a moral code or a judgment at the end of the day . . . I'm not a big believer in predetermination. I believe you can do whatever you want is my point. I don't think there is a punishment for it. If you want to become a mass murderer tomorrow you can. I don't know about fate; I don't know how I feel about that."

—ROBERT SEAN LEONARD

In "Wilson's Heart," Wilson is tortured because he doesn't know why Amber was on the bus with House, as if her intentions had any bearing on what happened. Thirteen is unable to participate fully in treating Amber because of her own fears about early death. But Kutner has perspective—he tells Thirteen his own parents were murdered when he was six. Life's not fair. As Amber is dying in the OR, Kutner watches TV and eats cereal. What's going on in Kutner's head will later leave the series' greatest unanswered question of all.

After Amber dies, House dreams or hallucinates he's on a bus with her. He says it should be him who is dead. Why?

HOUSE: "Because life shouldn't be random. Because lonely, misanthropic drug addicts should die in bus crashes and young do-gooders in love who get dragged out of their apartment in the middle of the night should walk away clean."

AMBER: "Self-pity isn't like you."

HOUSE: "I'm branching out from self-loathing and self-destruction . . . Wilson is going to hate me."

AMBER: "You kind of deserve it."

If House is having a breakthrough, it's a lesson hard learned. For a second, Amber is like House in "One Day, One Room," and House is like Eve, knowing the questions, lost for the answers.

AMBER: "Get off the bus."

HOUSE: "I can't. Because . . . because it doesn't hurt here. I lied. I don't want to be in pain and I don't want to be miserable. And I don't want him to hate me."

AMBER: "Well . . . You can't always get what you want."

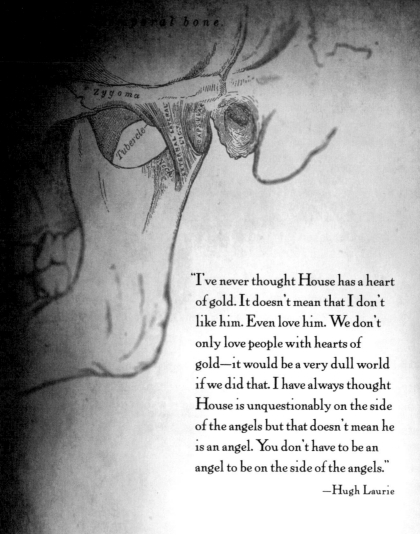

"I've never thought House has a heart of gold. It doesn't mean that I don't like him. Even love him. We don't only love people with hearts of gold—it would be a very dull world if we did that. I have always thought House is unquestionably on the side of the angels but that doesn't mean he is an angel. You don't have to be an angel to be on the side of the angels."

—Hugh Laurie

HOUSE

Hugh Laurie

At the end of "Resignation," House meets an attractive nutritionist, called Honey, in a café. House has treated her vegan boyfriend at the clinic and she thinks she's seeing House for a job interview. But she quickly realizes this is no interview; it's more like a date. Honey says she doesn't know anything about House although she's obviously aware he's a doctor. House candidly lists some of his qualities. He's on antidepressants; he eats meat; he likes drugs; he's not always faithful. Quickly she snaps back: "How miserable can you be saving lives, sleeping around, and doing drugs?" Good question. (House asks Honey if she was on the debate team in high school.) House also says he hates tea, and then orders some.

House is, of course, the story of House. "House is the key character," says David Shore. "You have the boss, best friend, subordinates and he is the hub of the wheel." House is in almost every scene in the show and the plot follows him around. As Chase tells House, he'll always be in charge whether he wants to be or not ("Instant Karma"). The other players help illuminate or reveal aspects of House's character: Cuddy and Cameron his relationship aversions; Wilson his conflicted need for companionship; Foreman and Chase his ambivalent attitude to helping people; Taub and Thirteen his need for control. Some people—Stacy, Cuddy, to some extent Cameron—get to him. Others—Vogler, Tritter, to some extent Cuddy—get on him. But it's all about him.

> "He is demonstrably an egomaniac in many ways but he is not a conventional egomaniac. He doesn't need conventional public applause for his good deeds."
>
> —HUGH LAURIE

As with most characters, the backstory is leaked out very slowly. When he's admitted after being shot in "No Reason," House's wristband gives a (reliable?) date of birth of 6/11/59. In "Three Stories," it's revealed what happened to his leg. We know House was at Michigan when Cuddy was there and that he was kicked out ("Known Unknowns"). In "Distractions," House exacts professional revenge on Professor Weber, who, like House, went to Hopkins and studied under the same professors and got an internship at the Mayo Clinic that House would have gotten if he hadn't been thrown out for cheating. House trashes Weber's medical research on migraine prevention. Offering clues as to why he might have been regularly relieved of jobs and places at med school, House disproves Weber by testing his drug, first on a coma patient, then on himself. Somehow House managed to qualify as a board-certified diagnostician with a double specialty in infectious disease and nephrology.

Just how many times has House been fired? In "Humpty Dumpty," Cameron says House is a great doctor, "But any other hospital administrator would have fired him years ago." "Four of them did," says Cuddy. "The question is, why did I hire him?" But she knows the answer. As she says in the pilot, "The son of a bitch is the best doctor we have."

Saving Lives

"Saving lives is just collateral damage."

—HOUSE ("UNFAITHFUL")

House is a truly gifted diagnostician. He can sometimes tell what's wrong with an apparently hearty patient just by looking at them. His knowledge of conditions and their symptoms is colossal and he is extraordinarily well read. (In "Fidelity" he reads in a Portuguese medical journal about someone getting sleeping sickness from their girlfriend; he found Weber's migraine research in *Neuroscience New Delhi*. Perhaps the only monograph he won't reread is the lupus textbook he used to stash his Vicodin in "Finding Judas.") House is unrelentingly dogged in his pursuit of the diagnosis. To an extreme degree. In "Last Resort," he gives the gunman holding him and Thirteen hostage his gun back so he can complete his diagnosis. With all this to take into consideration, is House actually a good doctor?

> Wilson: *"Some doctors have the messiah complex. They need to save the world. You've got the Rubik's complex. You need to solve the puzzle." ("DNR")*

House's interest in saving lives extends to solving the medical puzzle; about the patient House is at best indifferent. In the pilot Foreman asks, "Isn't treating patients why we became doctors?" to which House says, "No. Treating illnesses is why we became doctors. Treating patients is what makes most doctors miserable." All a patient is likely to do is lie and obscure the answer to the puzzle. Wilson explains House's position to Foreman more explicitly in "The Socratic Method":

> **WILSON:** "He likes puzzles."
>
> **FOREMAN:** "Patients are puzzles?"
>
> **WILSON:** "You don't think so?"
>
> **FOREMAN:** "I think they're people."

Foreman's interest is stirred because House is actually meeting a patient, Lucy, an apparent schizophrenic (who has Wilson's disease). Chase tells Foreman that House likes "crazy people." "They're not boring," Chase says. "He likes that." In "Lines in the Sand," an autistic child reacts to House, although House isn't really trying to make a connection. The boy hands House his game machine, an act of social interaction. But other patients, like Eve in "One Day, One Room," have to resort to extraordinary measures (an overdose) to get House to talk to them.

> "I think House thinks it makes him a better doctor by treating people as mechanical objects more than feeling ones. . . . He's more interested in his own issues. I think his comment was that if we worry about every death in society we wouldn't be able to function."
>
> —DAVID SHORE

If House were like Foreman, Wilson, or (especially) Cameron, he would be unable to make the wild throws of the dice he so frequently takes with patients' lives. "I take risks," House says. "Sometimes patients die. But not taking risks causes more patients to die. So I guess my biggest problem is I've been cursed with the ability to do the math" ("Detox"). House saves maybe fifty people a year; what about a guy who saves thousands? In "TB or Not TB," House meets Sebastian, the charismatic doctor who campaigns to cure TB in

Africa. Sebastian is media-friendly; House thinks he's pompous and just as selfish as the next person. Sebastian's drug protocol (it seems like he has TB) would cost ten thousand dollars so he turns it down—he won't accept treatment until similar meds are available to everyone in Africa, and he holds a press conference to say so. As far as House is concerned, saving lives is not a competition. Sebastian has a theory.

> SEBASTIAN: "You know, the difference between our jobs is not numbers or styles. It's that I know I'm gonna fail. Even if I save a million people, there's gonna be another million. You couldn't handle that. I think you resent anyone who can."
>
> HOUSE: "Can't we just agree that you're incredibly annoying."

For certain House wouldn't be interested if the diagnosis were always TB.

> "House has contradicted himself. He has said motives don't matter. If you are saving lives who cares why you're saving lives? If you are a great person in the sense of the best motives on earth but the results of your action is that people are dying then you're an ass. If you're the biggest ass on earth in the sense that your motives suck but you're saving lives, you're a good person. I think that attitude was severely challenged in 'TB or Not TB' because Sebastian fell into the latter category but it did annoy House, and I think Wilson pointed that out to him. That the guy was getting worshipped. House is a human being. He is not able to rise above his own personal biases."
>
> —DAVID SHORE

There is one that got away for House. When a boy comes into the ER and is diagnosed by Cuddy with gastroenteritis, House visits the boy and sees he's not able to grasp House's cane. In his office, House reaches down to the bottom of the file drawer to find a twelve-year-old file. He usually avoids cases but this is one he wants. House believes the six-year-old boy and seventy-three-year-old Esther, who died, had the same condition ("All In"). After Esther died, her family wouldn't let House perform the autopsy that he is convinced would have confirmed Erdheim-Chester, an incredibly rare disease.

Chase knows House has had this file out before (he mentions a case he was on before Cameron was at PPTH). Solving it is like finding the Virgin Mary for House. House's eureka confirms he's right—it was Erdheim-Chester in the boy and, QED, in Esther. The disease lied, or, rather, it played him by not showing up in places they had tested but spreading there later. It's notable that in a case he was unable to solve, House knows the patient's name.

In "Resignation," House is looped on antidepressants slipped to him by Wilson. House has diagnosed Addie, aged nineteen. Her outlook is bleak but House is pleased with himself because he's solved a particularly tricky puzzle.

> **HOUSE:** "Don't you see how incredible this call was, a protein deficiency. Can't be tested, can't be seen. I called it based on coughing blood."
>
> **FOREMAN:** "You're happy about this."
>
> **CAMERON:** "She's going to die."
>
> **HOUSE:** "That's not my fault. She's going to die anyway. Now thanks to me at least she'll know why."

Foreman asks House if he knows the girl's name. ("Dead sophomore girl?") Or her father's or mother's name? House asks Foreman if anyone's going to give a crap if he knows their names.

House goes to give the patient the news. "Addie, you're dying," he says. In two days or less. He starts to tell her about her condition but she cuts him off. "It doesn't matter." But House can't let it go. "This is what's killing you; you're not interested in what's killing you?" "Will it make any difference?" Addie replies.

> **HOUSE:** "What's the point in living without curiosity? Without craving the . . ."
>
> **ADDIE:** "So, I'm screwing up my last few hours because I won't listen to you?"
>
> **FATHER:** "Get out of here."
>
> **HOUSE:** "It's . . . It's like the dark matter in the universe . . ."

Addie looks at House. She thinks he's smiling. House sees his face in the towel dispenser and he has one eureka. House confronts Wilson and accuses him of dosing him with antidepressants. Guilty. But House says he wasn't smiling; the drug made him hazy, not happy. He can't get over the fact that Addie wasn't curious about why she's dying. Wilson says it's because she's miserable. No more than she's ever been, says House, who has another eureka. Addie is depressed—she tried to kill herself with cleaning fluid in a gel cap.

This is what patients get with House—he doesn't know their name, he doesn't care about their fate, but he will save their life. House doesn't offer a warranty with his service. He promises Addie he won't tell her parents that she attempted suicide and then tells them anyway so he's not burdened with the information. And when Addie's mom asks if she can call with any follow-up questions, House says no.

 ## ARE THERE REAL HOUSES OUT THERE?

Bobbin Bergstrom: "I would rather have an asshole treat me who knew what he was doing than someone who was going to pat me on the back and get it wrong."

David Foster says he gets this question all the time: "Is House like anyone you know?

"I say of course not; no doctor could really say these things and act this way. But if you talk to nurses, they say, 'That Doctor House, he's just about right.' Doctor House is more like doctors than doctors think he is."

DAVID SHORE: "I think that is one of the attractions of the show. I think we all work with people who are a pain in the ass and pain in the ass is in the eye of the beholder and we are probably someone else's pain in the ass."

BOBBIN BERGSTROM: "There was this horribly sad patient who had AIDS and had cardiac arrest and died and his lover was standing right next to him and the doctor came in and said, 'Got a double bagger,' right in front of the partner. There are Houses out there."

Sleeping Around

> "The perfect girlfriend for House is a question people ask me more than anything else. Not just out of the business but in the business, agents are pitching different actresses. Who is the woman who can heal those wounds? There is something incredibly romantic about that . . . Who will be able to see beyond all the baggage and celebrate what is beneath all the rough exterior?"
>
> —KATIE JACOBS

House has enjoyed a slightly more active sex life in his head than in reality. He fantasized about Cuddy stripping and hallucinated having sex with her and he was much better acquainted with imaginary Amber than the real one. There have been four women he's been romantically involved with: Cameron, Stacy, Lydia, and Cuddy. Then there have been women he's not romantically involved with, his hookers (his word), like Paula—"I'm looking for a distraction. You don't need to talk to do that, do you?" ("Distractions")—and the "actress" he hires to spring a trap on Kutner and Taub and their online diagnosis scheme ("Let Them Eat Cake").

> "There is a reason for tact in a civilized society but it is so rare and refreshing and heroic, a guy who just says what he is thinking not because it's on his agenda to make him like you or make you dislike him—he believes it is the right thing to say at this time so he's going to say it. That is so rare. Perhaps it should be."
>
> —DAVID SHORE

In "Sports Medicine," Wilson has dinner with Stacy the lawyer and House says he has no right to be upset. The audience knows nothing about Stacy but they do know House is taking Cameron to a monster truck rally. Is it a date? Yes, says House, except for the date part. Cameron makes it clear she's romantically interested in House but House, scientifically, is more interested in knowing why than in pursuing the idea. Cameron quits ("Role Model") and says she'll only come back if House agrees to go on a real date with her. But House and Cameron's date ("Love Hurts") is just another puzzle-solving session for

House. He figures Cameron is trying to replicate her experience when she married a man dying of cancer. "What I am is what you need," says House. "I'm damaged."

QUESTION: "Mira Sorvino [Cate, the Antarctic scientist in 'Frozen'] was the perfect girlfriend."

DAVID SHORE: "Yes. Because she was nine thousand miles away."

By the next episode, Stacy shows up at PPTH and is revealed as House's former partner whom he hasn't seen in five years. Cameron realizes she's outmatched and moves on.

QUESTION: "I was sorry to see that Stacy didn't work out."

DAVID SHORE: "He blew it. It's consistent with his character to blow it. Putting him in a relationship at that point would have been a mistake. You need him as that lone wolf."

Stacy has brought her husband, Mark, to be treated by House. In "Three Stories," through the course of his lecture, without saying it's about him, House reveals the story of what happened to his own leg: an aneurysm that clotted, leading to infarction. Muscle in the leg died. The problem remained undiagnosed for three days before the patient suggested it might be muscle death. House's partner at the time is . . . Stacy. House refuses to countenance losing the leg: He'll live with the pain. House is put into a coma so he can sleep through the worst of it. When he's under, Stacy invokes her medical proxy and has muscle removed from House's leg, the middle way between amputation and leaving the tissue in place. House is left with a bad leg and chronic pain and bitterness about it toward Stacy. "I saved your life," she says. "Yeah, maybe."

CAMERON: "What was he like before his leg?"

STACY: "Pretty much the same." ("The Honeymoon")

"I am not hanging everything on that leg. I suspect and we have alluded to this . . . He was brilliant but he had the same attitude toward humanity before that. I think he probably kept it to himself a little more before. He was an ass but he kept it to himself but what

I think happened was that when he became lame I think he realized he could get away with shit. That people would kind of forgive him a little bit."

—DAVID SHORE

House tries to diagnose Mark even if he's not sure he wants Stacy's husband to live. House and Stacy aren't over each other. At the end of season one she tells him, "You were the one. You always will be. But I can't be with you."

> Stacy: "What's so great about you is you always think you're right. And what's so frustrating about you is that you are right so much of the time. You are brilliant, funny, surprising, sexy.
> "But with you, I was lonely. And with Mark, there, there's room for me."

House merely says, "Okay," and they kiss. Until Cuddy, House has never told anyone he'll change for them: Here I am, take it or leave it. At the end of season one Cuddy offers Stacy a job, meaning she's at PPTH, ready to fall for House again. "I hate you and I love you," she tells House. "And I love Mark" ("Spin"). House manipulates and connives—he breaks into the therapy room to read notes of Stacy and Mark's sessions; he sleeps with Stacy after they get stuck out of town on a business trip ("Failure to Communicate"). But when Stacy tells House she's prepared to leave Mark, he tells her don't. Mark is willing to do whatever it takes; House isn't. He says he can't make her happy and down the road she'll need something he can't give her ("Need to Know").

Wilson is mad at House for letting the opportunity slide. House has to want to change and try to be happy, which is something he's not ready to contemplate:

> Wilson: "You don't like yourself. But you do admire yourself. It's all you've got so you cling to it. You're so afraid if you change, you'll lose what makes you special. Being miserable doesn't make you better than anybody else, House. It just makes you miserable."

"There is a line where Wilson says, 'You don't like yourself but you do admire yourself' and I think that's true. He doesn't like himself and I think he's scared out of his mind that if he lives his life like another person, he would still not be happy but he wouldn't only be unhappy, he would hate himself. He does admire the life choices he has made. He wouldn't respect himself in the morning."

—DAVID SHORE

In season five, House finally falls off the edge of the world when he hallucinates sex with Cuddy as he withdraws from Vicodin. In Mayfield Hospital, House watches a woman named Lydia come to the hospital dayroom to play piano for Annie, her husband's sister. Annie used to play cello in an orchestra but she's now locked in her own silent place. House and Lydia get close but House pushes her away because, he says, people always get hurt. But they find each other. Lydia has brought her friend's cello to the hospital in case she wakes up; House himself suddenly seems to have found a positive force in Lydia and they embrace, dance, and make love.

Lydia is looking for a miracle, and she gets one. House has moved toward realizing he wants to get better. He apologizes to the patient who calls himself Freedom Master, who was injured when House took him off hospital grounds to indulge Freedom Master's fantasy that he can fly. In the dayroom, Freedom Master unlocks Annie's silence by giving her a music box and Annie plays the cello again. House goes to Lydia's home—Annie's recovery will take her out of state and Lydia is going, too. She didn't tell House because she thought it ended perfectly between them. She's married—House was a fling. But House didn't want it to end.

House tells his psychiatrist, Dr. Nolan, "She left. And I'm lost." Nolan sees that House connected strongly enough with someone to get hurt, meaning he can leave the hospital. When he gets back to PPTH and Cuddy, House seems ready for a real relationship. He just hasn't earned it yet, maybe.

Taking Drugs

"House accepted for four and a half years that he was a Vicodin addict but he was okay with that. He thought it was the best of a crappy situation. He wasn't taking them recreationally in his mind, to get high, he was taking them to not be in pain so he could function in the day. Yes, he was addicted, and yes, it was taking a toll on

his body, but he didn't give a crap—this was working. It's a complicated question, which is what drives us here. I think he was fundamentally right about that, until he started having hallucinations
and not being able to tell what was real."

—DAVID SHORE

"No, I do not have a pain management problem, I have a pain problem."
This statement, as laid out in "Occam's Razor," is House's consistent position
on his drug use. His leg hurts, he takes drugs, he is able to get on with his life.
Not everyone agrees. "House is a junkie," says Foreman in "Son of a Coma
Guy," but is he a functioning junkie? In "Detox," Cuddy challenges House to
get off the pills in exchange for dropping clinic duty for a month. House suffers terrible withdrawal and smashes his hand with a pestle so the pain will
take his mind off the detox. House makes it a week and Wilson asks if he
learned anything: "Yeah. I'm an addict."

> **HOUSE:** "I said I was an addict. I didn't say I had a problem. I pay my
> bills. I make my meals. I function."
>
> **WILSON:** "Is that all you want? You have no relationships."
>
> **HOUSE:** "I don't want any relationships."

House's leg pain gets worse over time. In "Skin Deep," he asks Cuddy for a
shot of morphine to get some relief. But when he's shot by Moriarty in "No
Reason," House's leg feels better after surgery. Like Stacy, Cuddy had taken the
opportunity of House's unconsciousness to try to fix his leg, or at least lessen
his pain. House was put in a "dissociative coma" and his brain was rebooted,
an experiment tried on chronic pain patients. There's a 50 percent chance his
pain won't return. He denies it but House has the side effect of hallucinations.
Still, House is without pain for a couple of months. It doesn't last and in
"Meaning," House is writing himself a prescription for Vicodin on Wilson's
scrip pad.

When House sticks a thermometer in an annoying clinic patient's butt
and leaves for the day, it seems like something House would do and get away
with. But in Detective Tritter, he picked the wrong butt. Tritter tells Cuddy
that House is a bully and bullies don't back down till they meet someone

> "That's where I think the show lives at its best. There are no black-and-whites. When people say House is an asshole I don't even understand what they are talking about essentially. The writers are so nuanced and skilled that there is no black-and-white."
>
> —KATIE JACOBS

stronger and meaner. House won't apologize, so Tritter raises the stakes, pulls House over in a traffic stop, finds his pills, and arrests him for possession of narcotics ("Fools for Love"). With Tritter, the idea was "that House would finally get caught," says Katie Jacobs. Is House a functioning addict or an abuser of Vicodin? "We needed to deal with the issue of a pill-popping, lifesaving head of diagnostic medicine," says Jacobs. "I felt like Tritter gave us the opportunity to see both sides of that."

> "A lot of people thought Tritter was just the bad guy and I never perceived him as being just a bad guy. Tritter was so right in some ways."
>
> —DAVID SHORE

Tritter tries and fails to get anyone to give evidence against House until Wilson obliges. House goes to desperate measures to get his drugs, finally stealing a dead man's prescription. Tritter shows he's not vindictive about House—this is his way of looking to the greater good.

> TRITTER: "The pills distort reality. He is an addict."
>
> CUDDY: "He's not out robbing a liquor store, or—"
>
> TRITTER: "No, he's treating people. He needs to find a different way to cope before he kills somebody. If he hasn't done that already." ("Finding Judas")

Tritter is thwarted in court by Cuddy's bold lie on the witness stand in House's favor. Cuddy is making a deal with the devil here and acknowledges as much—"The only bright spot is that now I own your ass," she says. Tritter is magnanimous in defeat. "I hope I was wrong about you," he tells House. He wasn't. House's apparent rehab is shown to be a fake as an orderly slips him Vicodin and he's back to square one ("Words and Deeds").

In season five, the functioning-addict hypothesis finally falls apart. In "The Softer Side" House dangerously self-medicates on methadone and is pain-free and happy and quits his job. But House would rather take the familiar road: solving puzzles at PPTH, pain, and misery. "This is the only me you get," he tells Cuddy. Just before Kutner dies, in "Locked In," House admits he's seen a psychiatrist, perhaps a glimmer of hope. Then Kutner dies and House's need to know the answer drives him to the brink and over it. House can't believe Kutner killed himself: He's convinced Kutner was murdered. He starts hallucinating Amber. In a low point he sets fire to a cadaver in the morgue rehearsing Sambuca shots for Chase's bachelor party ("House Divided"). Then he hallucinates he has sex with Cuddy and he's on his way to Mayfield Hospital.

> "He went into the institution and it became much less about getting clean of the pills but how he should live his life. And recognizing his own flaws and limitations. Which I think he has on a certain level."
>
> —DAVID SHORE

....

House leaves Mayfield clean and out of a job. But he finds it impossible to stay away from his other addiction—to the puzzles. In "Epic Fail," when Vince the video game guy puts his symptoms up online and offers a reward for a diagnosis, House solves the case (and wins twenty-five thousand dollars). Dr. Nolan sees that the puzzles and the drugs work in the same part of House's head: He solved the puzzle and his leg stopped hurting. Nolan tells House to go back to work. There are demons there. "But maybe the only thing worse than going back is not going back."

QUESTION: "He is an addict."

DAVID SHORE: "It's hard to imagine he won't fall off the wagon at some point."

HOUSE'S LOOK

Cathy Crandall has photographs of Marlon Brando and Sean Penn up on her wall as inspiration for House's look. She reflected on House's irreverent personality: "We gave him a sort of couldn't-care-less look about his clothes, although the trick was we want him to look good."

Cathy gives House a neat, clean, tailored jacket and pairs it with a rumpled shirt, jeans, and one of the pairs of sneakers out of his vast collection of Nikes. But House's sport coats don't really fit—they're too small. "It tells a story," says Cathy. He's someone who doesn't really take a lot of time to get his clothes to fit perfectly. It's "subtle but noticeable," says Cathy. "Sometimes a character calls for ill-fitting clothes."

Don't be fooled—these are nice clothes. Most of House's sport coats are by Alexander McQueen and his shirts, "They still cost a whole hell of a lot of money. That's being in a hit show." As for House's T-shirts—"I try to keep them a little bit on the rock-and-roll side"—a lot are made to order. You won't find House's motorcycle jacket in a store, either. Cathy took a standard Vanson jacket and added the natty stripes on the sleeve herself.

The Empire Strikes Back

"What it is that Hugh does is really undoable, the idea that he can not only convincingly portray an American but then bring all the specificity to the performance at the rate that he goes, the number of pages that he does each day. I don't mean to be disrespectful to anyone else on TV but I don't think anybody comes close to what Hugh does."

—KATIE JACOBS

Hugh Laurie is one of a large number of Brits, Canadians, and the odd Aussie working on *House.* DP Gale Tattersall and other crew are English, part of a group of tens of thousands of Brits in Hollywood. Production designer Jeremy Cassells is Scottish; David Shore and David Hoselton are Canadians, Jesse Spencer is the Aussie. Hugh Laurie was already a very well-known actor in the United Kingdom, mainly for his comic work on shows like *Jeeves and Wooster, A Bit of Fry and Laurie* (with Stephen Fry), and the *Black-adder* series. In none of these shows did Laurie have to speak in an American accent.

House's customized biker jacket

"My dad's passed away and I told Hugh one day that I remember my funniest times with my dad were laughing hysterically to *Jeeves and Wooster* and *Black-adder.* I remember when I first met Hugh I just felt my dad up in heaven saying, 'Finally you're working with an actor I can respect.'"

—JEREMY CASSELLS

The only person not completely convinced by Hugh Laurie's accent is Hugh Laurie. "It comes and goes," he says. "I have good days and bad days and six years later, I can't work out why I have good days and bad days." He practices his accent on his way to the studio. If he's on his motorbike he'll see other drivers at stop signs wondering who he's talking to. "There are some days when I just can't get it," he says, and then corrects himself. "No, every day I can't get it." If he has to rerecord any dialogue he listens to himself.

"I might go in and only listen to one sentence but in one sentence I can hear three mistakes and I think, Well, if I am going to correct those three, that means in the whole show there are thirty-one thousand. What am I going to do? There come s a point when there just isn't enough time."

On the other hand, Gale Tattersall describes Hugh Laurie's accent as "flawless." Gale marvels at how Laurie remembers all his dialogue and the medical terms and all the physical details with the cane. "He is such a magnificent actor," Gale says. "It really is a joy to watch him and to be part of the team." Writers Russel Friend, Garrett Lerner, and Tommy Moran talk about Hugh Laurie's work ethic and what he brings to the show beyond what the audience sees. When House smashed Cuddy's toilet in "Let Them Eat Cake," Laurie figured out the best way to do it with the sledgehammer and did it in one take, at one point using the sledgehammer in place of his cane, an improvised little touch. The three discuss Laurie's sense of how a shot should develop. They agree how good his accent is. "I think it's flawless," says Garrett. "Sometimes he'll be hard on himself after a take and you'll go, 'Which word? I don't know what was wrong with that.'"

Garrett Lerner remembered Hugh Laurie from an episode of British cult comedy *The Young Ones;* Russel and Tommy were less familiar, and were completely convinced by the accent. Says Russel, "When we first met him and he spoke with a British accent I was like, 'Oh! Why are you speaking in a British accent?'" Tommy Moran had only heard Laurie speaking in an American accent, even during lunch. Then Laurie did an interview for *Good Morning America* from the set. "He's talking in the American accent right up to the point he's asked a question and he starts answering in a British accent and for a second I thought he's doing a joke accent."

TOMMY MORAN: "It doesn't sound like his voice. It seems odd to me."

GARRETT LERNER: "His British accent sucks."

Hugh Laurie on . . . *House*

QUESTION: "It's a great group here . . ."

"They're a lovely bunch, a lovely bunch. I'm not."

QUESTION: "You made the pilot and you have an expectation of what? Finishing the pilot? Making ten shows."

"That's it. I thought this will be an interesting two weeks. Bryan Singer is obviously an interesting fellow and at the end of it I will have an hour-long DVD I can show to my friends and say, 'See what might have been.'"

QUESTION: "But you know it was a good script."

"I did. I always knew it might be good. I'm being a little disingenuous. I always had a sneaking suspicion that it might work. I thought there is real worth in this, real value in this. You are at the mercy of so many things that have nothing to do with the show."

QUESTION: "How intense is the rhythm of the show?"

"It is intense and relentless. The quantity of it is mind-bending yet for all that, people are at the top of their game and things seems to move smoothly. It's an unmechanizable animal. You can't just hit a button and scripts churn out and you can't just hit a button and the camera unit shoots itself. Every week you feel like you are slightly reinventing the wheel. Every scene you are kind of starting from scratch thinking, How the hell are we going to do this in a way that hasn't been done? I suppose it would be possible to just fasten on things we think had been successful but what everyone is trying to do is the opposite—actors are trying to find things they haven't done and directors are trying to find shots they haven't shot."

QUESTION: "Do you feel pressure?"

"The strange thing about this game—which it isn't, it's not a game— is that ultimately of course it is only a TV show. But the paradox is that if you treat it as if it's only a TV show it wouldn't even be a TV show, it would be a canceled TV show. Everyone is obliged to be, paid to be, slightly obsessive over things. Of course, we know that we are not curing cancer. We're not even portraying people who are curing cancer but one is required to be obsessive and perfectionist about it even to have a chance of staying in the game. It's very competitive and audiences are very hard to come by and there are a million people wanting to do what we are doing. We can all feel the hot breath of failure on the back of our neck and it could all come crashing down."

QUESTION: "Not last season . . ."

"Very occasionally, I go on the Internet because I've got no other way of seeing what people think. I don't recommend it and of course it's absolutely deadly because people just complain. I'm not dismissing people's criticisms, you can't do that, but I think a large part of what people find unsatisfying or objectionable is actually in themselves. It is part of their own organic progress. They can say, 'Season two was so much better.' Well, was it really or was it that you were newer to this? So the audience was the audience they were when they first saw the show. I actually think that some of the things we are doing now are better than anything we have done."

QUESTION: "Even at this point, do you read this and think, that's cool?"

"I really do. And of course we are often accused of being formulaic but that is the nature of television. You have to build a number of sets and reuse them. That is the first and most practical consideration. You can't do a TV show which doesn't recycle its physical properties. As soon as you have set a thing in a place, usually a workplace, there must be a regular structure to it; otherwise it is uneconomic. I think we are much less formulaic than the cop shows that catch the bad guy every single week."

QUESTION: "You're the most popular show in the world. How about that?"

"I don't know what that means. But it appears to be weirdly successful in other parts of the world. I am very surprised by that because it is such a verbal show. We don't have many car chases or exploding helicopters or rooftop chases."

QUESTION: "You do get punched."

"I did get punched. That probably plays in a lot of cultures."

"Treating patients is what makes most doctors miserable."

QUESTION: "You had it coming to you."

"I did. I have had it coming every week."

QUESTION: "Chase punched you out last season . . ."

"There was a line in the premiere where the psychiatrist says something about people getting just desserts and House dismissed that idea, acknowledging the fact that if there is any justice he would be repeatedly gang-raped by his patients. He accepts that his behavior is provocative."

Hugh Laurie on . . . the Philosophy of *House*

QUESTION: "It's a key theme: You don't get what you deserve, you just get what you get."

"You just get what you get. It is sort of anti-television, it seems to me, particularly in this country. Films and TV serve to reassure people that there is such a thing as justice, that virtue is rewarded and evil is punished and the boy meets the girl. There are satisfactory resolutions to things and *House* stands resolutely foursquare against that. Even though of course we have to acknowledge that we are a TV show and by and large people do survive the terrible illnesses and there are happy endings. House as a character is very dismissive of the whole idea of justice. People watch TV shows because they know their lives are so haphazard and unfair. They switch on the television to see fairness, to see bad people getting caught and good people getting applauded."

QUESTION: "What about the hedge fund guy who gives away his money?"

"There is a sort of psychic moral economy that he must redress."

QUESTION: "That isn't going to appeal to House."

"No it isn't, but oddly House goes relatively easy on him. He is exasperated but not unsympathetic. Because there is a sort of harsh Protestant streak to House, I think. He regards the easy answer or the comfortable answer as being essentially suspect. If it is easy there is probably something wrong with it and it sort of equates to that guy's dilemma. He is so successful in so many areas of his life there must be something wrong somewhere. There is a price to be paid."

QUESTION: "House is not materialistic."

"He is so many things. But he has a sort of petty childish acquisitiveness to take money and toys. Those are just ways of keeping score for House."

QUESTION: "Do you think it's an attractive quality, that if it's on House's mind, he'll say it?"

"Of course. It's like the Icarus myth, the dream of being able to fly—it is a kind of social weightlessness. If you're not weighed down by the gravity of 'I mustn't say this,' 'I mustn't say that,' 'I am constrained by this.' This character just doesn't obey the laws of gravity. He is allowed to soar and that is an exhilarating prospect. It is unattainable."

QUESTION: "It's all about making it through the day because it is hard to get through the day."

"It is hard. And House is suspicious of the idea of intrinsic good. There was a script by Larry Kaplow called 'Autopsy' and he won the Writers Guild Award for it about a young girl with a brain tumor and everyone in the hospital is marveling at this girl's morale and state of mind, the bravery, and House is skeptical of the notion of cancer and bravery. It's one of the ways in which we defer to cancer by saying anyone who has it is brave. House is very skeptical. How brave can she be? Are there only brave cancer victims? If everybody is brave the word *brave* doesn't mean anything.

"Then he fastens on the idea that her bravery is a symptom; her personality has been affected by the cancer and that is how they are going to treat it. And the genius of the script is that he is wrong. He is wrong in such a way that leads to a better solution for how to treat her. It is an absolutely fabulous script—philosophically so intriguing, as they all are."

QUESTION: "There are some wonderful Housean ailments—the guy who is abusing cough syrup in order to become stupider." ("Ignorance is Bliss")

"Absolutely brilliant. I think it is painful to him and it threatens him to see someone surrender their intellect in order to achieve happiness because he has cherished the intellect over his own happiness at every turn. But he can see that it is at least a tenable position and he winds up accepting that ignorance is bliss."

Hugh Laurie on . . . Lucas

QUESTION: "House's other potential friend showed up as a rival. Poor House."

"The younger man. In a funny sort of way it makes sense . . . House would be a lot rougher on some of the other prospective Cuddy mates. In fact he has been."

QUESTION: "He could get rid of those guys."

"But here is a guy who is serious. In a strange sort of twisted way, I can imagine him giving it his blessing. Of him approving of the relationship somehow. Not admitting to it but on some level approving."

Hugh Laurie on . . . Wilson

QUESTION: "This is one of the few shows that investigates male friendship . . ."

"I don't know why this horrible word *bromance* has become so current. I think men are very confused about how to behave toward each other."

QUESTION: "After Amber, you had to know who Wilson was seeing. You have to know what he is up to."

"Yes, because although it is a male relationship, it is also a male-female relationship. It doesn't mean that I fancy him and I don't want to portray Robert Sean Leonard as in any way effeminate or unattractive, heaven forbid, but there is definitely, as there was with *The Odd Couple*, there are male and female sides to all of us and Wilson tends towards the female and House toward the slovenly male."

QUESTION: "Robert Sean Leonard says Wilson is more screwed up than House."

"I think that may be so. And probably by season fourteen—I'll be long gone by then—it will be an exploration of Wilson's very screwed-up psyche. He is superficially so much more functional. House's dysfunction is so evident. That in itself is relatively more healthy than the subterranean torture of Wilson."

Hugh Laurie on . . . Hugh Laurie

QUESTION: "Do you watch the show?"

"I have watched them. It's actually more enjoyable to leave it for a while until I have forgotten who did it and also forgotten what I did. Sometime I can go, 'Oh, that was quite a good moment.' If it's fresh in my memory I think, 'I could have done that better,' or, 'why did I do that?'"

QUESTION: "Is learning lines difficult for you?"

"It isn't actually. That's a real blessing. It's a lot of stuff. When the show started, the producers and the studio people are wondering, 'Well, will anyone like it?' That is their first concern. Their second concern is, 'If they do like it can we keep making it?' Because if he can't remember his lines, we can't make it. Or, 'is he sober?' 'Does he turn up on time?' 'Does he carry a gun?' All these sort of things which to be honest have happened and probably are happening right now somewhere in Los Angeles: Someone is not showing up or [is] threatening to punch a director or kicking the furniture or is just so unprepared it takes them three hours to do something that should take one. They are all meaningful concerns."

"It's fortunate he can learn lines quickly. Watching it, it looks effortless. The definition of someone who is fantastic at what they do is that it looks as though they aren't even trying. But it is incredibly hard for him to keep that going."

—KATIE JACOBS

QUESTION: "From a British perspective people know you from *Fry and Laurie* and *Blackadder* . . ."

"If they know . . ."

QUESTION: "Of course they do. Were they surprised en masse by this great character acting?"

"I don't think they paid any attention at all. That is one of the odd quirks of the way the whole thing panned out, is that it made much less impression, if any impression at all, in Britain. We are the number-one show in Italy, Spain, Germany, Brazil. I have letters from people in Russia. Britain, it didn't really penetrate at all. It didn't particularly catch on. That's fine. That actually worked out rather well."

QUESTION: "Some Brits are ambivalent about America."

"British people are guilty of the most awful set of lazy prejudices about Americans. 'They have no sense of irony.' That's such bollocks. They have a much more highly developed sense of irony than we do in a large number of cases. Large chunks of their TV are nothing but irony. They are incapable of being unironic. . . . There are a lot of lazy and slightly snobbish assumptions."

QUESTION: "Do you live here and go back there?"

"I do. Necessarily I live here but I don't think of it as living here. I'm staying here. Although I have finally applied for a green card partly because the work permit legislation has got so tight recently that unless you have a green card it's so hard to work . . . I'm a great admirer of this country and am very fond of the people I work with."

QUESTION: "How difficult is the leg to do? It's not the loss of the leg, it's the arm."

"That got to me a little bit."

QUESTION: "Did I overhear you say your leg actually hurts?"

"I did something; I don't know what I did. It's more of a mechanical problem. Reading a file, opening a door, answering a phone while administering an injection. My problem, as it would be, is how would you handle the cane?"

Hugh Laurie on . . . House

QUESTION: "Stacy. You blew that pretty badly."

"David Shore writes absolutely fantastic dramatic scenes but he has an amazing gift for allusion. The offstage stuff he writes incredibly well. The way he refers to past relationship or past events or off-screen exchanges that have taken place is absolutely masterful. Including the way he introduced the previous relationship with Stacy almost like it was *Casablanca*. They met in Paris. The Germans wore gray, et cetera. And she walks back into Rick's Bar. Of all the hospitals in all the world. He has a wonderful gift for doing that. I wound up believing that history completely and being very intrigued by it."

QUESTION: "In season six, we're meant to think you are getting better."

"Well, an addict is an addict whatever he is addicted to—painkillers or depression or puzzles or whatever it might be—just torturing those around him. The addiction is just in abeyance but it never goes away. Alcoholics go to AA the rest of their lives."

QUESTION: "House doesn't have time to go to everything he needs to go to."

"It would be a full day."

QUESTION: "House supports Chase over Dibala: He says 'better a murder than a misdiagnosis.'"

"Which is partly a joke but only partly. He is aware of the apparent absurdity of how that sounds but it is true as well. It is both things."

QUESTION: "You have been in this position before, saving the life that's right here but we're thinking of thousands of other people that we don't know. Ron Livingston [Sebastian in "TB or Not TB"]. You really hated that guy."

"Jealous . . . On what scale do human beings make their decisions? Are they making their decision based on the people in the room with them?"

QUESTION: "Why does House have a cricket ball in his office?"

"It's just something I wanted to be able to touch every now and then. Also he's a well-traveled fellow and it always felt to me as if academia, inasmuch as House is an academic or has been an academic, is almost its own country. He would pick up all sorts of curiosities. He has a trophy from the CIA—an eagle that he stole from a woman's desk."

> ## "I don't think House's the devil; I don't think he's an angel."
>
> —DAVID SHORE

QUESTION: "You have a picture of Stephen Colbert."

"I was thrilled—because the man is a genius—to see that Colbert possibly ironically decided to a have a picture of me as House in the background [of his desk], I don't care if it is ironic or not. He has since accumulated lots of other ones and I can't actually tell if I am still there but I was there for a couple of years and I thought it was worth returning the compliment. I thought that House would probably enjoy Colbert. It seemed fitting."

QUESTION: "I loved the time you were smashing toilets."

"There is something very pleasing about seeing bright, accomplished, people behaving like five-year-olds. There is a five-year-old in all of us. It never goes away. Some other shows will attribute a single characteristic to a single character and say he's the hothead. He's the so-and-so. We are all hotheaded at times. We are all timid at times. We are all anxious."

QUESTION: "David Shore doesn't think House has a heart of gold that some think."

"He is capable of noble acts of self-sacrifice and he is capable of kindness. When he does do a kindness he doesn't necessarily need to be rewarded for it. It is one of the strange things and sentimental things about a lot of American TV, noble acts or kind acts need to be noticed and rewarded or applauded at least. It's amazing how many times the director or writer will stage a scene in such a way that the lovers are reunited or the bomb is defused or the heroic act takes place in a very public arena. The lovers reunite in a baseball stadium or at an airport or in a subway train with people clapping. It never happens in their bedroom. House is unusual in that he is okay to have good deeds going unnoticed and that is an admirable quality. That line of Kipling [from "If"]: "Risk it all on one turn of pitch-and-toss / And lose, and start again at your beginnings / And never breathe a word about your loss." Not breathing a word about your loss is a very noble thing. He does have that."

"I personally don't think he has the heart of gold that many people in the audience think. I do think he is a human being. I think that's one of the great things about the way Hugh plays it—it would be very easy to play as simply an automaton and we get that sense with Hugh that there is humanity behind those eyes. I think that's the only reason the audience forgives him for those things."

—DAVID SHORE

QUESTION: "He is never going to say that he cares."

"Right."

QUESTION: "Tritter really got House. He said everybody lies and also your actions lie."

"Policemen and doctors more than any other profession see mankind for what he or it is. See people in extremis. They probably develop a better sense of what humanity is all about and what we are capable of or not. That was very nuanced. As was the very subtle escalation. It began with a remark about 'you've been keeping me waiting,' which catches House at a bad moment so he comes back with a crack and then he kicks his cane as a way of physical bullying. It was so interestingly escalated."

QUESTION: "That was the only time you thought House might be overmatched."

"There was a very good line from Foreman. You realize Foreman has had a troubled youth and with a very wry experience says cops have a million ways to mess you up and it really is true. You don't want to make an enemy of a policeman. It can't end well."

QUESTION: "Cuddy saved your bacon."

"That was a beautiful moment. There are some things I am very proud to have been involved in."

QUESTION: "Twenty-five years from now, are House and Cuddy still pals?"

"I have absolutely no idea. Doctors tend to stick to their profession more than others. Having invested so much in acquiring that qualification they will continue to do the jobs they do."

QUESTION: "What would he do if he retired?"

"His leg hurts until he engages with a problem. Sherlock Holmes was a depressive until he had a problem."

QUESTION: "Music is important to you?"

"Absolutely to me. It is a release for House. I find him a tremendously romantic figure in a way and music is a part of that romantic side of him. There's the mechanical mathematical side of music that would appeal to House. I can imagine House being a very good student of Bach, understanding the mathematical progression of Bach and the perfection of it. But also there is a sort of jazz side of him."

QUESTION: "The free-form thinking. He riffs wonderfully."

"Seeing connections between things. Being able to improvise. Bach and Thelonius Monk can coexist in him."

"I always had a sneaking suspicion that it might work."

CONCLUSION

"We don't strive to be an okay show. We strive for
every show to be as good as it can be and hopefully
we succeed more than we fail. None of us is
studying for a B."

—KATIE JACOBS

In 2009, Eurodata TV Worldwide, a French organization that collates
television ratings from around the globe, declared that *House*
was the most popular TV show in the world with more than
81.8 million viewers in sixty-six countries. House is certifiably a
phenomenon that succeeds across the breadth of the world's extraordinarily diverse cultures. The show has generated mountains of literature ranging from academic discourses to the
modern cornucopia associated with Internet fandom. House's
gruff charm crosses barriers of generations and borders and every
demographic indicator dreamed up by international marketers.
House is forever ensconced in reruns on U.S. cable. It's safe to
say, *House* is a hit.

For the cast and crew of *House,* the daily commitment to excel-
lence hasn't changed since the pilot. Television is an industry in
which quality is no guarantor of success. *House* has managed to be
both enduringly popular and extremely good, a hard combination

to maintain. The show has consistently been heavily nominated for awards, showing that it's held in high esteem by critics and industry peers, as well as legions of viewers. Among the winners: Emmys for David Shore for writing "Three Stories" (2005); for Dalia Dokter, Jamie Kelman, and Ed French for prosthetic makeup for "Que Sera Sera" (2007); Greg Yaitanes for directing "House's Head" (2008); and Von Varga, Juan Cisneros, Gerry Lentz, and Rich Weingart for the sound mixing of "House Divided" (2009). Hugh Laurie won Golden Globes for best actor in a drama series in 2006 and 2007 and Screen Actors Guild Awards in 2007 and 2009; Omar Epps won Image Awards for acting in 2007 and 2008; Lawrence Kaplow won the Writers Guild Drama Award in 2006; and Russel Friend, Garrett Lerner, David Foster, and David Shore won the Writers Guild Drama Award in 2010 for "Broken"; and on and on.

Even if, after six seasons, the day-to-day work on the show is marked by continuing artistic and technical quality, the view from the bridge has shifted somewhat. Katie Jacobs describes challenges of the first season: "The first season was a really different exercise. You are working at a time where you feel like everything is a fight, and I don't mean that in a bad way. I have to fight to stay on the air; I have to fight for good promos; I have to fight for publicity; I have to fight for casting; I have to fight for everything. It's a competitive business."

She compares them with today: "Now, I am in a really different incredibly blessed position—I don't have to fight any of those battles anymore. I am on the air. I am staying on the air. I get good promotion—that I still work on. It's daunting in a different way."

··················

Standing at the center of this particular universe is the character of House. It's always has been and it always will be all about House. The way he has been established over the years means that he will continue to be capable of surprising the people who think they know him so well. According to the man who created him, House is different, and not like the rest of us at all.

"He is not an immoral person; he is a very moral person in the sense that he is constantly struggling to figure out what is the right thing to do. Societal guidelines are no solace to him whatsoever. He approaches every issue from a fundamental issue. He never says what does the law tell me to do? He says what do the basic ethical principles tell me to do? And he recognizes that a lot of the questions that doctors face are very, very difficult and complicated questions."

—DAVID SHORE

QUESTION: "House is not a bleeding heart."

DAVID SHORE: "To say the least."

House is only constrained by the writers' ability to find fresh challenges for him professionally and new torments for him personally and by Hugh Laurie's capacity to inhabit the character with such overwhelming force and conviction. Neither of these variables seem in any doubt.

....

As season six closes, House is self-medicating with alcohol. In "The Choice" he wakes up in an empty bed in a neighboring apartment. Wilson is paying House's team members $100 to take House out (Foreman characteristically holds out for $200.) House actually has a good time singing "Midnight Train to Georgia" in a karaoke joint with Foreman and Chase; Thirteen takes him to the Foxhole, a lesbian bar, an evening that Wilson says House can't fail to relish.

But dangling over everything as it has been from the start is House's relationship with Cuddy. Innocently (meaning Wilson hasn't paid her), Cuddy asks House out for a bite to eat. He says no. Cuddy pauses at the threshold—people say the most important things to their doctors when they have their hand on the doorknob.

CUDDY: "I just want us to be friends."

HOUSE: "Funny. That's the last thing I want us to be."

Suddenly House is facing what he fears most, being alone. Sam is moving in with Wilson so Wilson asks House to leave the apartment and Lucas and Cuddy are going to live together, too. "Baggage" follows House's real-time shrink session with Nolan. House is looking for distractions: Drinking and getting in fights, taking in his old Mayfield buddy Alvie, and actively seeking the case of an amnesiac woman whose search for her identity parallels Nolan's attempts to get to the root of House's latest malaise.

Nolan deduces that the amnesiac's husband is afraid of losing his wife and House is losing someone too—he knows House will always have Wilson so it must be Cuddy. Alvie pawned some of House's books one of which House goes to extreme lengths to retrieve, offering the buyer $2,000, then having Alvie steal it. The book is *Approach to the Acute Abdomen* by Ernest T. Cuddy, M.D., Cuddy's great grandfather, a volume that House intended to present to her on a special occasion. As Nolan uncovers what must be the truth, that House is mourning someone he loved, House walks out. He says he did what Nolan asked and he's still miserable but Nolan can only do so much—he only has access to House's psyche, not Cuddy's heart.

In the finale, "Help Me," House gives the book to a newly-engaged Cuddy. The message he writes in it is banal and quite unlike House: "To Lisa and Lucas. Here's to a new chapter ... Best, Greg. X." House detects some hesitation in Cuddy's response but even House has to wait: Cuddy must deal with a serious accident, a crane collapse, in Trenton. House follows and finds himself in an extreme One Day, One Room situation, helping Hanna, a woman trapped underground, her leg pinned by heavy debris.

Cuddy and House have been here before, in different roles. In "Three Stories," Cuddy tries to persuade House to have his leg removed—he has suffered muscle death and the safest option is amputation as it is for Hanna who has crush syndrome. As Cuddy argues they must take the leg, House desperately tries to buy time for Hanna. Cuddy thinks House is using Hanna to get back at her.

CUDDY: "I don't love you so just accept it and move on with your life instead of making everyone miserable."

HOUSE: "That's great. A life lesson from a middle aged single mom who's dating a man-child."

CUDDY: "Screw you. I'm sick of making excuses for you . . . I'm done."

House then tells Hanna he wishes he had allowed them to remove his leg. Keeping it made him a worse person. "And now, I'm alone." House's doctors screwed up and diagnosed bed rest and antibiotics which accounts for the state he's in; Hanna's doctor (House) did everything right in the emergency situation and after she is freed, she should have made it. While House insisted on keeping his leg and lives, Hanna agrees to lose hers and dies from a freak embolism on the way to the hospital. You don't get what you deserve; you get what you get.

In the face of fate, all the work House has done to change seems futile. Foreman tries to reason with him but he's inconsolable. He goes home and takes pills from his last secret stash, ready to throw away all he's gained. Before he falls off the cliff, he's saved by Cuddy who tells House she ended it with Lucas. She's in her new home with her fiancé and all she can think about is House. Their last shouting match was just more foreplay. "I love you," Cuddy says. "I wish I didn't. But I can't help it." After the last time, House has to check—I'm not hallucinating, right? He isn't—so something *has* changed, and they kiss. So sometimes, you get what you want.

Who knows where House and Cuddy will be two weeks or two years from now? In love or not talking, or in love and not talking. Stability is always fleeting and whatever crisis Thirteen is suddenly facing is happening right now. Taub catches her leaving a note for House. She's asking for time off.

TAUB: "Are you okay?"

THIRTEEN: "Obviously not."

Fans of TV shows, like fans of any fictional drama, root for the success and happiness of the characters they like and against the ones they don't care for. We want our favorite characters to make good decisions, to not reach for that bottle of booze or pills in the hope they can change their own fate and redirect their lives. We want them to stave off illness, whatever the odds. Perhaps, it's comforting to know that nothing is cast in stone, there's no predetermined outcome for this or that career, relationship, or life. Ask David Shore the same question that other House principals have been asked about where the characters may end up. You'll find that the future remains to be written.

QUESTION: "Twenty years from now House and Cuddy will be friends?"

DAVID SHORE: "I can't answer that question. I can't say whether they are going to be married or be enemies. I don't know. These people are kind of real in my mind and I am watching their life unfold as I am going along."

QUESTION: "But you're unfolding it."

DAVID SHORE: "I'm unfolding it, but I'm taking it where I find it interesting and what feels natural. I don't know how it's going to unfold."

House equipment on "New York Street" on the FOX lot
in Los Angeles

APPENDIX

The Episodes

Season One

ONE: Pilot

TWO: Paternity

THREE: Occam's Razor

FOUR: Maternity

FIVE: Damned if You Do

SIX: The Socratic Method

SEVEN: Fidelity

EIGHT: Poison

NINE: DNR

TEN: Histories

ELEVEN: Detox

TWELVE: Sports Medicine

THIRTEEN: Cursed

FOURTEEN: Control

FIFTEEN: Mob Rules

SIXTEEN: Heavy

SEVENTEEN: Role Model

EIGHTEEN: Babies and Bathwater

NINETEEN: Kids

TWENTY: Love Hurts

TWENTY-ONE: Three Stories

TWENTY-TWO: Honeymoon

Season Two

ONE: Acceptance

TWO: Autopsy

THREE: Humpty Dumpty

FOUR: TB or Not TB

FIVE: Daddy's Boy

SIX: Spin

SEVEN: Hunting

EIGHT: The Mistake

NINE: Deception

TEN: Failure to Communicate

ELEVEN: Need to Know

TWELVE: Distractions

Season Two (*continued*)

THIRTEEN: Skin Deep	NINETEEN: House vs. God
FOURTEEN: Sex Kills	TWENTY: Euphoria, Part I
FIFTEEN: Clueless	TWENTY-ONE: Euphoria, Part II
SIXTEEN: Safe	TWENTY-TWO: Forever
SEVENTEEN: All In	TWENTY-THREE: Who's Your Daddy
EIGHTEEN: Sleeping Dogs Lie	TWENTY-FOUR: No Reason

Season Three

ONE: Meaning	THIRTEEN: Needle in a Haystack
TWO: Cane and Abel	FOURTEEN: Insensitive
THREE: Informed Consent	FIFTEEN: Half-Wit
FOUR: Lines in the Sand	SIXTEEN: Top Secret
FIVE: Fools for Love	SEVENTEEN: Fetal Position
SIX: Que Sera, Sera	EIGHTEEN: Airborne
SEVEN: Son of a Coma Guy	NINETEEN: Act Your Age
EIGHT: Whac-a-Mole	TWENTY: House Training
NINE: Finding Judas	TWENTY-ONE: Family
TEN: Merry Little Christmas	TWENTY-TWO: Resignation
ELEVEN: Words and Deeds	TWENTY-THREE: The Jerk
TWELVE: One Day, One Room	TWENTY-FOUR: Human Error

Season Four

ONE: Alone	NINE: Games
TWO: The Right Stuff	TEN: It's a Wonderful Lie
THREE: 97 Seconds	ELEVEN: Frozen
FOUR: Guardian Angels	TWELVE: Don't Ever Change
FIVE: Mirror, Mirror	THIRTEEN: No More Mr. Nice Guy
SIX: Whatever It Takes	FOURTEEN: Living the Dream
SEVEN: Ugly	FIFTEEN: House's Head
EIGHT: You Don't Want to Know	SIXTEEN: Wilson's Heart

Season Five

ONE: Dying Changes Everything

TWO: Not Cancer

THREE: Adverse Events

FOUR: Birthmarks

FIVE: Lucky Thirteen

SIX: Joy

SEVEN: The Itch

EIGHT: Emancipation

NINE: Last Resort

TEN: Let Them Eat Cake

ELEVEN: Joy to the World

TWELVE: Painless

THIRTEEN: Big Baby

FOURTEEN: The Greater Good

FIFTEEN: Unfaithful

SIXTEEN: The Softer Side

SEVENTEEN: The Social Contract

EIGHTEEN: Here Kitty

NINETEEN: Locked In

TWENTY: Simple Explanation

TWENTY-ONE: Saviors

TWENTY-TWO: House Divided

TWENTY-THREE: Under My Skin

TWENTY-FOUR: Both Sides Now

Season Six

ONE: Broken (two hours)

TWO: Epic Fail

THREE: The Tyrant

FOUR: Instant Karma

FIVE: Brave Heart

SIX: Known Unknowns

SEVEN: Teamwork

EIGHT: Ignorance is Bliss

NINE: Wilson

TEN: The Down Low

ELEVEN: Remorse

TWELVE: Moving the Chains

THIRTEEN: 5 to 9

FOURTEEN: Private Lives

FIFTEEN: Black Hole

SIXTEEN: Lockdown

SEVENTEEN: Knight Fall

EIGHTEEN: Open and Shut

NINETEEN: The Choice

TWENTY: Baggage

TWENTY-ONE: Help Me

ACKNOWLEDGMENTS

Ian Jackman would like to thank, at HarperCollins, Matt Harper, Lisa Sharkey, Carrie Kania, and Michael Morrison; at NBC Universal, Kim Niemi and Steve Coulter; Stan Pottinger; Michael Yarish; Lindsey Jaffin; and everyone who was so generous at *House.* And thanks especially to Geoffrey Colo and Neysa Siefert who both went above and beyond, and to my crucial three: K, S, and L.

The hot seat

"House stands out by defying the conventions of network television..."
— *New York Times*

[H]OUSE
M.D.

MONDAYS **FOX**

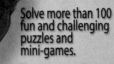